7-10 Split

My Journey as America's Whitest Black Kid

By

Michael Gordon Bennett

This print edition published by *Bennett Global Entertainment Publishing* 2015

Copyright Registered at the Library of Congress 2015

Cover design by *Nicole Anderson --- www.anobrainart.com*

Cover photography by *Chloe Green*

ISBN: 978-0-9864162-0-0
www.michaelgordonbennett.com

BENNETT GLOBAL ENTERTAINMENT
PUBLISHING

To my parents',

Richard Bennett

Dad, I know you're looking down from above thrilled at what I've accomplished. Despite our rocky relationship at times, know that it was you who motivated me to work hard, and it was you, who provided a foundation for my success.

Anita Bennett

Mom, I reach for the stars because of you. You've never waivered in your belief that I could do whatever I set my mind to. You provided love, compassion and the opportunity to learn and grow. I am honored to be your son.

CONTENTS

ACKNOWLEDGEMENTS

A big thanks goes to my dear girlfriend Cecilia Walters, more affectionately known as, my boo. You came along at a time in my life when I needed a path forward. You believed in me unconditionally, you supported my vision unconditionally, and you pushed me knowing I had something to offer. For everything you've done, and will do, I am eternally grateful.

My dear son, Michael David, you are the most precious person in my life. No father could be more proud of the man you've become. Reach for the stars; don't settle for mediocrity. You have a heart of gold and a mind second to none.

To my sisters' Karen and Amanda: You were both there for part of this journey. Thank you for being who you are, and the persons you've become. I couldn't ask for two better friends. I hope you've enjoyed being my sisters' as much as I love being big brother.

To my dear friend Anthony "Tony" Clarke: You, my friend, are one of the best writers I've ever read. Your encouragement, and that of your wife Krystyna is one of the reasons I continually pursued this story despite having doors slammed in my face. Enjoy living in Australia.

I submitted my first draft and synopsis of this book to over a hundred publishing houses and agents back in 2007. Most responded with the typical form letter, that read, thanks, but no thanks. Several responded with notes saying they liked my story, they just didn't know how to market it. But there were a handful that went out of their way to offer advice, and counsel on how to proceed. A few of you typed three-page letters of encouragement. I don't remember who you are, but I want to acknowledge publicly, not everyone in the publishing business hides behind gatekeepers.

Thanks to technology, I've chosen the self-publishing route. The timing, I feel, couldn't be better given current events of 2014. I hope you enjoy the read, and begin a dialogue decades overdue. You'll understand the dialogue I'm referencing once you turn a few pages.

AUTHOR'S NOTE

This story represents a part of my life as I remember it. It is a work of nonfiction that reflects my experiences and true feelings of the times. I've changed many of the names to protect the privacy of those who played a role in my life. To anyone whose names I do not recall, or omit, please accept my sincerest apology.

I hope, in some small way, my story encourages others to reject the insidious stain of racism that continues to plague the greatest country mankind has ever known. America will never realize its full potential until the wounds of hatred are eradicated. I encourage everyone to start a dialogue, and try to reach those who stubbornly cling to worn out paradigms. Reject leaders who play the divide and conquer game. Be honest about what's happening around you. We are a better people than the racial animus that continues to divide us.

PROLOGUE

I started this book ten years ago, not sure I would ever have it published. I thought my story was compelling, but I didn't write it for public consumption. I wrote it for me. Documenting my story was an attempt to remove the scar tissue of a terribly troubling, often confusing child-hood.

Recording my thoughts proved cathartic. Almost immediately, the burdens of my past disappeared. At long last, the cloud of confusion simply evaporated into a fine mist, falling harmlessly to the ground, never to form again. It is my sincere hope readers will find understanding, purpose, and a few life lessons so we might become better people, and an even better society.

In a country so racially polarized, it's difficult to walk around without an identity. When I heard the lyrics to the *CSI* television series, the song's producers and writers could have easily been talking about me---*Who Are You? Who, Who, Who, Who? CSI* uses an abbreviated version of the song *Who Are You,* originally produced by the rock band The Who, in 1978. Those simple lyrics seemed to capture the essence of my early existence.

I really wanna know (Who are you? Who, who, who, who?)
Tell me, who are you? (Who are you? Who, who, who,
who?)

My utter lack of knowledge about black America took me from a life of moderate privilege as a child, to homelessness by my late teens, all because I couldn't wrap my arms around my own identity. The transition to homelessness was truly startling in its abruptness. One day I had food in my stomach, a roof over my head, and the spoils of life pointing to college and a successful career.

The next day, I placed cardboard in my shoes to save my feet from scorching pavement, and slept in cars, or outdoors when weather permitted, scraping for food from friends, too ashamed to stand on a corner and beg.

I've often heard people of faith proclaim, God doesn't put something in front of you that you can't handle. My early life certainly put that belief to the test.

I was born to two eighteen-year-old kids on January 8, 1958. With bleak employment prospects on the horizon, Dad did what thousands of African Americans of the late 1950s did; he joined the armed forces. The military presented a way out of poverty for legions of those born into less than ideal economic circumstances.

At three months old, I joined the fraternity of military brats, when Dad raised his right hand swearing to protect and defend the constitution of the United States of America.

The Civil Rights Movement provided a backdrop to

arguably the most tumultuous decade in American history. Civil rights dominated the news cycle in my early years, to be supplanted by Vietnam War protests later in the decade.

Military families certainly weren't immune to the can of worms unleashed by this twin juggernaut, but we were insulated, allowing us to keep a respectable distance, often hiding our true emotions and feelings about the country at large.

The pinnacle of the Civil Rights Movement found the Bennett family living in Madrid, Spain. Dad arrived at Torrejon Air Base in the summer of 1962 following a brief eight-month stint in Morocco.

We met dad in Spain mid August of that year. I soaked up Spanish culture like a sponge, often thinking myself more Spanish than American. We were living the good life that included having a full time maid. America's civil rights struggles were not ours as long as we remained in Spain.

While in Spain we missed:

1963:

The March on Washington and Dr. Martin Luther King, Jr.'s, *I Have a Dream Speech*; the bombing of the 16th Street Baptist Church in Birmingham, AL; Chicago School Boycott; the Malcolm X Speech, *Message to the Grass Roots*; and the assassination of President John F. Kennedy.

1964:

Passage of the Twenty Fourth Amendment abolishing the poll tax; Freedom Summer---the massive black voter registration drive; President Johnson signing the Civil Rights Act into law; and the murder and eventual discovery of the bodies of civil rights workers James Chaney, Andrew Goodman and Michael Schwerner.

1965:

Malcolm X assassination; Bloody Sunday on the Edmund Pettus Bridge; passage of the Voting Rights Act; the Watts Riots; and President Johnson signing an executive order enforcing affirmative action for the first time.

Twenty-eight months after arriving in Spain, we moved to Loring Air Force Base, tucked away in Maine's northeast corner, fifteen minutes by car from the Canadian border. You couldn't get any farther from black America and still be in the lower forty-eight.

I have vivid memories of the breaking news reports announcing the assassination of Dr. Martin Luther King, Jr., on April 4, 1968. There seemed to be a sense of profound anger and sadness by many of the locals in this northern Maine hamlet. But, I also detected a sense of giddiness from others.

I knew absolutely nothing about Dr. King. Dad appeared reticent to share any knowledge he had of Dr. King, leaving me to figure out for myself, was King a good man, or evil, like I overheard some whites claim. It's hard to fathom how a ten-year-old, living in the 1960s, had never heard of Dr. King. In hindsight it's embarrassing.

In 1969, I got the first taste of my own blackness living in Atlantic City, New Jersey. We move to New Jersey to live with family while dad served in Vietnam. The experience proved an eye-opener, an entire black community, who knew? It seems silly now, but at age eleven, the striking contrast between my previous world and the black community scared me. My path to black oblivion had already been firmly established---I knew zilch about black America.

I'd lived in overwhelmingly white communities my entire life, indifferent to their presence in my surroundings, or the dearth of blacks. Most of my neighbors' were white. Most of my friends' were white. Most of my classmates' were white. Most of my teachers' were white. My parents' had several friends and co-workers who were white, and treated us as extended family with spare keys to their homes.

My skin color mattered little until Atlantic City. Even when I noticed the difference in living standards, it did little, at that moment, to alter my perspective on race in America. Initially I though my observations were an anomaly. I simply had no internal compass by which to measure.

When we arrived at Tyndall Air Force Base, Florida, for dad's new duty assignment in August 1970, I became part of the first group of students "bused" in the name of school desegregation. I didn't realize all schools weren't the same. I'd never heard of the Ku Klux Klan, knew nothing about "separate but equal," or what it meant to be a black person living in the Deep South.

Tyndall sits on the Gulf of Mexico in Florida's

panhandle, about one hundred miles from the Alabama state line. The beaches are beautiful, and belied the racism, abject black poverty, and subjugation that existed in the area at the time.

I learned, and learned quickly, my white world was a smokescreen not based in reality, but more on a unique set of circumstances that left me ill equipped for a time, to handle what lay in front of me. I'd been unceremoniously dumped into a Race 101 class without the prerequisite courses.

Experience can be the worst teacher, it gives you the test first, and instructions afterwards.

Four years later I'd found my way to what could easily be described as the make-believe set of the television series *Happy Days*---the quintessential white suburban school. Dad's new duty assignment in the fall of 1974, took us to the United States Air Force Academy (USAFA), Colorado Springs, Colorado.

It would be difficult to get any whiter than Air Academy High School. Air Academy had three African American students my junior year. By my senior year, I'd be the only black male in my graduating class. My new circumstances gave credence to my belief that I was the White's Black Kid in America. I was certainly the loneliest. I counted my friends at Air Academy on one hand. I hated what were supposed to be the best years of a person's life.

Things like dating, school dances, and sports were fraught with danger. I became persona non grata at most school functions for nothing more than having dark skin.

Then, in arguably the biggest mistake of my life, I moved back to Panama City a year after high school searching for friends, familiarity, and comfort. At a time when most upwardly mobile African Americans fled the South, I returned thinking it would be a launching pad to the future. I'd never heard of the Great Migration of the 1920s that led millions of African Americans north and west to escape Jim Crow. While Jim Crow was technically over, the migration continued.

Within six months I'd be homeless due to a series of bad breaks, unforeseen circumstances, and a tinge of racism. Eventually, I too joined the Air Force, much to my dismay. I had nothing against military service, quite the contrary, I was happy to serve, but I was supposed to improve upon the foundation dad laid, and become, at a minimum, a military officer.

Like many of you, I continued to grapple with America's ultimate sickness, seeking understanding, and ways to eliminate bigotry from my life. It took me years to realize, I couldn't control the habits and prejudices of others, but lord knows, I bumped my head hundreds of times trying. At times, based on my experiences, I felt preordained to carry this burden alone. Man, it's heavy. I'm glad I let that nonsense go, realizing we are all in this together.

As a teenager, it was difficult to hear some blacks chirping in my ear their collective disdain for whites. Then hear whites chirping in my other ear their misplaced hatred of blacks, as if I were a different kind of black. It has been my experience that goodness exists across all that makes up America. It's not hard to find, we just have to open our eyes, and accept what we see.

Unfortunately, the loud, boisterous, propaganda laced hate mongers garner all the media attention. Why, because hate sells.

I get deeply offended when politicians employ the "southern strategy" to separate voters along racial lines. Divide and conquer only benefits those in power. It stokes the flames of racism and keeps the ugliness moving forward.

I keep looking for messaging that would resonate with the electorate to eliminate the effectiveness of the southern strategy. I haven't found it yet, so I'll keep trying.

But this isn't a political book. It's a simple story of love and compassion crossing paths with ignorance, racism, and stupidity.

Take away what you will from my story, but the existence of entrenched bigotry is not intractable or unsolvable. We are better than this.

ACT 1

NAIVE BEGINNINGS

CHAPTER 1

LET THE GOOD TIMES ROLL

SUMMER 1963

Powerful jet engines roared to life. In a sudden burst of power, we reached speeds in excess of one hundred sixty miles per hour in less than a minute. The captain pulled back on the yoke thrusting us skyward on a gradual ascent in an easterly direction. The plane teetered back and forth ever so slightly as the sound of landing gear retracting could be heard under the constant roar of the engines.

The bright lights dotting the New York and New Jersey shoreline quickly disappeared from view. Ten minutes later, it was pitch black over the Atlantic Ocean, as we continued our climb to a cruising altitude of thirty-two thousand feet.

My head was on a swivel---one moment staring at the beacon lights flashing from the plane's wing tips silhouetted against the dark sky; the next, watching flight attendants scurry about in a controlled frenzy serving our evening meal. Anyone who bothered to notice knew this was my first time on a plane.

My twenty-three-year-old mother, with a five-year-old and a three-year-old in tow, were headed for a land we knew nothing about. That realization terrified Mom. Her only comfort, the man she loved would be waiting at the other end of this journey.

Even at age five, I delighted in my ability to read Mom's facial expressions. So I did what I did best at that age---talked to damn much. The more she screamed at me to shut up, the more she relaxed.

After a few hours, a deep sleep ensued, many snoring loud enough to violate the space around them irritating other passengers. Mom and my sister Karen were fast asleep. I stayed awake for an hour after the lights were dimmed, looking out into the abyss for stars. Eventually, I too dosed off, only to be greeted by sunshine splashing through my window after a few hours. Madrid was six hours later, making it mid-morning when we arrived after a seven-hour trip.

Our Pan Am flight carried a combination of U.S. military personnel and their families, American civilians, and Spaniards. Guessing by our collective reactions, most had never been to Spain. My eyes remained fixated on the ground, as earth grew closer by the second. Passengers grew restless when the fasten seat belt sign illuminated announcing our final approach.

My ears popped, followed by intense pressure and muffled sounds. I swallowed hard, yawned, and pretended to chew to clear the dulling sensation in my ears, nothing worked. The sensation of hearing loss persisted; it proved somewhat disorienting.

The plane hit the ground with a thud slamming my head into the seatback. The wind fought violently with the aircraft wings before the pilot applied the breaks.

Next thing I knew, we were standing in line at Spanish customs and immigration. With my ears still in recovery, I heard murmurs of a new language, one that seemed to elicited excitement and passion.

I spotted Dad standing just on the other side of a glass partition. It had been nearly a year since we last saw each other. He looked great, even out of uniform, just like I remembered in pictures.

Dad arrived in Spain a month earlier, having gone straight from Morocco, his previous duty assignment in 1962, to Torrejon Air Base, just outside Madrid.

We embraced for what seemed like an eternity among the throngs of people standing just outside baggage claim. We were exhausted, but that didn't seem to matter at the moment. Minutes later, we were whisked away on a bus headed to Torrejon, home for the next few weeks until our apartamento (Spanish for apartment) in Madrid was ready.

The breeze blowing through the bus windows provided a welcome relief from the stifling mid-August afternoon heat. Dad went into tour guide mode, providing running commentary on what appeared outside our windows. We stopped at the hospital where he worked as an administrator. I would have my tonsils removed in that very hospital the following year.

The next morning, Dad hired a driver who took us to view famous Madrid landmarks---The Alcala Gates (La Puerta Alcala), The Royal Palace (Palacio Real) and the

Plaza Mayor. I was mesmerized by the architecture and beauty of the city, even though I didn't truly understand the significance of what lay before my eyes.

We made a quick stop at what would become our new home located in a ten-story rectangular high rise across the street from a park.

We were greeted by the portero---Spanish for doorman, who doubled as the building superintendent. The portero escorted us to a spacious second-floor, two-bedroom unit with maid quarters. Expats, military families, and Madrileños all called this building home. Karen and I started running around like we owned the place. Our playfulness earned us a stern warning from Dad to behave in a voice only he could deliver.

Dad was born in Baltimore, Maryland, in 1939, to a fifteen-year-old mother. From the very beginning, his life took a series of twists and turns so completely unfair to any newborn; it's amazing he became such a warm and loving person. Dad's birth name was Richard Lee. On his birth certificate under "Fathers Name" it simply says "Baby Lee."

Dad's birth was an embarrassment to many in his family, and their treatment of him, except his grandfather and at times his mother, was harsh. The Lee family carried many secrets. One of those secrets would be the identity of Dad's biological father.

Dad passed away in 2012 of pancreatic cancer never knowing who fathered him. This glaring omission haunted him for life. He continually pressed his mother and other family members for the information, only to watch them stiffen in their resolve, often becoming downright hostile. It became even more difficult for Dad to accept the hole left in his genealogy, when his mother married, and had two more sons.

Not knowing his father was insult enough, but race reared its ugly head early, and often, in Richard Lee's young life. It wasn't because his skin color was too dark. Dad is what many in the black community call "high yellow," a pejorative meant to reflect a lack of dark pigmentation.

Dad endured years of verbal abuse, some opinions downright vicious, for having light features. Many blacks thought he was Caucasian. This ignorance transcended generations as my sisters' and me faced a series of contentious incidents from blacks and whites, all over the shade of a man's skin. Some whites couldn't understand how he married a black woman.

Dad was eventually shipped off to Philadelphia to live with Aunt Sue, who adopted him, and changed his last name to Bennett. While his life improved temporarily, Dad led somewhat of a nomadic lifestyle, going from one relative to the next, before landing back at Aunt Sue's. In addition to the mental abuse, Dad suffered beatings meant to enforce discipline with a strap used to sharpen razor blades.

Dad attended Catholic schools, where, as he put it, punishment was swift for the slightest of infractions. The beatings he described to me at the hands of the nuns would be deemed child abuse today.

Dad and Aunt Sue eventually made their way to the Atlantic City area, where he graduated from a Catholic high school in 1957, met and married into the only truly loving family he had ever known. The Hicks family loved Dad, and he loved them with every once of his being, even after my parents' divorced.

Dad was not one to suffer insolence or insubordination; quick to punish us kids for any acts he deemed inappropriate, which included spankings. As part of my punishment, I often went to bed without dinner, only to have Mom sneak into my room after he'd fallen asleep to feed me.

When Dad joined the Air Force, it provided the structure he so sorely lacked growing up. Dad loved the military, yet the demons of childhood persisted and manifested themselves in how he treated his family at times.

He loved us all, no doubt, and constantly tried to do the right thing. Dad just lacked a complete set of tools in his toolbox. He had no mentor or role model, forcing him to fly by the seat of his pants when it came to rearing children.

So when Dad said stop, I froze in my tracks, for justice Richard Bennett style was equally as swift and harsh as his upbringing, and in some cases came without explanation or cause.

❦

The apartamento had an outdoor central courtyard. It was just wide enough to run clotheslines between buildings on a pulley system connected to a pole anchored in the center. I stuck my head out the window and looked up. Everyone had clothes hung out to dry, not something I'd seen in America.

Our apartamento was just off a busy thoroughfare dotted with tapas bars, mercados (markets), restaurants, and other small businesses. Street parking in our neighborhood proved especially chaotic at night when all the bars and restaurants were open.

Consuelo joined our family as a live-in maid within a week after we moved in. When we went on picnics or other family outings, she was there. On the mornings Mom couldn't walk me to the bus stop for school, Consuelo provided escort. If we needed things from the mercados, Consuelo usually took me along for the journey and taught me Spanish.

I'm not certain how old Consuelo was. If I had to guess, I would say in her early twenties. She had a youthful look about her and very energetic. She needed all that energy to chase two toddlers around. Consuelo also provided discipline when needed, but like Mom, punishment was balanced with love and affection.

We settled quickly. I began kindergarten at Royal Oaks Elementary School two weeks after our arrival in Madrid. I don't remember much about the place, but it was the first time I'd been away from Mom for more than a few hours. The Royal Oaks area is where all the Americans attended school, K-12.

Life rolled along until November 22, 1963. That was the day the earth just stopped rotating on its axis. I'm not sure what time of day President John F. Kennedy was assassinated, but Spaniards, known for late night meals and robust nightlife, were glued to small black and white television sets, and tiny radios for any news from the United States. The streets were eerily quiet that night.

That quiet lasted for days.

Our portero hugged every American exiting the building, in a display of love and affection I'd never witnessed in a stranger. His swollen red eyes and moist shirt revealed the depth of pain he felt for all of us.

The typically noisy morning traffic of Madrid, even on a Saturday was replaced with stone cold silence. A cool breeze blew through the park across the street whipping up dirt and dust clouds, only to settle and start all over again. I sat, staring into the distance, unsure what the death of President Kennedy meant to me, or my family.

Consuelo and I walked to the mercados to buy food and supplies. Somber faces greeted us, followed by offers of free candy and soda from the storeowners. The merchants tried everything they could think of to cushion the devastating loss of our president, but at age five, I was simply too young to grasp the impact and importance of President Kennedy's assassination. It was a sad time in our little piece of paradise, brightened by a group of people whose compassion was truly genuine, and much appreciated by all Americans.

Dad came home from work long after I had gone to bed on the day we lost President Kennedy. I heard my bedroom door open ever so slightly. He peeked inside as I feigned sleep. Just as softly as the door opened, it closed again, submerging the room in total darkness. He and Mom chatted briefly, then as suddenly as he appeared, Dad left, not to be seen again for several days. Only later did I learn the military had been put on high alert.

Life at Royal Oaks was anything but normal for weeks. Teachers seemed nervous and scared. Even as a kindergarten student I took notice. Teachers tried their best to bring a semblance of stability to our young lives. It worked for those less observant than me. The upcoming Christmas/New Years recess couldn't come soon enough.

As spring 1964 acceded to the demands of summer, my many friends, Spanish and American, trolled the streets of our neighborhood looking for anything to keep our six-year-old minds occupied. We hit up merchants for free food and candy, or played amongst the piles of lumber from the construction site across the street when the workers left for siesta.

Siesta is a long-standing tradition in Spain. It started as a short nap of fifteen to thirty minutes, taken in early afternoon just after lunch. It's a great way to combat that post lunch drowsiness and hot midday sun. Through the years, siesta morphed into a three-hour sleep fest. Between the hours of 2 p.m. and 5 p.m., Spain, or at least Madrid, shut down. Shops and restaurants were closed; once bustling streets, deserted.

Bored with sitting around the apartamento, I used siesta time to explore the city, traveling as far as my feet would carry me. I wandered blocks in one direction, then another, ignoring Mom's admonition not to amble off too far. I have no doubt I was lost on occasion, but the one or two people I found on the streets, pointed me in the direction of home. I felt totally safe in Madrid.

Mom often sent Consuelo to find her wayward son, but to no avail. I mastered the fine art of getting lost. By the time I arrived home, both Mom and Consuelo took turns screaming, yelling, and administering some mild form of punishment. As long as they didn't say, "what till your father gets home," I was cool with whatever punishment they meted out.

Mom was a softy compared to Dad, yet, I feared disappointing her more than any corporal punishment Dad dispensed. Mom had a way of getting a point across, seldom raising her hand, or voice. For her to scream meant whatever transgression I committed was a serious violation. After a few weeks of trying to track and contain my movements, Mom and Consuelo gave up.

Anita Bennett – nee Hicks - was born December 1939, in Atlantic City, New Jersey. She is the second oldest of four siblings. Mom was a quiet child, a trait she still carries, now in her seventies. She could sit in a room for hours and not say five words, but when she spoke, it was usually something profound. To hear her tell it, she was just an average student with a love for reading. As an adult, I could always find Mom reading three books simultaneously, switching from one to the other, and back again, until she devoured them all. I loved our weekly trips to the bookstore.

Mom was born and raised in a predominantly African American neighborhood, in a city that still practiced segregation. Chicken Bone Beach, the euphemism for the black only beach, was located on a two-block stretch of oceanfront on Missouri Avenue at the famed Atlantic City Boardwalk, minutes by foot from her front door. It was the only beach where blacks were allowed during parts of Mom's childhood, yet, I never heard her say a word about segregation.

Ironically, prior to 1900, blacks and whites lived side-by-side. African Americans used the beaches without restriction. To appease the influx of southern tourists, hotel owners pushed local leaders to establish Chicken Bone Beach as the black only spot. The beach held its designation until the Civil Rights Act became law in 1964.

Hundreds of black leaders and celebrities hit Chicken Bone Beach to entertain, or be entertained. Sammy Davis, Jr., the Mills Brothers, Jackie "Moms" Mabley, Sugar Ray Robinson, Dr. Martin Luther King, Jr., Billie Holiday and Sarah Vaughan were among the many notables who spent time on Chicken Bone Beach.

Mom is stunning in her beauty. Had she been five feet eight inches tall or taller, instead of five feet three, she could have easily been America's first black supermodel (no disrespect to Beverly Johnson). According to my aunt, most of the high school students in AC were envious of my parents'. They were the "it" couple, with all the good looks to match. While Mom defined introvert, Dad was the life of any party---the ultimate alpha male extrovert. If opposites attract, their relationship was truly magnetic.

Unlike Dad, Mom was born into a great family. Hard working and determined to provide for their family, my grandparents' Harry and Helen Hicks were married for seventy-three years until they both passed away at age ninety-five, forty days apart---the love affair of all love affairs.

When Mom and Dad were "courting" as Dad liked to call it, he spent more time at Mom's home than his own. The Hicks family embraced Dad as if they had given birth to him. My aunts' and uncle adored Dad.

My parents' courtship led to my birth two weeks after Mom's eighteenth birthday.

With a family to support, Dad joined the Air Force in March 1958. When he returned from basic training and technical school, Mom and Dad married. For some reason, it remained a big secret for years that I was born seven months before their marriage. I confronted Dad in my thirties about the secrecy. He asked me how long I had known, I replied, since age ten. He simply laughed and went on about his business. I guess that old habit of maximum secrecy instilled by his family proved hard to shake. Dad's family would have made great CIA operatives.

My parents' entertained a great deal in Madrid. Karen and I would awaken early the morning after one of those famous Bennett parties, and treat ourselves to leftover potato chips, peanuts, finger sandwiches, soda, and whatever non-alcoholic beverage we could find. It was the ultimate breakfast of champions. Poor Consuelo had the unenviable task of cleaning up the mess---a tough job when you have two brats running around.

Never one to shy away from a good time, Dad relished the nightlife of Madrid. During the summer between kindergarten and first grade, Dad often took me with him on one of his many early evening excursions along the cobblestone streets of Madrid's bar life.

Dad set me up at a table outside with a bowl of hot Spanish peanuts, and all the soda and candy I could consume without getting sick. It served as a distraction while he went inside to party, occasionally peeking his head outside to make sure I hadn't wandered off. That repeated itself many times during the summer of 64.

The señoritas that frequented these bars would spend hours sitting with me drinking and baiting men to sit and buy round after round. The ladies often bought my dinner, or made the men pay for it. Those ladies smelled good, were always nicely dressed, and pampered me like I was their child.

The señoritas hugged my narrow frame so tight at times I could lick the lotion off their partially exposed breasts. I looked forward to these excursions, constantly harassing Dad to take me along.

Dance and music is a way of life in Spain. Restaurants and bars often treated their guests to Flamenco dancers, and other forms of Spanish dance. Some performed on the street right in front of where I sat. The colorful dress and toe-tapping music drew huge crowds. The dancers often noticed me sitting alone, grabbing my hand to participate and teach.

Flamenco originated in the Andalusia region of southern Spain. Over time, it migrated north into Madrid, before spreading globally. Flamenco is a blend of Spanish folk music and dance, performed with amazing grace and power.

The clacking of castanets interspersed with powerful tap dance movements against the cobblestone streets, told stories I didn't understand. The well-choreographed lively movements left open to interpretation a particular dance, and its true meaning. Those who really knew the art formed discussed it for hours afterwards.

The señoritas usually walked me home because Dad simply forgot, too caught up in his own revelry. I lied to Mom about how I got home so Dad wouldn't get into trouble.

First grade came much too quickly for me, but provided Mom a semblance of comfort, knowing I couldn't hangout with Dad any longer.

Like Mom, I read everything I could get my hands on. I had an insatiable appetite for knowledge. During my preschool years, Mom often sat me down in the kitchen while she cooked dinner, or baked a cake, teaching me the alphabet. Once I mastered letters, she put basic words together until I could read cooking instructions. The cakes were always the fun part. Mom rewarded me with batter when I met or exceeded her expectations.

When I entered Royal Oaks, I was light years ahead of most of my classmates. The last hour of each day was devoted to Spanish lessons, but because I'd been in Madrid for over a year, the lessons came easy. The combination of Mom's teaching and Spanish exposure had me so well prepared; I grew bored with the pace of instruction. Instead of seeking a more useful outlet for my energies, I became a class clown of the highest order. My shenanigans ended when my butt had an encounter with the wrong side of Dad's belt.

Earlier that year (February 1964), the British rock group sensation The Beatles made their way to America for the first time. It certainly didn't go unnoticed in Madrid. The Beatles film *A Hard Day's Night* was released that summer. Dad treated us to the movies, the first time I'd ever been in a theater. The simplicity of a big screen showing a projected image in a darkened room captivated my imagination. The crowd became energized as Beatle mania swept the theater, many standing, clapping, or snapping their fingers to the beat.

Dad, the ultimate movie buff missed the opportunity to attend more films while we lived in Spain. He could recite word for word, lines from movies such as *Casablanca*, and the film's star, Humphrey Bogart.

"Here's looking at you, kid," and *"Where were you last night? That's so long ago, I don't remember,"* were among Dad's favorite lines. He used the last one on Mom when he stayed out too late.

Dad captured Bogart's voice, intonation, and mannerisms in exquisite detail. He had a special affinity for that particular film since he'd been stationed in Morocco, although the movie wasn't shot there.

Dad also had an infatuation with Latin music. He loved the drama, rhythms, and style the music evoked. It would be a toss up between Latin music and R&B for Dad. He brought back music from Spain often regaling us with his excellent vocals. He could have easily been a professional singer had his life taken a different direction.

I didn't know any of the Latin artists Dad followed in Spain, but later in life he shared with me his love of José Feliciano, the early music of Carlos Santana, and the Spanish language albums of Linda Ronstadt. Some time in the 1980s, I bought Dad Ronstadt's *Canciones De Mi Padre*, *Mas Canciones,* and the *Frenesi* album for a Christmas present. He memorized them all in Spanish and sang loudly and proudly over the phone.

Madrid represented everything one would want in life---freedom, love, excitement, and adventure. The food was great and the people were even better. Dad took to Spain like fire to dry brush; we all did. It fed his partying lifestyle, but just as important, it helped him relax. Spanish culture meant life was to be enjoyed and Dad submersed himself in it like no other.

One early afternoon, Dad made the trip to Pamplona to run with the bulls after having a little too much Spanish fun. For his exuberance and heightened state of inebriation, he was gored in the left leg leaving an ugly gash that took minor surgery to close. As much pain as he endured, his bruised ego suffered more. Dad was the only one in his group of drunken airmen who came away with a scratch.

With first grade now over, another summer of fun was upon us as Dad once again took his personal escort to the latest Madrid hotspots. Nightlife had returned to normal in my world, the señoritas rubbing their perfumes and sweaty bodies all over me.

Just before the start of second grade, Dad delivered disturbing news to our family. Orders had come; we were headed home. Dad's new assignment would deliver us to one of the coldest places in America; Loring Air Force Base, just minutes from the Canadian border, in Maine's northeast corner.

Dad's disappointment at our imminent departure nearly destroyed him psychologically. Our love affair with Spain had come to an unceremonious conclusion. It never occurred to me that life in Madrid could end, but end it did in November 1965, but not before the Gods of Madrid sent a few subliminal messages that suggested we should remain in Spain.

Mom was seven months pregnant with my little sister Amanda, the month we were set to travel. Against her obstetrician's rather stern advice, Mom decided she was going to travel with her family, ignoring pregnancy complications. Dad tried to convince her otherwise, looking for an excuse to either stay in Madrid, or come back. Mom wasn't swayed in the slightest.

On our last day, Dad gave Consuelo a rather substantial sum of money, which he had me deliver. At first she refused. Dad insisted, like a true salesman, that she take the money. With heavy tears flowing down her face, Consuelo accepted, hugging him for several minutes. I don't know what became of her, but she would be sorely missed.

As if we needed one more reason not to leave Madrid, our plane was at full throttle set to liftoff, when the pilot slammed on the breaks, bringing us to a screeching halt. Passengers were tossed about like rag dolls despite being strapped into our seats. Mom almost gave birth on the spot.

Armed security boarded our aircraft, grabbed a man by the collar and escorted him off the plane. His crime, he smuggled a small dog onboard.

Decades later, Mom admitted she was hesitant to come home. She knew just enough about the Civil Rights Movement to feel trouble loomed on the horizon, especially for me. At the time she couldn't predict how truly isolated living in northern Maine would become, shielding all of us from events in the South.

CHAPTER 2

IT'S FREEZING UP HERE

NOVEMBER 1965

We arrived at Loring Air Force Base just before the Thanksgiving holiday. A stiff breeze shot through the door of our temporary living quarters, as if, an EF-5 had stalled, frozen in place. The bitter cold and stiff wind penetrated everything it touched, chafing bare hands and stripping paint from buildings.

The outdoor temperature sat in the upper twenties with a wind chill hovering around the low single digits. A light snow had fallen leaving the roads and sidewalks somewhat slippery, but not impassable. Winter announced its impending arrival.

Our family needed to settle in quickly. Unfortunately, most of that fell on Dad's shoulders. Mom's pregnancy, and the fact that she didn't know how to drive, severely restricted her movements.

Dad had to register two kids for school, start his new

duty assignment, purchase more appropriate clothing for our new surroundings, help Mom find a doctor, start looking for furniture, Christmas shop, and eventually move us into more permanent housing. All of that needed to be done in less than a month.

We were ill prepared for the drastic change the cold wrought upon our bodies. By January, temperatures seldom reached twenty degrees, falling well below zero at night.

My parents' spent a small fortune on clothing at the BX (short for Base Exchange), the military version of Sears, JC Penney, or Target. Students here walked to school, making warm, waterproof clothing an absolute necessity.

Loring is tucked away in the northeast corner of Maine near a small town called Limestone. I could throw a snowball from my bedroom window on a windy day, and it would land somewhere near the border that separated Maine from the Canadian province of New Brunswick.

Loring is about as remote as one could get and still be in the lower forty-right. Interstate 95, the main north/south artery along the eastern seaboard, ended in Houlton, sixty miles to the south, before the road veered off into Canada.

Presque Isle, the areas largest town housed one of the only major department stores, a Sears, about twenty-five miles away. The population then, and now, stood at well under ten thousand.

Aroostook County is home of the famous Maine

potato. Numerous festivals commemorated the potato harvest before winter snows set in.

The beautiful wilderness featured caribou, eagles, deer, and great fishing. All this wildlife meant a robust hunting season, where I witnessed more than one hunter skinning and cleaning their trophies.

Winter sports, such as skiing on nearby Mt. Katadin, and snowmobiling along the many trails were one of life's great pleasures in this part of the world. We used the golf course at Loring for snowmobiling. The contours of the course, now buried under fifty, to one hundred inches of snow, provided easily identifiable trails to follow.

Established in 1947, Loring was carved out of those potato fields, much to the dismay of farmers in the area. The base proved of great strategic value during the Cold War.

Loring featured the longest runways in the United States and played host to a squadron of B-52s. Flying the shorter routes of the northern latitudes made it easy to reach the United Kingdom, other parts of Europe, or the old Soviet Union in hours instead of days.

At forty-six degrees north latitude, the winter solstice sunrise occurs around 7:15 a.m., setting before 4 p.m. leaving us eight hours of sunlight. That meant walking to school just as the sun peeked over the eastern horizon and heading home under the cover of darkness.

It also meant trudging through chest deep or higher snow if we didn't stay on cleared paths, all while battling wind chills at times well below zero. Snow accumulation is often measured in feet when a Nor'easter slams into the region. Average annual snowfall is one hundred fifty two inches. That's fifth on a list of snowiest places in America.

Snows can start in September, ending as late as early May.

During the summer solstice, bright sunlight poured through my bedroom window at approximately 4:30 a.m., setting around 8:30 p.m. with rays of sunlight lingering on the horizon for an hour or more after sunset.

We didn't have time to dwell on our heartache at leaving Spain. I joined my second grade class at Harrison Elementary a week after arriving at Loring. Fear of my new surroundings quickly evaporated. Friends came easy. We were just a bunch of bright innocent faces accepting life as it comes.

We celebrated Thanksgiving dinner at the NCO Club (Non-commissioned Officers Club). It would be another two weeks before we moved into 156 Foulouis Drive.

Fifteen days after entering our new home, my little sister Amanda was born---December 23, just one day after Mom's birthday. Mom came home with this new bundle of joy on Christmas Day.

I marveled at this tiny person gripping my little finger. I sat by her basinet for hours ignoring my gifts. This little soul who invaded my house slept quietly. Mom placed her in my arms for a few minutes. She fidgeted ever so slightly before returning to a deep and restful slumber. I'd never held a baby. When she got older, I teased her that I accidentally dropped her on her head, how else to explain her stubbornness.

Two black babies born in Maine six years apart, in two different parts of the state. My sister Karen was born in 1959, at the naval hospital in Kittery located in southern Maine. We were stationed at Pease Air Force Base, New Hampshire early in Dad's career, but the military hospital was located at a Navy base across the state line in Maine.

Our new home was a two-story attached structure on one side of a squared-off, U-shaped cluster of homes. The open end faced the street. Each leg had ten houses. The middle of the U was a grassy area about the size of a football field. During the winter months, snow piled so high, we could only see the rooftops of most homes from one hundred feet away.

Our particular building was an ugly off yellow edifice with red wood trim. On the front door of each home appeared a nameplate, painted yellow with black lettering. Engraved on the nameplate, the name and rank of the military member who occupied the premises. Ours read, "SSGT R.L. BENNETT" in all caps---Staff Sergeant Richard Lee Bennett.

Icicles the size of large stalactites hung from awnings and facades, often crashing to the earth either because of weight, or the winter thaw, making it especially dangerous if a jagged or sharp edge struck any part of the body.

Our garage was a detached, single-car, single-story structure just outside the back door. The garage sat just far enough away to make any wintertime journey treacherous. These garages were seldom used. Snow and ice accumulation left vehicles trapped for days.

Finally, turning back to the Christmas tree, I opened the most prized gift of my childhood, a beautiful white telescope with a black eye piece.

Our living room featured a huge window, a good five feet wide, four feet tall. I sat that telescope in position anxiously waiting nightfall. With the telescope came a book of easily identifiable points of interest, starting with the moon. Dad and I went from crater to crater, matching my book with the pictures.

After several minutes, I made out the Little Dipper, the Big Dipper, and Polaris, known by its more common name, the North Star. During the Apollo 11 lunar landing four years later, I wouldn't let the movers touch that telescope.

January typically brought with it the bitter cold. School was cancelled on my birthday in 1968, when the high temperature for the day reached a robust minus eleven degrees. Wind chill clocked in at fifty below.

Living so far removed from the rest of the United States, this region of Maine was like living in Canada. The locals didn't place much importance on racial strife, other than that brought to the area by U.S. service members.

My friends ran the gamut of racial and ethnic diversity. Only one kid was prohibited from playing with me, it just happened to be my next-door neighbor.

Once I got adjusted to the weather, cold ceased to restrict my activities, frequently risking frostbite in exchange for fun. No one ever explained to me the consequences of frostbite. I guess my parents' thought I would simply come indoors when I got too cold.

The thawing process started as a slow warm up, like stepping into a nice bath. It wasn't long before my extremities felt like someone had pounded needles into them. The pain from near frostbite was excruciating, lasting several minutes, yet I continually risked life and limb.

Snowmobiling, tobogganing, sledding, skiing, and digging tunnels under the snow were our favorite wintertime activities. Our slanted garage roof made an excellent launch pad, with snow accumulation so high; we just walked to the highest point and slid down.

Dad took to parking our car on the street avoiding the garage at all cost. Not only could a car get trapped in the garage, the alley that connected all the garages to the street were often piled with snow higher than the garage structure itself.

On the streets, snow blowers, in an attempt to clear the roads, buried everything in its wake. At times, cars and trucks were invisible, even with orange scuba diving flags attached to a vehicle's radio antenna. We gently poked through the mounds of snow with a long stick or pole until we hit something hard, then we started digging, an arduous, but necessary evil.

One particularly heavy snowstorm lasted for days. We couldn't open the front or back door to our house. Dad and I forced open an upstairs window; then took turns shoveling. It took us hours to reach the front door, at which point we had to use an ice pick to chip away the frozen stuff to open the door. For a nine-year-old, lifting heavy snow proved exhausting. I slept for a week afterwards, every muscle in my body screaming, no more.

During the snowmelt season, April, May, and June, we often ventured into the nearby forest and became trapped by deep ravines of impassible water runoff. The dark soft mud acted like quicksand swallowing anything that weighed more than a few pounds.

The streets of our neighborhood were often running torrents of water and slush by day, only to freeze at night leaving hazardous road conditions.

Dad started working part-time at the NCO Club to bring in extra money. His base military pay in 1966 was a whopping $278 a month. That's approximately $2,100 in 2014 dollars, not nearly enough to support a family of five.

Late one evening, as Dad drove home from work, he hit a large patch of ice left by that day's snowmelt. He slid across the road, slamming his powder blue Cadillac with the fish tail fin rear lights, into a huge pine tree. The accident totaled the car and nearly killed him. Dad was more hurt by the loss of that car, than the injuries he sustained. His reaction reminded me of the bullfight disaster in Spain.

For some reason, which to this day I can't explain, I became addicted to baseball. Living in Spain, I'd never seen a game on television. I guess since my friends played the sport, I did too. This was pre-Super Bowl days and the National Basketball Association (NBA), outside of Boston, New York, Philadelphia, and Los Angeles wasn't on the national radar.

One of our two television channels carried Boston Red Sox games from Fenway Park. Carl Yastrzemski, Jim Lonborg, Tony Conigliaro, George Scott, Rico Petrocelli, Reggie Smith---they were my team and became more so after the 1967 World Series loss to one of my childhood idols, St Louis Cardinal pitcher, Bob Gibson.

It pained me to learn years later, the Boston Red Sox were the last team to integrate in 1959, and even after that integration, it was alleged that racism played a role in the trading away of many black ballplayers.

My parents' bought me every baseball book they could find, quenching my thirst for everything baseball. I frequently read baseball encyclopedias with a flashlight under the cover of darkness after being sent to bed. It turned me into an eight-year-old baseball statistician. I could recite numbers and figures with the best baseball announcers.

Sports announcers and writers had a way of telling stories that captivated my imagination. Shakespeare, move over. I particularly loved the biographies of the famous old baseball players like Babe Ruth.

Dad found me a book about Jackie Robinson. I devoured its contents in one eight-hour sitting. The story of Robinson's life served as an introduction to black America. I realized, for the first time, black Americans hadn't always been welcomed, not only in sport, but society at large. It horrified me to learn how much abuse he tolerated just to play a game.

Baseball is how I learned everything. The sport was

my conduit to the outside world. I learned how to understand numbers and their true meaning from reading box scores. I practiced division and decimals calculating batting averages on reams of paper, killing my fair share of trees. I learned geography by studying maps once I discovered the city or town of a particular team.

I learned racial injustice through the story of Jackie Robinson. I also learned about the Negro Leagues and other black ballplayers denied opportunity, solely based on skin color. I didn't know what to do with this newfound piece of information about Robinson, other than to be thankful he blazed a trail for others to follow.

One year blended into the next as thoughts of Spain occasionally appeared in my subconscious. With no Spanish speakers around, I quickly lost the bilingual abilities my parents' were so proud of.

April 4, 1968 shattered my insular world once again. Dr. Martin Luther King, Jr., was murdered while I played at a friend's house. We had our army toys spread out on the floor while the television played in the background. A news flash announcing King's assassination appeared on the screen.

My playmate's father rushed to the television set, stepped over me as if I were a piece of dog excrement on a city sidewalk, and turned up the volume. "It's about time someone killed that nigger," he said. I'd never heard the word nigger. It took me a few minutes to process this man's contempt for Dr. King. If he hated that black man, what would he do to the little black boy sitting in his living room?

My playmate's mother, quickly realizing the error of her husband's ways, grabbed my coat and escorted me to the door. She hugged me as I exited their house, assuring me everything would be okay. I thought to myself, okay from what.

Mom's eyes were a shade of red I'd never seen before when I arrived home. She had just hung up the phone after speaking to Dad about the King assassination. I wanted to ask her what nigger meant, but now was definitely not the time. I simply ate dinner and went to my room and read baseball books.

That word gnawed at me for days. The next day at school was one of utter confusion. My fourth grade teacher wasn't sure how to handle a question from one of my classmates about Dr. King. Prior to his assassination, I'd never heard of Dr. King. For all I knew, he could have been a physician at the hospital where Dad worked.

I felt dumb for the first time in my life. I prided myself on being one step ahead of everyone. I hated the idea of not knowing. It was rather obvious my teacher, an African American woman, and several classmates knew about Dr. King.

I arrived home that evening determined. Who was this Dr. King fella, and why should I care? That probably sounds blasphemous to those in the black community. I bolted through the front door and made a beeline for Mom. "Who is Dr. King?" She patiently explained all she knew about this great man. The conversation lasted about an hour or so as she prepared dinner.

Dad arrived a few minutes later to eat. He changed out of his uniform into a suit for his night job as club manager. I figured dinner would be a good time to pop the big question. Dad was well read. In my mind, he knew everything.

I blurted out, "What is a nigger?" Mom made an audible gasp. The look on her face was one of sheer horror. Dad, slightly agitated, asked me where I heard the word. I told him, up to and including how my playmate's father uttered the phrase, "It's about time someone killed that nigger," with emphasis on "nigger" and the glee he felt at the death of Dr. King.

To Dad's credit, he took the time to explain nigger to me, causing him to be late for work. My parents' never used the word nigger at home. This would be the first and last time I ever said that word in our house. Use of the word nigger made Dad's blood pressure boil.

Dad's mood changed in a nanosecond. One minute he was cool, calm, and collected, explaining nigger to me; the next, his vein bulged from his head in fits of anger. "How dare that son-of-a-bitch use that word around my son," he said, as he cursed repeatedly for several minutes until leaving for work.

My friend Kevin, who sat next to me in class, either never understood his father's ugly comments, or didn't care. We played together outside the confines of his home as if nothing ever happened. Our friendship ended when his father was transferred later that summer.

Unfortunately, I wasn't done dealing with the "N" word. I played organized baseball for the first time in my life that summer. I wore those famous Yankee pinstripes proudly. During one of our games, a white woman, whose son played on our team yelled from the stands, "strike that nigger out." The words rolled effortlessly off her lips as if they'd always been there.

Dad, and many others in the stands, black and white were enraged by this woman's audacity. Dad was itching for a fight, but he certainly didn't believe in striking a woman. Mom grabbed his arm holding him in place. She'd decided to let the white parents deal with this woman, and deal they did.

The umpire stopped the game and had her escorted from the diamond. Whew! Disaster averted, Dad avoided a night in jail. As for my poor teammate, he sobbed uncontrollably like the ten-year-old he was, shocked at his mother's outburst. Poor kid never escaped his mother's transgression. At school, kids avoided him like the plague.

On our way home Dad launched into a tirade about the "N" word. I'd never seen him so passionate and angry simultaneously. He knew black people used that word as a sign of affection for one another. Some claimed using the "N" word took the sting and stigma away.

Dad wasn't having any of those shallow arguments. "That word ghettoizes us," he shouted at no one in particular. Dad thought blacks' use of the "N" word was a form of self-loathing. He looked into the rearview mirror at me sitting in the back seat, "If I ever hear you say that word, I will," Mom cut him off. It would be a few years before I heard the word nigger again.

Mom picked up the game of bowling at Loring when cold winter months forced most people indoors. The bowling alley was a cavernous dungeon partially submerged underground, to better protect the lanes from the bitter cold. Once or twice a month Mom and I bowled for fun. She taught me what little she knew at the time. Dad hated bowling. He thought bowling was for punks and not worthy of being called a sport.

After a few months, I found myself in a Saturday bowling league. My average that year was a measly 78.

Something about bowling had me hooked. *Was it a bond Mom and I shared? Could I ever excel at bowling?* I didn't have the answers, but I begged Mom to take me as often as time and finances permitted. After Saturday bowling, I ate lunch at the cafeteria until the afternoon movie matinee, a short, but cold walk from the lanes.

For $2, I could watch a double feature, and eat all the popcorn and candy my stomach could handle. I loved Juicy Fruits and root beer barrels. This was my ritual every Saturday from the fall of 1968 through spring 1969.

On Sunday it was off to church and Sunday school for Karen and me. We were raised Catholics, much to Mom's chagrin. She married into a Catholic family and agreed to raise us as such, despite her strong ties to the African Methodist Episcopal Church.

Dad, the product of the Catholic school system never set foot in a church with us, and Mom refused to attend Catholic services. So it was just the two of us, indoctrinated into something neither one of us understood, with absolutely no guidance.

I received my first communion at Loring, but understood nothing of its significance or meaning. *Who or what is God? What did it mean to me? Did Jesus truly die on the cross for our sins?* Religion remained a vacuum for years.

I walked into the confessional one day after school, having no idea what I was to confess too. I hadn't done anything wrong that warranted a confession. I made up a few lies to tell the Father just to play along. I thought confession was required, and I would get in trouble if I didn't confess to something.

My penance; a series of *Our Father's*, *Hail Mary's* and *Act of Contrition*. When I finally got to the *Act of Contrition*, I looked around at the dozen or so people in various states of prayer. I thought, *what's the point*, got up, and walked out. That would be the last confession I'd ever attend.

The best part of the whole church experience for me was the music---a blend of folk music and soft rock, with heavy guitar rhythms. The music were rewrites of many of the 1960s popular songs, such as Bob Dylan's, *Blowin in the Wind.*

The church services were stoic affairs filled with Catholic rituals. Parishioners sat ramrod stiff in the pews, like someone had administered a sedative upon entering. I felt detached; my mind drifting aimlessly from one thought to the next until the music started.

Sunday school started right after church services. Even as a ten-year-old, I felt manipulated and brainwashed. None of these teachings made any sense. Instructors skipped around from one part of the Bible to the next, struggling themselves, to make sense of it all. I often wondered; *why didn't they just start at the beginning with Genesis and move forward?* That was the way every other class I'd taken was taught.

By the time I hit my early teens, I presented an argument to Mom that relieved me of attending Catholic Church services ever again. Instead, I voluntarily attended a weekly youth gathering of high school students at the church that focused more on fellowship.

When not involved in bowling, baseball, church, or school, I participated in Cub Scouts. My precocious nature loved the challenge of earning those merit badges and the praise of my scoutmasters.

Our annual camping trip, the only one I participated in before we moved, took place during spring break, 1969. The snowmelt at lower elevations was in a full affect as rivers of water cascaded down slopes and mountainsides.

The rivers we crossed during our three-hour bus ride looked like whitewater rapids, even from the safety of the bridges.

Our cabin sat next to a lake. In contrast to the running torrents of snow runoff, the water near our cabin was placid and clear as glass. The sun glistened off the water surface, blinding anyone who dared peek without shading his or her eyes.

Nightfall brought a chill so deep we slept fully clothed inside our sleeping bags. We joked about using the outdoor facilities for fear our urine would freeze into icicles as it exited our bodies.

The smell of breakfast emanating from the clubhouse on a cool, crisp morning was the only thing that could move me from the warmth and comfort of my sleeping bag.

By noon, we were receiving instruction on paddling a canoe and what to do if it tipped over. Moments later we donned life vests and shoved off. The only disturbance to the peace and tranquility of this setting, fifty scouts screaming in excitement. I expected the lake to be partially frozen, but much to my surprise it was ice-free.

The only ripples in the water were our paddles calmly stroking the surface.

After a series of afternoon games, we sat around a campfire roasting marshmallows for hours. Our camp guides took turns telling us kids stories---some true, others only believable if you had the most vivid of imaginations.

As summer 1969 rapidly approached, Dad appeared restless. We spent four years in the Maine wilderness. I think the isolation made him stir crazy. He also hadn't been promoted in five years, something unheard of in the mind of Richard Bennett, a man possessed with drive and determination to succeed in the military.

Dad had reached a crossroads. He sat down with Mom to discuss his options. Leaving the military was out of the question; Dad an eleven-year veteran at that point. Nine more years and he could retire with benefits for life, not to mention, he had nothing else planned.

Dad knew he would be reassigned soon, but where. Dad went to the personnel office and submitted a list of eight places he would like to be stationed. In the Air Force, it's known as a "Dream Sheet." The military would try to assign you to a place of your choosing, provided the needs of the government were met first.

When nothing materialized, Dad made the decision to volunteer for Vietnam. How he convinced Mom, I have no idea, but she went along. It was highly probable he would be sent there anyway. As a hospital administrative type, he wouldn't be on the front lines, but close enough to smell death. A tour in Vietnam meant sure promotion.

CHAPTER 3

GOING HOME

JULY 1969

The God's of Creation fell in love with Maine. How else to explain the tapestry of exquisite beauty whizzing by as we drove south on U.S. Highway 1, headed for Interstate 95. The road cut through dense forest of Eastern White Pine trees as far as the eye could see, interrupted by the occasional river, creek, or small quaint town. The distant mountains, with light snow-covered peaks, looked spectacular silhouetted against the bright sky.

The lush vegetation my youth hadn't allow me to appreciate four years earlier, lay in front of me to soak in, as Dad expertly drove our Olds 98 toward New Hampshire.

Six hours later, we stopped in Portsmouth, home to Pease Air Force Base. We drove around reminiscing for an hour before nightfall stole our visibility. Dad found our old house, the drive-in movie theater, and the A&W we frequented so often during those early years. This was an old school A&W, with food delivered to our vehicle on a tray suspended from the car door by a couple of plastic-coated hooks so as not to scratch the paint.

Dad kept asking me if I remembered, of course I didn't, but I told him I remembered the smell of the A&W burgers, which was partially true. I was three-years-old when we left New Hampshire.

The following morning, Dad detoured to a nearby lighthouse overlooking the ocean where he took Karen and me as infants. We sat on rock cliffs as the crashing waves of the Atlantic Ocean roared through the cracks beneath our feet. The ocean mist dampened our bodies and obscured the view for a brief moment leaving behind a colorful rainbow. The ebb and flow of Mother Nature's awesome roar drowned out sound for hundreds of feet in any direction.

Approaching noon, Dad announced it was time to go. We had four hundred miles to cover---the distance to Atlantic City. We were all in good spirits, Dad especially, but lurking in the recesses of my mind, Vietnam. In less than three weeks Dad would be gone. *Would he come back injured? What would become of us if he didn't come back? How would Mom handle the bad news?* The fear of losing Dad became my constant companion.

Vietnam supplanted the Civil Rights Movement as the lead story on the nightly newscast. Dad, the quintessential information junkie left us strict instructions not to disturb him during the *Huntley Brinkley Report.*

My mere presence at home during the news hour made it impossible to ignore the all to frequent reports of dead U.S. soldiers. It's as if the war were fought in our living room. Vietnam stories were typically followed by war protest reports from cities and college campuses around the country.

Unlike the Civil Rights Movement, I was now old enough to understand Vietnam in all its ugliness and brutality. Death is final. *Why had Dad volunteered for duty in Southeast Asia?*

Muhammad Ali's outspoken and defiant stance against the draft, would soon find its way into my conscious. Up until now, I knew nothing about Ali, but Aunt Ethel quickly solved that problem. We would be staying at her house the year Dad spent in Nam.

Aunt Ethel, my father's aunt, was an avid boxing fan. Saturday night fights were a ritual in her home, and one she allowed me to share. With no DVRs in 1969, all she had were her memories of the "Greatest of All Time." Despite his exploits in the boxing ring, and his dashing good looks, Aunt Ethel was most impressed with Ali's stance against the war. She made it known to all; this was his greatest contribution to mankind.

The stench of marshland announced our arrival on Absecon Island, home to the towns of Margate, Ventnor, Longport, and Atlantic City.

We arrived in AC a few hours after dark. My eyes settled on the bright lights of the biggest city I could remember since Madrid. Dad found a radio station that played everything from the Four Tops and Temptations, to Diana Ross and The Supremes, and Stevie Wonder.

He cranked up the music and belted out song after song performing a live concert in the car. Dad had a great voice, and together, my parents' formed the perfect duet.

A few moments later we parked in front of 1307 Drexel Avenue. The hugs and kisses, the my mys and lordy lordys created a halo of love and goodwill over my grandparent's home, the likes of which I'd never experienced before.

My grandmother seemed particularly fixated on me, probably because I'd grown so much in four years. While short in stature at less than five feet, Granny had a presence about her that made it feel like she could look Kareem Abdul Jabbar in the eye. Love poured out of her, making it nearly impossible to quit hugging her long enough to let someone else enjoy her company. I was in a trance the minute we made eye contact.

Grandpop was a rock. A quiet man by nature, the pride that swelled in him at the sight of the wonderful family he and Granny raised exploded from his body. If I had to use one word to describe Grandpop, it would be integrity. He was honest, smart, hardworking, compassionate, and above all else, worshiped my grand-mother. We were indeed fortunate to have been born into such a wonderful family.

Granny was the undisputed matriarch by sheer force of personality. As the pastor noted during the eulogy at Grandpop's funeral service, Granny led Grandpop to heaven. Granny passed away in late January 2011, just forty days later, Grandpop followed her home. They were married for seventy-three years.

After a wonderful visit we headed to Cedar Inn. Cedar Inn was located off a busy four-lane highway called

Black Horse Pike in Pleasantville, about twenty minutes away. The property sat back about one hundred yards off the road, amongst a thicket of brush and a forest of evergreen trees. The marque announcing the inn was shaped like a huge Christmas tree trimmed in green lights, offset by red lettering. The nearest neighbor: a good half-mile away.

The gravel driveway had enough room to easily park seventy-five cars. Aunt Ethel and her family had owned Cedar Inn for decades. The inn attracted the black working class of the 1940s, 50's, and 60s. This three-story property had a rustic green exterior trimmed in brown wood.

The bottom floor featured a long wrap-around bar with enough seating for a dozen. Two pool tables dominated the cavernous space, with tables and chairs spread throughout. A jukebox and piano sat in one corner. There was enough floor space for fifty or more to dance the mash potato.

The second floor had twenty-seven rooms, a humongous kitchen, an elegant formal dining room, and a front room we used for television. The wooden floors were covered in some durable linoleum the squealed violently under the weight of an average sized human being.

Aunt Ethel was a fair-skinned black woman in her late seventies. Due to her advanced years, Cedar Inn had ceased being an inn a decade earlier. Those rooms sat vacant, piled with junk, beds, and assorted pieces of furniture at least twenty years old.

The third floor family quarters are where we lived. It had three large bedrooms and a bathroom the size of a full house. The bathroom featured a cast iron clawfoot tub that had seen its better days.

For the next two weeks we traveled back and forth between Pleasantville and Atlantic City, with occasional trips to the Boardwalk to enjoy the beaches, saltwater taffy, cotton candy, and the Steel Pier amusement park.

The day we all dreaded finally arrived, August 16, 1969. We watched Dad board a Trailways bus headed for McGuire Air Force Base, near Wrightwood, New Jersey. Next stop, Bien Hoa Air Base, Vietnam.

My parents' embraced for a long time forcing the bus driver to hurry them along. I tried to choke back tears, but I lost it, salty liquid streaming down my face. No sense in trying to hide my obvious grief. Gripped in fear, we all remained motionless until the bus moved well out of sight. Mom trembled. The reality of Vietnam had just become tangible.

Bien Hoa Air Base sat twenty miles outside Saigon---today Ho Chi Minh City. Saigon, the largest city in then South Vietnam, had a population well over five million. Bien Hoa received an inordinate amount of media attention due to its proximity to Saigon and the international airport---the jumping off point for many U.S. service personnel.

Saigon marked the point of entry for the reporters I had grown to despise for bringing so much death into my living room. Yet, it was these reporters I depended on for any news of Bien Hoa. I'd adopted Dad's habit of watching the nightly news. Mom stayed away from television news, quick to retreat to one of her books during the broadcast.

In 1969 troops starting leaving Vietnam in droves.

First, it was thirty-five thousand the month after Dad arrived, then another fifty thousand that December. In April 1970, President Nixon ordered another one hundred fifty thousand troops out within a year. I prayed Dad would be on the first list, but his recent arrival guaranteed he wouldn't be headed home anytime soon.

Days after President Nixon's troop reduction announcement, he ordered an incursion into Cambodia. Now, I worried Dad's tour would be extended, but by June 1970, he had orders in hand to come home.

In the year Dad served in Nam, nearly nine thousand of our nation's bravest warriors lost their lives. Dad said he survived twenty-two direct rocket attacks; otherwise, he shared nothing of his experience in Vietnam with the family.

H. Russell Swift Elementary sits in a rural community about six miles from Cedar Inn, near a golf course where Dad caddied and performed various clubhouse duties as a teenager. The owners of this white's only golf course had no clue Dad was at least part black. Dad was able to "pass"---light skin color, straight hair, and perfect English.

Three of the thirty-three students in my sixth grade class were black. Some classes had no black students. Friends were hard to come by, in large measure because of our rural setting. Jimmy was my only friend in the early days. His parents' owned a business similar to Cedar Inn that catered to the white working class.

Once or twice a week after school, I hopped on my bike for the thirty-minute ride to his house risking life and limb on the shoulder of Black Horse Pike, where cars flew by at fifty-five plus miles per hour. We played for a few hours, before I made the trek back to Cedar Inn under the cover of darkness---a very dangerous journey without lights in dark clothing.

Jimmy's place looked a lot like Cedar Inn. By the time I arrived, the working class whites had already filled the tavern. Jimmy's parents generally ignored me; probably satisfied he had someone to keep him company. He never made a trip to Cedar Inn, which had me curious. *Were we friends? Did his parent's think I lived in a black community, and Jimmy would therefore be unwelcomed? Or was it simply a matter of safety concerns given the distance between our houses?*

Recognizing our relationship turned into a one-sided affair in more ways than one; I curtailed my ventures to his house. Not once did he inquire why I stopped coming. I guess I had a premonition I might not have been welcomed.

I spent hours standing on the front porch in solitude swinging a baseball bat pretending to be the game's top players---Roberto Clemente and Hank Aaron one minute, Mickey Mantle and Willie Mays the next. I studied their swings as if conducting a science experiment. I adopted every mannerism, up to and including pretending to wear spikes, obliterating the chalk marks of the batters box, or spitting, if that's what a famous player did.

Boredom doesn't being to explain life at Cedar Inn for a twelve-year-old. Heidi, our dachshund was about the only thing that broke up the monotony. This twenty-pound dynamo put the fear of God into anyone who dared to enter Cedar Inn, scaring off many of Aunt

Ethel's patrons. But this beautiful, short brown-haired, four-legged critter was a precious soul who wouldn't harm a flea. That's what all dog owners say, but in Heidi's case, it was true.

My weekends, when we didn't go to AC, were spent in front of the television watching baseball. I had lots of games to choose from in addition to the Saturday game of the week. Philadelphia was just forty-five minutes west, New York City two hours north, and Baltimore three hours south.

The Philadelphia Phillies of 1970 were a less than average squad, finishing near the bottom in their division. I became a fan anyway, catching most of their games on one of the Philadelphia channels broadcast in Atlantic City.

I continued bowling while living at Cedar Inn. Not wanting to burden Mom at 8 a.m. on a Saturday morning, I hung my bowling bag around my bicycle handle bars, peddled down Black Horse Pike arriving at Northfield Lanes sweating, freezing, or out of breath.

After league play concluded, I spent whatever money remained practicing alone. Bowling had unwittingly become my companion. I didn't care about improving; it was an activity that for a few brief hours provided a respite from isolation and lack of consistent human contact.

I spent the remainder of my time reading books or putting two thousand-piece puzzles together. Mom and I read so much; our frequent trips to the bookstore were measured in days not weeks. Between the two of us we came home with a dozen books.

Cedar Inn was no place for kids, especially someone

accustomed to roaming freely. I felt like a caged animal under sedation with no means of escape.

After school, but before the evening crowd of workers arrived for their nightly libations, Aunt Ethel had me help her stock the bar. That included going into a dark, dingy, spider and rat-invested cellar buried in the woods behind Cedar Inn, to retrieve cases of beer and anything else that need refrigerating. She had no dolly, so I had to roll the kegs on their side to a spot behind the bar, and then the two of us would lift the heavy liquid-filled metal containers into their proper place.

The loud music and drunken patrons stumbling out of Cedar Inn on Friday and Saturday kept me awake more times than I can count. Aunt Ethel allowed those revelers too drunk to drive, to crash in one of the empty rooms free of charge. The following morning a parade of strange disheveled men rushed home to explain to their significant others where they slept that night.

Some of their wives didn't wait for an explanation, making their way to the Cedar Inn parking lot for a direct confrontation. I saw more than one man get the daylights slapped out of him from my bedroom window.

Aunt Ethel also cooked for her patrons on weekends. Chicken wings were by far the favorite dish, especially during Saturday night fights. About once a month she busted out a pot of chitterlings. If it wasn't the boisterous bar patrons who ran us out, it was the God-awful smell of chitterlings cooking on the stove.

On chitterling Saturdays we escaped to my grandparents' house, followed by a date Sunday morning with St. James AME Church.

Granny worked at St. James for thirty-five years as

church secretary and Sunday school teacher. Unlike the somnambulant Catholic services at Loring, St James was festive. Jesus was being celebrated.

The screaming and hollering, primarily from the women of the church, startled me at first. I actually thought someone had fallen or gotten hurt. I'd never witnessed the explosion of emotion of a black church.

When the spirit moved them, parishioners unabashedly rose from their seats. Some symbolically passed out in front of me as if being hit by a bolt of lightening from the hand of God. Others lifted their arms, palms pointed skyward in a symbol of acceptance of God's teaching.

The pews were full of people who saved their best outfits for Sunday. The ladies of the church were adorned in colorful hats, with equally beautiful dresses; some doused in more perfume than the human nose could handle choking everyone in the vicinity. Men wore the finest suits they owned, shoes polished to a fine sheen, pocket-handkerchiefs perfectly positioned.

No matter what happened Saturday night, Sunday was meant for prayer and worship. Our Catholic services lasted an hour. At St. James, if the service ended in less than two hours, parishioners acted as if they had been cheated.

Like my previous church, music provided the glue that held everything together. The choir, led by Granny, one of the four soloists, was a harmonic masterpiece of gospel music. We jumped out of our seats with such ferocity the floor shuddered like we'd been struck by a magnitude seven earthquake. The sound of music reverberated from the walls of the church, cascading onto the street for those outside to enjoy.

St. James was the epitome of the true black experience; the energy palpable, spirits high, and everyone appeared festive as they worshipped. Weekdays I played a rural black kid in a predominantly white school, on Sundays it was the black church; followed by a sumptuous meal Granny spent hours preparing the night before.

For the first time in my life I though I understood a little about black America. The north side of AC had very few whites unless you walked to the Boardwalk where the tourists hung out, and even then, no one bothered us, we simply blended in as if race never mattered.

After dinner we crowded onto the front porch to rest and observe the happenings along Drexel Avenue. More often than not, Granny, Grandpop, and Mom dosed off in their chair, snoring on occasion drawing a quick round of laughter from those still awake. Grandpop always broke into laughter when Granny's body fell limp from exhaustion, her neck practically snapping off at the shoulders as she snored loudly.

The kids across the street played music loud enough to rattle neighborhood windows, but no one seemed to mind. The Jackson 5 burst onto the scene that year and even the adults could be found taping their feet. During more quiet times, Grandpop would disappear indoors to play his prized collection of music from the Big Band and Swing era. Something about the sound fascinated me. Like the church experience, it was rich and alive. The music told a story.

I'd never seen this many black people in my life. These kids weren't rioting in the streets as depicted on the nightly news reports; they were just living life to the fullest.

Television news had few positive portrayals of African Americans. Unlike the music industry, news and television struggled to find a voice, an appropriate balance between the growing black consumer base, and its programming.

A couple of exceptions: the television series *Julia*, starring, Diahann Carroll debuted on NBC in 1968. It was the first non-stereotypical role featuring an African American woman in television history. Carroll played a nurse and single mother who lost her husband in Vietnam. Talk about hitting close to home. Mom's eyes stayed glued to the television screen on the night this program aired.

The other exception to the lack of positive portrayals on television: *I Spy*, starring Robert Culp and Bill Cosby. It went off the air in April 1968 after three years, but before Dad left for Vietnam, they were *I Spy* fanatics. Dad felt a certain kinship to Cosby since they both spent part of their youth in the same Philadelphia neighborhood, although, to my knowledge, they never met. Cosby is two years older than Dad.

The Tom Jones Show was another Mom favorite. His program debuted on ABC in 1969, and was must see TV for Mom. I still remember the diamond-studded ring Jones wore on the show's opening scene---a tight shot of his hand as he grasped the microphone. His pants were so tight it left little to the imagination. Censors of that era must have had some heated discussions behind closed doors. The show featured virtually every top performer of the day from Bob Hope to Stevie Wonder, Ella Fitzgerald and Janis Joplin.

Candice was the definition of a tomboy and my best friend in sixth grade. This beautiful white girl with blond hair that always smelled freshly washed had my back.
She was a pint-sized Madea who always fought to protect me from harm. The two of us made a dynamite team, hitting as hard as we got hit. She was tough with no fear of boys twice her size.

The attacks on me usually started when the school bus arrived, and extended to recess, during lunch, and occasionally on the bus ride home. It was always the black students who delighted in making my life miserable, pummeling me with any hard objects capable of inflicting maximum pain.

Mom hated fighting; in fact, she might have been the ultimate pacifist. Dad on the other hand was a brawler. Any punch thrown in my direction must be countered with a barrage that left no doubt the outcome. If I didn't fight back, I knew Dad would punish my inaction in ways I can't even fathom.

Mom's dam of passivity broke two months into the school year when a boulder found its way to my mouth at the hands of one of my assailants. My surgically repaired face required several stitches from lip to chin. My gums had wire stiches and four teeth were reset. I sucked food through a straw for days, followed by soft foods until my stitches were removed. Mom was furious. A trip to school offered a brief respite, only to have the assaults begin again in earnest once my face healed.

Mom gave me her permission to fight back. I felt liberated. During recess, teachers organized a game of flag football. Knowing I would be a target for a different kind of sport, I decided then and there to make my stand.

I found a target, the kid who disfigured my face. Without his friends to protect him, I made a beeline for his chest barreling into him with the full force of my one hundred thirty pound frame. I flattened him in a fit of rage I didn't know I possessed. His head hit the ground with an awful thud. My rage quickly turned to fear thinking I killed him, but I wasn't all that remorseful. I stood over him for a moment as teachers rushed to his aid.

The next thing I know, Mom's straight "A" student was sitting in the principal's office looking for an escape. Mom arrived with my three-year-old sister in tow. The target of her venom wasn't me; it was a school system that allowed her son to get beaten on a daily basis without consequences. She had me lift my shirt to show the principal my bruised ribs. After a few more questions, I was sent into another room while the principal and Mom spoke.

Unsure of the exchange between the two, I assumed I would be suspended, or worse yet brought up on criminal charges---neither happened.

Candice took it upon herself to be my bodyguard sitting next to me on the bus ride to school the following morning. Not sure what to expect, she came prepared just in case, carrying nunchucks in her bag. The tomboy in her itched for a brawl.

Exiting the bus, we were both on high alert. Nothing happened. Teachers positioned themselves at strategic locations around the buses and ushered everyone to class. School policy now prohibited anyone from congregating around the bus drop-off zone, the place where most assaults began.

Candice stayed by my side for the remainder of the school year. We stayed connected even after school, finding places to meet, hold hands, and remain in constant physical contact. She even took my baseball glove home with her at night as a keepsake, bringing it to school in time for a game at recess.

The black students took to calling Uncle Tom so many times, I truly wondered if I had an uncle named Tom. I didn't even know what Uncle Tom meant. Despite all the books I'd consumed, I'd never read the one book that could have shed light on the intended insult, Harriet Beecher Stowe's 1852 classic novel, *Uncle Tom's Cabin.*

It took me years before I figured out why I'd become so reviled. The well-dressed, smart, tall black kid, and teacher's pet had inadvertently appeared arrogant and condescending to every black student in school, often embarrassing them in front of others.

I was neither arrogant nor condescending. I simply didn't know any other way to behave. Dad drilled in me to always do my best, for Richard Bennett, second place may as well have been last place.

I didn't have anything in common with my black classmates except skin color. I rubbed their face in my early life benefits oblivious to what I had done, naïve to think everyone had my life advantages. Yet at the end of the day, some of their problems were my problems---a lesson I soon learned the hard way.

Eventually the deep freeze of hatred thawed. While not everyone embraced the tall kid from the other side of the tracks, I found myself making friends. Some parents even approached me about tutoring their kids, a task I relished. Now these kids were on my turf and I made the rules. Of course kids being kids, we spent most of our time goofing off and acting silly.

Payment for my services took the form of friendship and lots of well-cooked meals. Unfortunately, those who sought me out for help became the object of scorn and ridicule enduring the same taunts and cries of Uncle Tom as I had.

Mom usually received letters from Dad once a week. They were lengthy affairs, difficult to read. Dad's handwriting made that of a doctor look like a Picasso painting. Mom finally convinced him to type, which he dutifully did.

By early May, with school winding down, Mom received her weekly letter. She ripped open the envelope and devoured it's content in minutes, then handed me one page to read. It said, "Pack your bags, we are moving to Tyndall AFB, Florida. I have to report by August 30, 1970."

Mom and I shared a look as only mother and son could. Our year in isolation had an end date. We quickly shared the news with Aunt Ethel, my sisters', and Granny and Grandpop.

Later that evening we visited AC for a family meal, when I finally asked the obvious question, "Where is

Tyndall Air Force Base?" None of us knew. I learned geography through baseball. I sifted through newspapers daily, paying particular attention to location usually located in the byline---"AP-New York" or "UPI-Boston." When I didn't know about a city, I grabbed a map or encyclopedia, studying the city and surrounding community for hours. I learned all fifty states and their capitals because of baseball, but I'd never run across Tyndall in my readings.

Grandpop went to the front room and pulled out an atlas. He quickly turned to the Florida page and left me to discover the whereabouts of our new home. After a few minutes, he reappeared noting the look on my face. I was stumped. Grandpop realized Florida was so large and awkwardly shaped the panhandle section was on a different page.

Grandpop flipped the page, and in less than a minute, he found Tyndall. It sat just outside of Panama City, right on the Gulf of Mexico. Mom and I were ecstatic---a warm weather climate had come our way. Atlantic City had great beaches, but it got cold in the winter.

At school the following Monday, I found it difficult to contain my excitement. Parole was imminent. Candice on the other hand took our impending departure hard. The thought of ending our budding relationship had a little sting to it. Like most young kids with good intentions, we vowed to stay in touch since I would always have a connection to the area through family. Yet I knew, like all previous military moves, I would never see her again. Moving from place to place proved a difficult concept to grasp for those unaffiliated with the military.

As the final days of the school year approached, Aunt

Ethel told Mom she sold Cedar Inn. The news caught us off guard. Aunt Ethel had decided to retire. We had two weeks to find a place until Dad returned.

Next thing I know, we found ourselves jammed into my grandparents' Drexel Avenue home. Granny and Grandpop's home was a two-story row house common in many east coast cities, with a narrow alley out back to allow for trash pickup and other city services.

Crime in the area was rampant. Most homes, like theirs, had a dog in the backyard to alert owners of potential intruders. Somehow Karen, who I affectionately call the "Dog Whisperer," managed to tame Sugar enough to sit on the paved back porch and visit for a few minutes every day. Sugar was a black mixed breed of some kind with a ferocious bark that belied her small stature.

A few blocks away sat a Sunbeam bread store. The pleasing aroma of fresh baked bread wafting through the open doors and windows, elicited a warm homey feel to an already warm and loving home. Granny shopped at Sunbeam on occasion with me in tow. We brought home day old bread and an assortment of sweets meant to feed the Hicks and Bennett clan's voracious appetite for sugar and pastries.

Just down the street, less than a block away from our home sat the typical vacant city lot. The fenced lot had weeds and trash so high one needed a helicopter to see the other side. Across from the vacant lot sat a Miller beer distributorship.

Directly across the street from my grandparents' home was a faded red brick building that looked more like a warehouse. It appeared abandoned most of the time, but, was in fact, a Pentecostal church.

Several streets leading from Drexel Avenue to the Boardwalk featured more run down lots, dilapidated or abandoned buildings, and several bars with drunken patrons pouring onto the streets. All of this was unfamiliar territory. I grew to be somewhat fearful and warned on several occasions not to wander from home alone. I ignored Mom's admonition twice earning myself two weeks of house arrest.

Atlantic City did have its good points. AC was host city for the Miss America pageant and parade, a parade we proudly attended in 1969. The city's large convention center played host to boxing and special events such as the Ice Capades. AC is also famous for the board game Monopoly. Most of the streets on the game are Atlantic City landmarks.

But the most popular landmark in the BC era (before casinos) was, and is, the Boardwalk. The amusement parks on Steel and Million Dollar Pier, cotton candy and taffy shops, nearby hotel nightclubs, and the cool waters of the Atlantic Ocean, made the Boardwalk the place for entertainment and fun along the eastern seaboard.

Grandpop worked for the Public Works Department as head foreman for the Boardwalk division. He was partly responsible for keeping the Boardwalk operational.

Time flew by once we moved to AC. My cousins from Cleveland came for a visit. Sharing a bedroom with five girls was torture, but I learned so much about life outside a military installation just by hanging with them. We were family getting along like we'd lived under the same roof our entire lives.

After they left, I took to playing with a girl next door about my same age. She was sweet, smart, and very proper---the most beautiful black girl I'd ever met. When she rubbed up next to me, the scent from her body lotion lingered in my clothing for hours. We spent weeks sitting on the front porch talking about my life beyond Atlantic City. She was dreaming, making plans for the future.

By far the best memories of those few months in Atlantic City took place in the wee hours of the morning. Grandpop arrived at work around 4 a.m. Once or twice a week, he would roust me from a deep slumber and feed me breakfast. Afterwards, I escorted him to work, making small talk with his co-workers until sun up. Sunrise meant freedom to explore.

Grandpop gave me $5 to enjoy the sites and sounds of the Boardwalk with instructions to return by 1 p.m. for the walk home. Not much was open at 5:30 a.m. One bike rental facility cracked its doors just long enough to provide me with transportation, most of the time free of charge.

I made my way to the north end of the Boardwalk where a lighthouse sat by a small inlet leading to the open Atlantic. I watched quietly as fishermen headed out for the day with a flock of birds hovering above looking for a free meal.

By 7 a.m., I'd made my way to the other end of the Atlantic City Boardwalk, about four miles. On my return, I'd stopped in donut and pastry shops for a quick bite and told it was on the house. I was Harry's grandson. Shop owners, white and black loved him, and as an extension me.

I made it to Steel Pier as shops, restaurants and amusement ride owners prepared for their daily activities. Often, I would help carry boxes and supplies making myself useful in exchange for their companionship. My reward was usually free rides and food.

By 10 a.m., beach lovers and sun worshipers had taken to the sandy shores. At age twelve, I began to feel urges I later understood to be puberty. Bikini clad women as far as the eye could see.

I didn't know anything about sex, but the bulge in my pants told my mind something it couldn't quite comprehend. I found myself somewhat embarrassed by my body's reaction to women twice my age.

By noon, every tourist on the planet must have descended on the Jersey Shore. No longer able to ride my bike, I returned it to the shop and assisted the merchants with little errands until time to walk home.

When I handed Grandpop back most of his money, he assumed I didn't have a good time, quite the contrary; I had a blast all thanks to him. The freedom being on that beach, while lonely at times, allowed me to appreciate my surroundings and study human nature like never before.

Seeing black and white families side by side enjoying AC made me happy. This was how things should be.

Dad returned in early August. His physical appearance hadn't change, but even from a distance, I could see his countenance had.

After hugging Mom for a few minutes, he embraced us kids one by one before entertaining Granny and

Grandpop for hours, but he looked haggard. Jet lag had supplanted the adrenalin rush of seeing his family. He needed sleep.

For the next two days I never saw Dad for more than five minutes. Even Mom kept her distance, allowing his circadian rhythm to adjust to an eleven-hour time zone change. Constant fear and a steady state of alertness had given way to deep REM sleep.

Unfortunately, little sister was too young to understand what Dad had gone through. She received the spanking of her four-year-old life for screaming at the top of her lungs when everyone told her to be quiet. I'd never experienced Dad's wrath like that, spanked yes, but this seemed particularly brutal. *Was that the remnants of war affecting his behavior? Would this be what we could expect in the future? How did someone adjust to a more tranquil environment after experiencing firsthand so much death and carnage?*

I stayed out of Dad's orbit, even after his body adjusted to Eastern Standard Time. I think he recognized my fear; playfully grabbing me around the neck, tenderly punching me in the gut. It was the first time he called me "big daddy," a term of endearment that stuck with me for the rest of my life. That was the man I knew.

I'd grown seven inches the year Dad spent in Nam. We were now both six feet tall. That must have been disconcerting to him; it most certainly was to me. My growth spurt served as a constant reminder of all he'd missed. *How do you get a missed year back?*

With a week of rest under his belt, Dad prepared to head south, but not before a visit to his Aunt Doris in Philadelphia. She was one of the many who helped raise him. We spent three days in West Philadelphia. There were so many black people around I thought we drove to Africa.

Aunt Doris ran a foster care center with eight to ten kids at any given time under her care. She was a disciplinarian of the highest order, quick to get a belt for any infraction of the rules---a display of power she executed right in front of me to an eight-year-old who stepped out of line. Aunt Doris weighed in excess of three hundred pounds. The size differential added to the macabre scene played out before my eyes. Mom and I were appalled at the ferocity of the spanking.

We didn't venture from Aunt Doris' house for three days. Dad, knowing I was a fish out of water forbade me from leaving the front porch. I simply read books and played with my younger cousin Vanessa, who I met for the first time.

The huge petri dish of poverty I witnessed driving in sickened me. Never had I seen so many poor people, and they were all black. Houses leaning to one side from slipped or cracked foundations, drunks and drug dealers sharing the same corner with babies in strollers, boarded up buildings, trash strewn about, lawns in dire need of care, and stray dogs roaming the neighborhood scavenging whatever they could find to eat.

My cushy Leave it to Beaver-esque life just received a jarring reminder of the fragility of life and how fortunate I was Dad joined the military. While AC had its poverty, nothing compared to what I witnessed in Philly. It looked like the forgotten corner of hell.

ACT 2

SCHOOL'S IN

CHAPTER 4

THE UNKNOWN FAMILY

AUGUST 1970

My breathing was short and shallow, the air heavy. It was an utterly miserable day along the South Jersey shore. Flags hung limp from high atop their perch. Perspiration flowed freely drenching my cloths. Not even the typically cool Atlantic Ocean breeze offered respite from the scorching mid-morning sun, because on this day, there was no hint of the slightest zephyr. What's a beach without a breeze? The drive south in a car without air conditioning would push the misery index to an all time high.

We packed the car with a hundred pounds of luggage and new stereo equipment Dad shipped from Vietnam. My profound sadness at saying goodbye to my grandparents' was tempered somewhat, by what I perceived to be an exciting new adventure on the horizon.

Dad drove west to pick up Interstate 95 near Philadelphia. We were headed to his birthplace, Baltimore, to visit his mother, a stranger to everyone but Dad. We completed the journey in three hours arriving early afternoon.

Grandma Jean looked radiant in a colorful floral patterned dress, perfectly highlighting her light black skin, and long flowing locks of salt and pepper hair. Tears of happiness dampened her cheeks at the sight of Dad. Behind her effusive praise and outpouring of love for our family, I detected a sense of sadness in Grandma Jean's eyes.

Dad succeeded despite the many obstacles before him. He had a good family, married into a great family, had a satisfying career, and was highly intelligent, all with little direct help from his mother. Grandma Jean appeared to be experiencing a collision of emotions uncertain which should take the dominant position.

Grandma Jean married several years after Dad's birth to a gentleman with the bedside manner of a rabid pack of wild dogs. While he did his best to remain cordial during our one-night stay, it proved a struggle. He treated us with a measure of reserved contempt.

Dad had two half-brothers. One I bonded with immediately despite our different backgrounds. The two of us were less than a year apart in age.

They lived in a two-story townhome with a full basement located in West Baltimore, the epicenter of the city's black community, not far from Martin Luther King, Jr., Blvd., on Gwynn Falls Parkway.

Two years earlier, Baltimore suffered through four days of rioting following the murder of Dr. King. When all was said and done, over eleven thousand Maryland National Guard troops were called into the city, many in this neighborhood.

I overheard a brief discussion about the riots amongst the adults. It wasn't a pretty picture. Grandma Jean's husband John carried lots of residual anger. He made some rather disparaging remarks about white people that made my parents' cringe. His comments were better left unchallenged, lest we plan to spend the night in a hotel.

The route Dad chose to bring us into Baltimore featured lush green rolling hills, wide streets with grassy medians, and row house after row house of mostly manicured lawns.

Then we arrived in the black community. Remnants of the riots were evident; rows of burned buildings, boarded-up homes with black soot extending up the façade and trash-covered lots. This scene was marginally better than what I observed in West Philadelphia a few weeks earlier.

I wondered if Baltimore, Philadelphia, and Atlantic City were the true black America I'd been shielded from my entire life? *What was expected of me? How did I fit in?* I screamed inside for someone to provide direction.

Later that afternoon, Dad went to see his hero, my great grandfather. This was the one person Dad talked so much about over the years, I felt like I knew him before our arrival. It would be the first and only time we met. This man was everything Dad bragged about and more. He had a gentle gracious spirit about him that soothed my troubled soul. Seeing the two of us together might have been the most gratifying moment of Dad's life.

Grandpa Lee was in his late seventies, born just before the turn of the twentieth century. This distinguished looking man with fair complexion had features that left little doubt he and Dad were kin. Grandpa Lee's wavy white hair sat perfectly cropped on top of a narrow six-foot frame.

Grandpa Lee and Dad would sneak into white-owned movie theaters and other establishments around Baltimore in the 1940s because they could both "pass"---the benefit of looking white in a segregated city.

I'm not sure what Grandpa Lee did for a living, but at one point in his career he worked at Memorial Stadium, the old home of the Baltimore Orioles baseball team.

As the sun started to set, we left Grandpa Lee's, but not before he gave me a gift I cherished for years. He presented me with a rather expensive pair of sunglasses. These weren't just any sunglasses; these were the designer pair perched on his nose when we met a few hours earlier. As he handed me the glasses, he cupped both my hands with his warm gentle touch and told me, "take care of them." He pulled his hands away sobbing uncontrollably.

I wore those glasses all the way to Florida then stored them away never to be worn again. I stood sentry over those glasses like a security guard watches over the nation's gold reserves at Fort Knox. Two years later Grandpa Lee would be gone shattering Dad's world.

When Grandma Jean became pregnant with Dad, at age fifteen; it was Grandpa Lee who insisted she carry Dad to term, no other option existed, especially for a Catholic family. It was Grandpa Lee who advocated for Dad's adoption by an adult family member to protect him from harm, and provide a nurturing home. Dad spent the school year with Aunt Sue and summers with Grandpa Lee and his mother.

The big mystery still remains, the identity of Dad's

biological father. Grandpa Lee, his mother, and other family members took that secret to their grave, emotionally scaring Dad forever. This gap in Dad's family tree became the perpetual sore that never healed. Given Dad's skin complexion, many assumed over the years his father was white.

It's equally true his father could have been a person of color. Both his mother and grandfather were of fair complexion with features typically associated with Caucasians. While both were darker than Dad, somewhere in our lineage, like most black descendants of slaves, its highly probably someone is the progeny of a slave master.

Dad's love of Latin music predated our arrival in Spain, especially Latin Jazz and ballads. His affection for Latin music was only surpassed by his total immersion in Motown and R&B. Many mistakenly thought Dad was a Latino, especially when we lived in Spain, due to his musical tastes. Spanish was one of several languages he spoke fluently.

I also heard Dad called Puerto Rican, Cuban, and Italian. If the ignorant among us discovered Dad had been stationed in Morocco, I'm certain they would have added Arab to the mix of mistaken cultural identities. People were quick to try to place Dad in a category, and they all missed the mark.

When Dad filled out the myriad paperwork of a government employee, the forms always asked racial identification. When he checked the box marked black, or Negro, as we were called back then, a sergeant thought he ticked the wrong box. It angered Dad at times that others couldn't wrap their brain around Dad's blackness; nevertheless, Dad wore his African American heritage with pride, never shy to share his true lineage.

CHAPTER 5

WELCOME TO DIXIE

Dad decided to drive us downtown for a history lesson before departing Baltimore. Located on the banks of the Patapsco River, Baltimore's inner harbor has been a major seaport for centuries. Generations of early Americans, including slaves ships, navigated this offshoot of Chesapeake Bay.

Dad, the world's foremost history buff, delighted in sharing the story of The War of 1812 and Fort McHenry, where Francis Scott Key penned the Star Spangled Banner. "Babe Ruth was born here," Dad said. Baltimore is also the one time home of abolitionist, author, and orator Frederick Douglass.

Thirty-five years later, I introduced Dad to Frederick Douglass IV in the Fells Point section of Baltimore as part of a television program I produced. Talk about the spitting image of his great great grandfather. Dad almost fainted.

Dad knew a great deal about Baltimore's black

history, but chose not to share the ugly parts, drifting off into momentary silence as he reflected back. He did drive us past the white-owned movie theater he and his grandfather frequented during his youth. He laughed uncontrollably at the memory like he'd gotten away with a high stakes robbery.

With the tour now complete, the "Bennettmobile" headed to Dixie. We traveled south once again on Interstate 95. The rolling green hills of Virginia had my attention, eyes riveted to each passing landmark. Dad was the only one in our family to have ever traveled south of the Mason Dixon Line.

The smooth pavement cutting through these hills seemed a minor disturbance to the peace and tranquility of Mother Nature's creation.

The warm breeze blowing through the windows felt refreshing in contrast to the ninety-degree temperature and high-humidity.

Just south of Richmond, we transitioned to Interstate 85 towards Charlotte, North Carolina. We drove several hours after nightfall before Dad decided he had had enough for one day. He found a roadside hotel just off the interstate near Greensboro. Nothing fancy, just a nice clean room with two beds and an outdoor kennel for dogs.

I always hated hotels when we traveled as family. Mom and Dad had one bed; my sister's got the other, me, the floor. My lower back screamed its displeasure the following morning.

All was quiet around 10 p.m. when Heidi let the world know she was none too happy stuck in an outdoor kennel. A call from the front desk jolted us awake.

Management called to complain about our temperamental pooch. The non-stop barking and that call prompted Dad to embark upon a covert rescue mission. He managed to sneak Heidi into our room undetected, where she remained for the evening, happy to snuggle next to Karen.

The following morning Dad and I quickly packed the car and headed to the restaurant to join Mom and my sister's for breakfast. We entered the restaurant where a noticeable hush settled over the crowd of patrons. All eyes were intently focused on this presumed white man with a tall black kid on his heels. If looks could kill, we just died a hundred deaths.

We were the only black people in an otherwise packed hotel restaurant. When Dad checked in the night before, he entered the front lobby alone. It wasn't planned, it was circumstances; someone had to stay in the car and watch us kids. I remain convinced Dad knew nothing about Greensboro and its recent history of racial animus, despite his knowledge of history.

Settling in for breakfast, we were greeted by a rather pleasant waitress. A plump white woman who appeared to be in her thirties, with a white apron, a pencil stuck behind one ear, and another acting as some sort of bobby pin holding her hair bun in place. The southern charms of her voice were welcoming.

As she took our order, one patron stared intently to the point of annoyance. The lady talked to the gentleman she shared a table with; then returned her steely blue eyes to our table. I'm certain we were the topic of their conversation.

Her interest in us became so intense she missed her

mouth with a glass of milk dousing her blouse in white liquid. "Damn it," she shouted at no one in particular. Mom and I laughed uncontrollably while filling Dad in on the happenings behind his back. Dad started to get a little belligerent, then thought the better of it, and joined us in laughter mumbling the word bitch under his breath.

The irony of it all was the place Dad chose to sleep that night. Greensboro was home to one of the most famous sit-ins of the Civil Rights era. On February 1, 1960, four black college students from nearby North Carolina Agricultural and Technical College sat down at an all-white Woolworth's lunch counter and demanded service. When service was denied, the students refused to leave. Hundreds of additional students continued the protest that lasted for months.

The year prior to our arrival, Greensboro was engulfed in an uprising that would become the largest in North Carolina history. Student protestors at North Carolina A&T exchanged gunfire with police and National Guard over a civil rights issue at the segregated James B. Dudley High School. One black student bystander was killed.

The North Carolina Advisory Committee to the United States Commission on Civil Rights found the authorities reaction to the incident to be the classic law enforcement overreach, something we've become all too familiar with today.

Our journey south continued through Atlanta, the mecca of black achievement, and birthplace of Dr. King and

Ebenezer Baptist Church. What a waste of a precious moment to learn more about black history. An opportunity for a closer look at Atlanta flew by at fifty-five miles per hour. Dad's love of history would have most certainly compelled him to stop for a closer inspection had he been more in touch with the Civil Rights Movement.

They only thing I knew about Atlanta were the Atlanta Braves. Another of my childhood heroes, Hank Aaron played for the Braves. I followed the exploits of Hammerin Hank religiously. Only after I read the Brave's box score, would I stop and read the article, often, two, or three times, if Aaron had a good night. I gravitated towards players who carried themselves with grace and dignity; Aaron was all of that, and more.

We stopped for gas on the outskirts of Montgomery, Alabama. Something alerted Dad to danger lurking. He wouldn't even allow me to use the restroom demanding that I "get my ass back in the car." He later told me some white males were harassing black patrons who dared stop at this particular gas station. We eventually stopped a few miles down the road on a desolate stretch of U.S. Highway 231, where I finally relieved my bulging bladder in the bushes, just out of view of passing cars. It was the dog and I hiding in the woods.

In a span of twenty-four hours, we traveled the Heart of Dixie, driving through, or by some of the most memorable destinations in the struggle. First, it was Richmond, home of the Confederacy; then Greensboro.

We drove through Atlanta before coming within one hundred miles of Birmingham---or "Bombingham" as it became known for the frequent church bombings, including the one at 16th Street Baptist Church that took the lives of four little girls.

We stopped near Montgomery, home to what many consider the birthplace of the modern Civil Rights Movement, when Rosa Parks defied southern sensibilities refusing to give up her bus seat to a white man.

We were less than fifty miles from Selma, the scene of "Bloody Sunday" on the Edmund Pettus Bridge. It was here civil rights marchers were attacked and beaten by law enforcement, the Ku Klux Klan, and other locals. The marchers were headed to Montgomery, the state capitol, to protest voting restrictions. One distinguished member of the protest group is current U.S. Congressman John Lewis of Georgia, who received a fractured skull on that bridge. *Who, or what, was the Klan?* I'd never heard of them or the Citizens' Councils, the group of white supremacist who did all they could to oppose racial integration.

Many of the highways we traveled were used by Freedom Riders of early the 1960s. The Freedom Riders, a combination of blacks and whites, many college students, road the buses to test southern states' compliance with bus desegregation mandates issued by the Supreme Court. Congressman Lewis also participated in those Freedom Rides.

I'm ashamed to admit as a twelve-year-old, I'd never heard of Rosa Parks, the Freedom Riders, "Bloody Sunday" and all the people who sacrificed and died so my family could make this journey to Florida without fear of being lynched.

For the first time since Spain, I actually felt like we were in another country. I didn't recognize this America. It started with the language. Southerners spoke a form of English that required a new dictionary and lessons in elocution. Their speech and colloquialisms represented a linguistic nightmare for a kid who'd spent four of the previous five years buried in New England, a region with its own unique dialect and accents.

The long drawn out words, incomplete sentences and cutoff words, accents and syllables in the wrong place, and misplaced contractions were just the tip of the iceberg.

It's "laud" instead of lord, "bidness" instead of business, and "hawg" instead of hog, or "purdy" instead of pretty.

But the two words Dad detested the most were "y'all" and "ain't." It just offended all his sensibilities. He smacked me upside the head on numerous occasions for using words not found in the dictionary.

I earned a Ph.D. in Southern. I just couldn't use my expanded vocabulary within earshot of Dad.

Continuing our journey south down U.S. Highway 231 from Montgomery, Dad announced we would be arriving in Panama City before nightfall. The verdant colors, rolling hills, and red clay of northern Alabama had given way to less dense forest of pine trees embedded in sand.

Then a different sort of poverty materialized as we

passed through a series of small towns. Unlike Philadelphia or Baltimore, this dystopian environment of rusted our cars, trailer parks with over grown weeds, and trash strewn about, made those two northern ghettos look like the Upper East Side of Manhattan. The few people we saw, both black and white, were poorly dressed, many with tattered clothing and shoes that had seen their better days.

We crossed over a road that would eventually become Interstate 10 in the Florida Panhandle, when I spotted two signs. One sign read "Black Entrance," the other "White Entrance." They were discarded on the side of the road. They appeared to have only recently been dislodged from their former perch, the lettering and coloring of both signs in pristine condition. Those signs swirled around in my head for the next ninety miles. *Is this how we would live, separated along color lines?*

Closing in on the Gulf Coast, my parents' took note of the low hanging clouds on an otherwise beautiful day. They appeared close enough to touch.

No sooner had they commented on the clouds, we were greeted by one of those fifteen-minute southern monsoons, better known to southerners as liquid sun-shine. Rain pounded the earth in a fusillade of heavy drops. The noise effectively drowned out the sound of any normal conversation in the car. We quickly rolled up our windows prepared for a certain steam bath.

Dad struggled to maintain control of the car, nearly ditching us more than once. The sun never truly disappeared behind the clouds, but the monsoon like rain reduced visibility to zero. The wiper blades swept furiously, but proved no match for the deluge. Then, as if

Moses himself appeared to part the Red Sea, the storm beat a hasty retreat. The world reappeared as quickly as it had disappeared moments earlier.

Cars were scattered about in a sea of brake lights, some stuck it grass covered drainage ditches on either side of the road.

Intense rays of sun refracted off the pavement creating moments of temporary blindness, followed by a thick fog-like steam rising from the asphalt. The mixture of warm rains colliding with an even warmer roadway created a mysterious and eerie tapestry reminiscent of a scene from the old black and white television series, *Twilight Zone*.

Any preconceived notion of what I thought the Florida Gulf Coast and Panama City would look like before our arrival, soon vanished. This didn't look like any part of Florida I saw in picture books, in fact, it looked down-right depressing.

Dad made the left turn from U.S. Highway 231 onto U.S. Highway 98, a four-lane divided thoroughfare that formed the main east/west artery along the Florida panhandle. Tyndall sat twenty minutes east of downtown Panama City, a city of twenty thousand and the government seat for Bay County.

We passed through a series of small towns that looked like *Mayberry*. I expected Andy, Barney, Opie, or Aunt Bee to coming running towards our car any minute. Our journey took us past, or through, Cedar Grove, Springfield, Callaway, Parker, and a sign pointing to Wewahitchka twenty miles.

They all looked like sleepy southern plantation towns minus the plantations that I read about in history books. We passed by grayish-colored wooden shacks that were still inhabited. They looked like old slave quarters.

While lost in thought, a dreadful odor invaded our surroundings. The combination of rotten eggs and sulfur felt strong enough to destroy my olfactory senses. I started breathing through my mouth, a defense against actually having to process the smell any longer. The source of this highly toxic odor: the St. Joseph Paper Mill. If the wind blew in from the Gulf of Mexico, this noxious odor would linger for days, causing headaches for anyone inhaling its harmful fumes.

Panama City sits along the shores of St. Andrews Bay, separated from direct access to the Gulf of Mexico, by a series of small barrier islands. Farther west, the town of Panama City Beach opened directly to the Gulf of Mexico. This is where the spring break crowd of college students, primarily from Alabama, Mississippi, and Georgia hung out. During the winter locals had the beaches to themselves.

The town's moniker, "World's Most Beautiful Beaches," was indeed well deserved. The white sand dunes supported by sea oats gave way to expansive powdery white sandy beaches, perfectly silhouetted against the turquoise waters of the Gulf of Mexico. I'd never seen sand so white and so fine. This mosaic was breathtaking.

Some refer to this stretch of U.S. Highway 98 west to Pensacola as the Redneck Rivera, or LA, Lower Alabama. These less than flattering euphemisms target the people of the region, not its natural beauty.

We continued east towards DuPont Bridge, crossing over an offshoot of St. Andrews Bay, known as East Bay. Across this half-mile long cement and steel structure is Tyndall Air Force Base. I noticed a drawbridge just to the left as we crossed Dupont Bridge. The draw part of the bridge had been cutaway turning the remaining sides into a rusty fishing pier.

U.S. Highway 98 was the first time I'd seen a military base bisected by a U.S. highway, with no true guard gate to signal government property.

To the north, as we headed east, sat a series of houses, one of which would become our home for the next four years. To the south, a shallow forest perched on a bed of sand, followed by a road veering off towards the Gulf. Then Tyndall Elementary School appeared on the south side of the highway. Both my sister's would school there in about two weeks. The school was followed by another housing development.

Tyndall is located on a peninsula that juts into St. Andrews Bay to the west. East Bay forms Tyndall's northern boundary, the Gulf of Mexico, its southern border. Mexico Beach, Tyndall's land connected eastern border lies on a desolate stretch of highway twenty miles from Tyndall's main entrance. Mexico Beach sits just inside Central Standard Time.

Three miles after crossing Dupont Bridge, we arrived at a traffic signal. To the north, a manned guard gate giving military members and authorized personnel access to the flight line and Tyndall's fighter jets. To the south, a two-lane road that housed Tyndall's support functions---police headquarters, a movie theater, BX, commissary, the hospital, barracks, bowling alley, beaches, and the Gulf of Mexico.

Dad turned south stopping at police headquarters for directions to our temporary housing. After twelve hours cramped in the back seat, the returning blood flow to my lower extremities was a welcomed relief. Too amped for sleep, I lay awake long after normal bedtime watching television.

Local news featured a sea of white faces, but I learned a lot from my fifteen minutes in front of the small screen. I would start my first year of junior high school in less than two weeks. Tyndall didn't have a junior high school, so none of us were certain at the moment where I was headed.

Panama City's two local high schools, Bay and Rutherford, had already started football practice. Prospects for a successful season were bright for both squads according to the sports anchor.

Then a local military member in full dress blues appeared to give the *Tyndall Report*, a brief summary of the happenings at Tyndall, and how military personnel interacted with the community.

Like most military bases located in small towns, Tyndall is one of the region's largest employers, so anything that happened at Tyndall, affected the greater Panama City area. A growing number of military retirees brought a much-needed economic shot in the arm to the local economy. I finally drifted off, anxious, and somewhat fearful of what lie ahead.

CHAPTER 6

LOST SOUL

Dad arose early the following morning, put on his uniform, and made his way to the hospital where he would work as an administrator. He returned at 11 a.m. with a sergeant he introduced as his sponsor, charged with helping us get settled.

The first order of business, find more permanent, albeit, temporary shelter. Dad was on the list for government housing, but our new home was still occupied by another military family. That home wouldn't be available for three months.

Our sponsor took us to a place called Treasure Cove Cottages, located on U.S. Highway 98 just off base. We met the landlord, a genial white woman who made her living catering to military families. She appeared unfazed by our family rainbow.

We toured a two-bedroom, single bath cottage and signed a rental agreement on the spot. The cottage sat less than ten feet from the highway in a thicket of trees covered with Spanish moss. There were approximately fifteen detached cottages with a shared U-shaped gravel driveway. The grounds were mostly sand and light brush. The landlord's property sat centered at the back overlooking East Bay, approximately twenty feet from the waters edge.

The cottage was fully furnished with some of the cheapest accessories I'd ever seen. The linoleum floors were warped, peeling back from rotted wood. The carpet was a dingy threadbare off-yellow shag that had been trampled flat. The place smelled musty. The living room sofa bed, my place of rest for the next three months, had a mattress so thin it left indentations in my back and legs. The floor might have been better for sleep were it not for the nasty bug-infested carpet.

Next came school registration. My sister's were registered first since there was no doubt where they would attend school. I waited until mid-afternoon when our sponsor revealed the name and location of my home away from home.

Rosenwald Junior High School is located in what was then the poorest section of Panama City, smack dab in the middle of the town's black community. A normal bus ride to school took thirty to forty minutes depending on traffic. All military kids were bused to Rosenwald, even though Everitt Junior High School, the one attended the previous year, sat much closer.

We were initially told Rosenwald was the school of choice to alleviate overcrowding at Everitt. That, I quickly discovered was a fabrication of the tallest order. We were being bused in the name of school desegregation.

This would be the first year Florida instituted "forced busing" to desegregate public schools. But the need for busing, and its eventual evolution and implementation, went back nearly a century.

Following the Civil War, America entered an era known as Reconstruction. Part of that era included three constitutional amendments that became known as the Reconstruction Amendments.

The Thirteenth Amendment granted citizenship to anyone born on U.S. soil. In 1868, the Fourteenth Amendment became law of the land. One of the many provisions of that amendment granted total rights of citizenship to all U.S. citizens, which of course included former slaves.

Two years later, the Fifteenth Amendment became law. It prohibited the practice of denying citizens the right to vote, based on race, color, or previous servitude.

The Reconstruction Era came to an abrupt halt with the Compromise of 1877 that led to federal troops being withdrawn from southern states. Immediately following the troop withdrawals, southern state governments began passing what became known as Jim Crow laws. These laws prohibited blacks from using the same public accommodations as whites.

Then in 1896, the United States Supreme Court codified into law Jim Crow in the case of Plessy vs. Ferguson. By a seven to one vote, "separate but equal" became the law of the land. This decision, combined with the rise of white supremacists groups such as the Klu Klux Klan and the Citizens' Councils stymied black progress for decades.

Politicians, business leaders, and others in power used their newfound authority to keep their foot on the necks of Negroes. "Separate but equal" was not restricted to southern states; many locales across America enforced some form of this doctrine.

With white America controlling all levels of government, they also controlled the purse strings that determined how much money was allocated to the black community. The result, inferior everything for black Americans, that included public schools.

The move to dismantle "separate but equal" took root in the early 1950's. In 1951, a class action suit was filed on behalf of thirteen Topeka, Kansas, parents and their twenty children. The suit called for the school district to reverse its separate but equal schools. All Topeka high schools were already desegregated. The suit targeted those schools below the high school level.

This case was combined with four others that became known collectively as Brown vs. Topeka Board of Education. The U.S. Supreme Court, in a unanimous decision, ruled that separate "educational facilities are inherently unequal." As a result, "separate but equal" facilities violated the Equal Protection Clause of the Fourteenth Amendment to the Constitution passed during Reconstruction. With this 1954 ruling, the desegregation of all public facilities, including public schools was born.

But the initial ruling fell short on specifics. The court didn't order integration with the first Brown decision; it simply ordered an end to discrimination in enrollment. How to implement Brown would come one year later in

Brown II, on May 31, 1955. This short seven-paragraph ruling, gave wide latitude in implementing Brown.

Due to some nebulous wording in a clarification to Brown I that included the phrase, "all deliberate speed," the implementation of Brown dragged on for years as states and local communities were allowed to set their own timetables. This proved to be an excuse to maintain the status quo. If things were going to change it would have to be forced upon white America.

The Civil Rights Act of 1964 outlawed racial segregation in schools, public places, and employment. The act, initially conceived to help blacks, was later amended before passage to include women, and whites. This act invalidated once and for all, all Jim Crow laws. Title IV of the act encouraged the desegregation of public schools and authorized the U.S. Attorneys General to file suits to enforce its mandates.

By 1970, many communities still had done little to desegregate schools. That year, a U.S. judge in North Carolina ordered white students who lived in predominantly white neighborhoods, to be "bused" to black schools, and black students who lived in predominantly black neighborhoods, to be bused to white schools.

A year later, the U.S. Supreme Court, in Swann vs. Charlotte-Mecklenberg unanimously upheld the North Carolina judge's use of busing to desegregate schools. That U.S. Supreme Court decision unleashed a torrent of judicial and political intervention to use busing as a mechanism to desegregate the public schools in both the North and South. Those baby steps now turned into a full-fledged sprint.

Fortunately, my little corner of Florida took to

desegregation a little sooner than other parts of the country, and with little, to no violence that plagued other communities across the country in the 1970s.

Busing and desegregation were foreign concepts to me. All my previous schools had been desegregated. The first time I heard of the Brown decision or the term Jim Crow, was in relationship to my attending Rosenwald. At the time, I didn't understand the greater purpose being served.

The reason us military brats were chosen for this new adventure was simple. Most of us attended integrated schools our entire lives and we were transitory. After three, or four years, we would move on to our next duty station. The second reason, Tyndall was ninety percent white, making it easy to bus us without displacing local kids.

When we arrived at Rosenwald to register for school, we were taken aback by the dilapidated housing directly across the street. While it might not have appeared substandard to its occupants, this was new to us.

Homes that predated the turn of the twentieth century stood on cinder blocks with wooden slates so warped, I could see into some of the rooms. Some leaned left, others right. Around the corner sat another row of houses, somewhat more colorful, like one would find in the Caribbean, but in equal states of disrepair.

To the right of the school, behind a chain linked fence indicating school property sat a well-worn oval-shaped dirt running track, with patches of greenery sprouting up through cracks in the earth. The center of the track offered patches of trampled grass and knee-high weeds. The red brick exterior of the school, along with the sign announcing Rosenwald Junior High School, looked to be in good repair compared to the surroundings.

We entered the hallway and made our way to the administrator's office, which sat right inside the front door. The faculty, staff, and principal were friendly enough and went out of their way to reassure Mom I would be in good hands. Mom looked skeptical.

Rosenwald, prior to busing, stood as an all-black high school established under Jim Crow in 1937. The black students that still remained from those high school years were absorbed into either Bay, or Rutherford High Schools, leaving both integrated.

Rosenwald was named after Julius Rosenwald, a descendant of Jewish immigrants from Germany. He was born just blocks away from President Abraham Lincoln's house in Springfield, Illinois, while Lincoln occupied 1600 Pennsylvania Avenue.

In 1908, Rosenwald became president of Sears, Roebuck and Company. A noted philanthropist, Rosenwald gave away millions of dollars through the Rosenwald Fund to build black schools, especially in the South, including the famous Tuskegee School for the Normal, better known as Tuskegee University.

The fund, established in 1917 would be completely exhausted by 1948. In total, this fund provided over $70 million in philanthropic causes, including black schools, a tidy sum of money back then.

Rosenwald considered the plight of the Negro, and lack of quality education, one of the great social blunders of our time, "the horrors that are due to race and prejudice come home to the Jew more forcefully than to others of the white race, on account of the centuries of persecution which they have suffered and still suffer."

The trip to school that first morning had taken forty minutes. Wilson, the bus driver was black, probably in his early fifties. We became instant friends.

For the next three years, Wilson greeted every kid who boarded his bus with a kindly "good morning my friend." If he recognized you on the street, the greeting was always the same. Everybody was his friend, even if they didn't reciprocate in kind. This man loved transporting us kids and it showed.

Since we didn't have a permanent home, Dad had to make arrangements to drop me off at the motor pool each morning to catch my ride to school. Wilson and I would spend several minutes in his office joking amongst the other drivers. I was one of the boys for a brief moment. They were all older than my parents'. All had grown up in the Jim Crow south. It's an era I could never appreciate or comprehend. Yet, the black and white bus drivers I observed, on the surface at least, had a bond, a friendship I couldn't account for, but that I thoroughly loved being a part of.

I always took the seat right behind Wilson so we

could talk on the way to school. He was my counsel and security blanket.

The black students who witnessed our arrival that first morning of seventh grade looked befuddled. They kept a respectful distance, unsure what to make of these insurgents to their community. The chasm created by the blacks was not out of fear, or respect, but one of strange curiosity. What were they to make of six big blue Air Force buses, mostly of white kids, pulling into the school parking lot this early September morning?

Mine was the second of those buses. When we arrived, the students from the first bus were already stepping out of the shadows onto their new campus. They were a festive group, laughing among themselves in light colorful clothing consistent with the warmth of the Florida sunshine. They appeared impervious to the gaze of their new black classmates.

I delayed my departure from the bus a few minutes, letting others pass. I couldn't get a handle on my emotions. If my bladder had anything to excrete, I would have wet myself. I was paralyzed with fear. I couldn't shake the notion racing through my mind, that the horrible experience of sixth grade would be tame in comparison to what lay in wait at Rosenwald. The moment of truth had arrived and I couldn't move.

After several more seconds of contemplation, I rose from my seat and meandered towards the exit. My normally steeled nerves were being attacked. I began shaking uncontrollably; beads of perspiration dripped from my forehead. I coaxed my legs and feet forward, one small step at a time. Between the humidity and my nerves, the shirt I wore was soaked in fear.

I'd procrastinated long enough. After a little nudge from Wilson, I finally exited the bus into the land of the unknown. I glanced over my shoulder as I descended the final step, making eye contact with Wilson one last time. His smile provided reassurance, but did little to cure the menacing jitters now in charge of my movements.

Their eyes bore into me before my foot hit the landing. *What were my new black classmates thinking? Were they simply being curious teenagers, or was there something more insidious and sinister on their minds?* I kept my head down, eyes glued to the pavement for fear mental paralysis would stop me in my tracks. My tongue and gut were tied in knots.

While walking to my first period class, I made my first friend, a white kid named Adam. He arrived just moments after we pulled into the school parking lot. He walked up and introduced himself like a good politician on the campaign trail. We chatted for a few minutes, navigating the halls towards our assigned lockers, and homeroom. Lucky for me, Adam and I shared the same homeroom and several classes.

As Adam and I made our way through the throng of kids towards homeroom, I began to notice what I'd missed on registration day, the interior of the school and its various stages of disrepair.

Bathroom doors were missing. Several spots on the ceiling, those that actually had tiles in place, showed the moldy residue of a water leak. Pipes were exposed. Walls and light fixtures were either broken or missing. Some of the restrooms were disgustingly filthy, easily qualifying as health hazards. Rusted metal fixtures were the norm in environments with a heavy concentration of salt air, and Rosenwald was no exception. A year later it was determined that asbestos was a serious health hazard and Rosenwald looked to be ground zero.

Several classrooms had broken desks piled in the corner. To make matters worse, the school lacked air conditioning, except in the teacher's lounge and the administrator's offices. The heat at times could be unbearable, making for a difficult learning environment, especially in early fall and late spring when temperatures soared into the nineties, with a humidity to match. Most students fell asleep in the stifling heat. Others used books and notepads as fans to stimulate air movement. Rosenwald was living proof the word equal in "separate, but equal" was pure fiction when it came to the appropriation of funds.

Despite all my initial observations, someone had taken the time to clean and wax the floors, the wooden desks, while covered in ink marks left by previous students, were clean to the point where I didn't notice gum stuck underneath the chairs and table tops. The windows were spotless; a slight smell of cleaning solvent still lingered. School officials tried to take care of what little they had.

I arrived in homeroom and took a seat in the back. Adam and I were both six-footers. I slumped down in my chair, a feeble attempt to hide, and blend into my surroundings. Adam sat up straight showcasing his confidence and good posture. My effort to blend into my surroundings lasted all of two minutes as Ms. Jones took roll. She noticed my slumping posture. Sounding like a drill sergeant, Ms. Jones gave an order, "young man sit up straight." I complied unfolding my longer slender frame.

Thinking she would move on to the next person, I relaxed for a split second, but Ms. Jones had other ideas. In rapid succession came a series of questions. *Where are you from? How many different places have you lived? What does your father do? What are your interests outside of school? How are your grades?* It was interrogation at its finest. The best lawyers on the planet had nothing on Ms. Jones.

I almost swallowed my tongue attempting to answer her questions. My vocal chords became constricted. I tried to moisten my lips but the saliva needed to do so must have found another home.

When I finally mustered the courage to answer. The sound emanating from my mouth sounded like the babbling of a two-year-old. She admonished me to speak up, but the lump in my throat prevented all coherent sound.

The piercing eyes of my classmates caused me to squirm and shake. I noticed a faint smile come across Ms. Jones' face that relaxed me somewhat, followed by a wink. It was a look that only the two of us shared, since all heads and eyes were fixated on me. I cleared my throat and proceeded to methodically answer all her questions.

As the other students listened to my answers she pried deeper and deeper. Her demeanor changed from that of a tough drill sergeant, to one full of empathy and compassion. Ms. Jones took great delight in listening to my New England accent, my proper use of the English language, and, as it turned out so did the other students, especially my black classmates. One kid jumped in and asked, "Are you American?" Many thought my voice sounded exotic.

Ms. Jones spoke with all the mannerisms of someone born and reared in the South, but she was nobody's fool. This highly intelligent person turned out to be a great teacher, who understood the fine art of connecting with a student regardless of background.

A couple years later, Ms. Jones told me she'd chosen to question me long before I walked into her class. She read my transcripts. I was the only black student in her first period class who'd ever left the cozy confines of Panama City. She wanted the other black students to know, according to Ms. Jones, that the outside world wouldn't harm them.

The rest of my day came nowhere close to that first period grilling. Between classes, the halls were so crowded it looked like a busy New York City subway. All the black students went one way, whites the other, only touching when it couldn't be avoided.

For the remainder of the day, I chose a seat in the back corner, perfectly positioned to size up the rest of the classroom. It provided a great vantage point where I could avoid being the center of attention. If someone wanted to look, they had to turn. I hoped to find a friendly face. Every few minutes a black student would turn for a quick glimpse. Those who dared to look quickly turned back avoiding eye contact at all cost.

Coach Collier, or simply Coach, played an integral role in my life for the next ten years. We met that first day of seventh grade in the gym during roll call. For most boys, physical education was a class not to be missed. For me, I could've cared less, until now.

This affable black man, in his early thirties had a great rapport with all students. Coach, dressed in his African safari shorts and wide-brimmed hat, took roll like no other. At times, his raspy voice hollered names putting inflection on the wrong syllable in a deliberate attempt at humor. At other times, he sounded like a basketball play-by-play announcer, complete with his own set of sound effects. My name was "Benneeeeeett." In the ten years we knew each other, I don't think he ever called me by my first name.

Coach had one of those engaging personalities that just consumed you over time. You couldn't help but love him. Through that gruff exterior was a man who accepted the challenge of molding young men into responsible citizens. He possessed the perfect blend of compassion and discipline.

We were assigned gym lockers and began dressing the part for physical activity changing to shorts and t-shirts. Like most pre-teen boys, stripping down to your underwear while others gawked could be a little disconcerting. Students avoided this unpleasant task by wearing gym shorts under their street clothes.

I arrived early for physical education that first week, when I discovered Coach joking with a group of white students. Everyone in their circle was in fits of uncontrollable laughter. When the black students arrived, they didn't know what to make of the frivolity. I overhead one kid trash Coach for talking to "whitey." *What was the man supposed to do, ignore half the class?* I mumbled idiots under my breath just a little too loudly. Fortunately, my audio fell on deaf ears.

After roll call each morning we ran four laps around

the track. That one-mile was a tension release I thoroughly enjoyed. Another kid and me finished a full two minutes ahead of everyone, so Coach allowed us a drink of water. The student who ran with me was black, about four inches shorter and muscular for a thirteen-year-old. I introduced myself, but that overture was not reciprocated.

After we got back to the track, Coach divided us into teams for a little flag football. I was the ultimate neophyte having never put my hand on a football. Thanks to television, I knew basic football rules and responsibilities, but playing is so different.

Coach split each team almost evenly along racial lines. It didn't escape anyone's attention that the teams were desegregated just like the school. Coach guided our team, one of his assistants, the other. The kickoff traveled less than thirty yards skipping end-over-end along the dirt field. The receiver had his flag ripped off immediately.

Coach drew up a play in the dirt. We all watched intently as he went over the play a second time. The black and white students still hadn't made eye contact with each other; that proved to be an ominous sign of things to come.

Almost immediately a light bulb popped on in our collective heads. As we approached the line of scrimmage, the white and black students realized they were going to block each other, which meant close contact and touching. The first play went off and not one person blocked. The pass, intended for me, fell incomplete.

When we got back to our respective huddles, the coaches rode us hard for lack of effort, never once succumbing to the elephant on the field. As the hour wore on, play improved. Racial fear and hostility had given way to teamwork. The students, regardless of race, were actually speaking to each other for the first time. After class, Coach walked up to me in front of the group extolling my superior play. That was a bad joke and everyone knew it.

Once we entered the locker room, it was back to normal---blacks in one group, whites in the other, me, the outlier sitting by myself.

Our gym had showers, and we were all instructed to take one, but not one student made a move in that direction. We were all too embarrassed and afraid of ridicule about the size of our anatomy. The most anyone did was wash up in the sink. This was our gym routine for six months. The only thing that changed was the sport.

Coach prodded the black students to interact with their more willing white counterparts. They warmed up to the idea at glacial speed. While we were on the athletic field, it was as if the Olympic Gods descended upon us, encouraging good play and sportsmanship. Afterwards, the Gods disappeared, replaced by the Devil of Bad Intentions.

When I arrived home after that first day of school, Dad peppered me with questions. I wasn't sure what to make of my experience. Rosenwald was the ultimate riddle that needed solving---it was a paradox of epic proportions, cold and distant one minute, warm and inviting the next.

Since we hadn't moved into our house yet, the white kids had no vested interest in learning more about their new classmate. I was just the kid on the bus. The black student body had much the same reaction. Not one black student spoke to me my first day, a trend that continued for nearly a month outside of gym class.

My rapid growth spurt the year Dad spent in Vietnam caused considerable physical pain to my knee joints---seven inches in a year, most in the last three months, had taken a toll. My feet had grown from a size nine to a twelve. Poor Mom spent a fortune replacing my clothes and shoes.

The acute pain emanating from my knees caused me to collapse on numerous occasions for doing nothing more than walking. If felt like someone slammed my patella tendon and the surrounding soft tissue with a sledgehammer. Time to see a doctor.

The doctor took x-rays of both knees. Before I knew it, my left leg had been placed in a cast from hip to ankle. Mom blamed herself for not taking me to a doctor sooner, taking my predicament hard. The x-ray revealed a broken bone just below my kneecap, or at least that's what the orthopedist told my parents'. I knew that couldn't be the reason, my other leg ached just as bad. I certainly hadn't broken both legs. I went with the doctor's explanation never revealing my thoughts about the diagnosis.

Mom, bless her heart, did everything she could to make me comfortable, including relieving me of the chore of washing dinner dishes. Dad on the other hand wasn't having it, making me do as much as possible. No way would he allow me to give into the pain.

While my parents' went back and forth practicing

what each thought was best for my wellbeing, I had to deal with a far bigger problem. With the only respite from an otherwise lonely day, my gym class, now gone for the foreseeable future, how would I handle my angst?

Wilson bent over backwards to make my transition from home to school a comfortable one. No student was allowed to sit next to me. I couldn't bend my knee so I definitely needed the bench seat to stretch out. He carried my books even though I didn't need, nor ask for his help. I wasn't on crutches. Bearing my own weight wasn't a problem, although my other knee, which was already aching, took the brunt of the stress.

My misfortune turned into a godsend. When the white students boarded the bus and observed my added appendage, they all took note of my predicament. Several expressed their sorrow for my circumstance. A few actually moved closer to the front, better to hear me explain to Wilson how I found myself in such dire straits. *Was this the break through I had been looking for, all because everyone thought I had a broken leg?* As it turned out, lugging a cast around was the best thing that happened to me in seventh grade.

White students started to speak. Friendships were being formed, although it would be several months before any of us really bonded. I didn't care; the process had begun. The girls flocked to me, first out of sympathy, then genuine concern. These young ladies were the honey that drew the bees. My new friends were named Joey, Susan, Sharon, Dorothy, Chuck, and Lonnie. The attention bolstered my spirits.

My fellow riders allowed me to get off the bus first volunteering to hold my books while I limped down the steps. My black classmates took note of this white plaster showing through the seam of my pants. Some seemed shocked, some curious; others just gave a blank stare of indifference.

My first period class sat on the opposite end of the school making for a long and labored walk. Teachers stopped to ask the usual questions, how, when, does it hurt? I should have issued a press release. For the next month, my teacher's had an extra desk for my leg. I never asked, nor expected special treatment, the teachers just took over, often at the expense of fellow classmates, but no one held it against me.

When I arrived for gym class, I thought Coach was going to lose his mind. He thought I hurt myself in his class. After I explained my history of knee problems, a look of relief washed over him, his blood flow returning to normal.

For the next month I became a spectator and cheerleader. Coach made me responsible for roll call and other little projects that didn't require much movement. When I called roll the other students were forced to respond. That was about as much conversation as I got out of my black classmates.

I needed to get to know them. It was a matter of pride and personal development. My black classmates were the windows into the history of my own people. They could help fill in gaps about black life that my parents', either couldn't, or wouldn't. Coach noticed the cold-shoulder treatment and tried to intervene, but those stubborn kids wouldn't budge. I needed an audacious plan to get them to open up. What that entailed, I had no clue.

The dehumanizing affects of Jim Crow existed in Panama City, like no place I'd ever been. Were there worse places, absolutely, but my orbit never stopped in those other places, for me this was it.

I realized no one would separate me from other African Americans, no matter my background. For some in America, color mattered and to pretend otherwise would be the height of stupidity and ignorance. I needed to accept my blackness.

How I handled matters of race would determine my future. Would I succumb to second-class citizenry, or excel, and create my own vision for the future? I needed a mentor. I needed guidance.

Unfortunately, we never discussed race in our house. One could debate the merits of never having that discussion, but in hindsight, I believe my parents' didn't know how to have the conversation.

I shouldered the blame of my ignorance for years, when in fact, the chasm in my knowledge of black history could easily be spread to family, and a school system that avoided the issue altogether. At age twelve, I should have known more about black life than slavery, especially given the times.

Dad's Catholic school upbringing kept him in integrated schools. He never grasped the magnitude of forced busing until he saw the unrest in Boston years after we left Panama City. Consequently, he offered no help in dealing with my reality.

One thing remained certain, busing and segregation would not be used as an excuse in our house for poor academic performance. Dad reminded me of my academic responsibility often. "This is where you can level the playing field, " he said.

CHAPTER 7

THE REVELATION

The relationship with the black student body remained frozen more than a month into the school year, when a slow, almost imperceptible thaw commenced thanks to the love and kindness of a total stranger.

The lockers at Rosenwald had three air vents in the door making it easy to slip small scraps of paper through the opening. I opened my locker causing a folded piece of paper to fall gently to the floor. At first, I thought it was a message from the principal, or one of my teachers.

My junior detective license told me immediately after retrieving the correspondence that it didn't come from a person of authority. The note, laced with a zesty perfume, infected everything it came in contact with---my hands, the air I breathed, and the books in my locker. Those with lockers near mine inched closer at the site of the note and smell of strong perfume. They knew someone had taken a liking to me. Too embarrassed to read its contents in front of prying eyes, I stuffed the letter into my shirt pocket, and made a beeline for class.

Since I ate lunch alone that would be the perfect place to read uninterrupted. But curiosity was killing the cat. I couldn't wait for lunch, still three hours away. Not to mention, the odor emanating from my shirt pocket sucked the oxygen out of my immediate airspace.

While the teacher called roll, I peeked at the letter looking for a name. The sender chose to remain anonymous. Oh well, at least someone wanted my attention, and that would suffice for now.

The letter covered two pages front and back. I'd never written a school paper that long. Its contents were flattering referencing my intelligence and dashing good looks. The word intelligence jumped off the page, leading me to believe we shared a class, how else would she know I had a functioning brain. The final line asked if we could talk.

Could it have been a person in the lunchroom with me right now? I started looking around; my head on a swivel, but no one seemed to be paying attention. I continued to eat slowly while attempting to scan the room undetected, hard to do with my leg in a cast. I made eye contact with several young ladies, black and white. Some girls smiled, others ignored me probably thinking I was somewhat foolish for having the audacity to look in their direction.

The next day, I received another note, and on Friday, another. The only discernable pattern in the delivery of the note was the time of day of its arrival in my locker, between first and second period. I wanted to excuse myself from class to use the restroom and patrol the hallways, but I thought Ms. Jones would send an escort.

Each day's correspondence proved more romantic than the last. She intimated rubbing my leg once the cast was removed. Her words could easily put the day's best romance authors to shame. Three months shy of my thirteenth birthday, I knew nothing about romance, except what I watched on television, and even I knew that stuff was fairy dust.

I read my collection of love letters nightly after my parents' fell asleep. I had a crush on Miss Anonymous, sight unseen. What did she look like? I started to construct this model like figure in my mind, but I couldn't tell if I should make her black, or white. It was a fuzzy image of a girl with a warm smile, tall, with soft hands and beautiful eyes.

My dream of beauty would be reinforced the following day when Dad decided to take the family for a beach outing, our first since we arrived in Florida. The five of us loaded up the car and drove to Panama City Beach.

The gentle waves of the Gulf were like a mother covering a baby with a blanket. The blazing hot white sand burned the soles of our feet until we got closer to the waters edge. The temperature, in the mid eighties, with a slight breeze, made for one gorgeous afternoon.

Dad played with my sisters' in shallow water. Since I couldn't get into the water, Mom filled plastic beach buckets with the salty liquid and poured its contents on my cast-free leg, and used the remainder to rub my back and shoulders. I turned several shades darker in less than two hours. The peeling skin caused by my first sunburn lasted a week.

The only people on our portion of the beach that day

were white; some of the prettiest women I had ever seen. All were shapely and tanned, some to the point of looking black or brown. Several noticed my cast and stopped by to cheer me up. The men were just as complimentary as the women. They approached without pretense showing genuine concern. These white strangers caught me off guard at first. After a moment of reflection, I remembered, this is how I grew up. *Had my two months in Florida already clouded my perspective about white people? I vowed not to let that happen.*

As the girls walked by, I was reminded of the letters I'd been receiving. I kept putting heads of younger girls on the bodies of mostly college-aged women lying about in their skimpy bikinis. It made the day pass faster.

When I returned to school on Monday, I expected, and received another note inquiring about my weekend.

Adam, of all people, caught the anonymous author as she slipped a note into my locker. He was giddy at the prospect of revealing the identity of Miss Anonymous.

He didn't know her name, but Adam milked her description for all it was worth. Adam began slowly, "she is short," you might not like that, he opined. He talked about her smile and shapely legs. He even described her breast as melons in a testosterone driven description that turned more salacious afterwards. It sounded weird coming out of the mouth of a twelve-year-old. By the time he finished I needed a bib. Then, as an afterthought, he told me she was a cheerleader, in ninth grade, and she was black.

When he mentioned she was black, my countenance changed to one of shock, followed by terror. *Could this be a joke? Was I being setup?* I became immediately suspicious. Despite my skepticism, I decided to return the favor the next day and put a note in her locker. I knew her identity from the description.

I went home and worked on my magnum opus for two hours. It sounded corny when I read it out loud to myself, but it would suffice. I signed my name.

The next day, before first period, my note was delivered through the vent, into her locker, the one right next to mine. Then I got nervous. She was definitely among the more popular girls in school and very attractive. What could she want with a tall skinny black kid with crooked teeth from the "wrong" side of the tracks?

Then my mind went back to thinking I was being played for a fool.

The time had come to get a status report on my leg. I knew the cast would come off eventually, but this silly piece of plaster and I had become an item that I was reluctant to have removed.

I propped my leg on the exam table and waited what seemed like an eternity for the orthopedist to show his face. After nearly forty minutes, the doctor entered with x-rays in hand, and a smile on his face. He extended his hand towards mine for a handshake while telling Mom he had good news, and bad news.

The doctor told us I didn't have a broken leg. The bad news, I had something called Osgood Schlatter's Disease (OSD). *What the hell was that?* The disease, he explained, typically occurs in boys between the ages of ten and sixteen. It's a growth spurt and overuse disease. The pain and inflammation is caused by frequent use and stress at the point where the patella tendon attaches to the shinbone, just below the kneecap.

If you continue to place pressure on the leg through physical activity, it could cause tiny fractures in the shinbone. That explains why doc thought I had a broken leg. It also explained why I had pain in both knees. The doctor told Mom I would outgrow OSD in a few years, and no later than my eighteenth birthday. The doctor wound up being partially correct. I did get rid of the pain, but not until I hit twenty-five. My rickety knees affected every sport and leisure activity I pursued for the next fifteen years.

With the diagnosis now complete, the doctor told Mom the cast could come off. But before the doctor took the cast off, he cautioned me to rest my legs anytime the knees got sore, or he would invite me back for another four weeks of misery, a new cast from hip to ankle. That was a common way to treat Osgood's back in 1970.

Doc pulled out a saw and turned it on, the whine of the tiny motor filling the room. He started on the outside part of the cast near my ankle, and made a thin cut all the way to my hip. The cast fell softly to the floor.

A nurse cleaned up the cotton and plaster stuck to my leg, bathing it in warm soapy water. Her gentle touched reminded me of Mom washing my little sister in the kitchen sink.

With the cast gone, all I thought about was rejoining my gym class. The orthopedist's admonition to take it easy had fallen on deaf ears. While lost in euphoric thought, the doctor reappeared with Dad on his heels. I made some offhanded comment about playing ball again. The doctor warned me once again to take it easy.

As if to prove a point, he dared me to jump off the table. Doc taunted me in such a way, that had I not been consumed with excitement, I probably would have noticed his evil intent. He had a smirk on his face winking at both my parents' as he issued his challenged. *What the hell was he up to?* Without giving it a second thought, I jumped off the table, and fell flat on my face nearly breaking my nose.

The room erupted in laughter. I have to give doc credit, the man put on a convincing performance worthy of an Oscar. My knee was so stiff it wouldn't bend and the leg had atrophied. The muscles needed strengthening.

The doctor wrote the school administrators a note excusing me from physical activity for another three weeks while I started rehab.

The cheerleader actually had a name; Amanda, just like my little sister. She actually signed her note this time. At the bottom she wrote "congratulations" making reference to the fact my cast had been removed, an obvious addition to a letter she had already written.

During lunch, I picked up my tray and made my way through the line towards my lonely seat in the corner, when a beautiful young lady's voices came up from behind, "you need help carrying your tray?" She was as pretty close up as she was from a distance. I declined the offer but summoned the courage to ask her to join me.

We sat across the table from one another engrossed in

deep conversation, eyes locked on one another barely touching our food. She explained how I never found her in the lunchroom, always positioning herself a few tables behind me, which meant I would never see her unless my head rotated like Linda Blair's character in the movie, *The Exorcist*. The conversation, despite my stuttering and stammering, went well.

While we were talking I took a moment to take in my surroundings. Students gawked in disbelief. The black students seemed particularly taken aback by the two of us engrossed in discussion. Little did they realize, we were actually joking about them, and how they'd treated me the previous months.

My guardian angels; the ladies who ran the lunchroom, all quietly applauded giving me that Good Housekeeping Seal of Approval smile. A heavy burden had been lifted. The loneliness of the past few months hurt more than I realized, or, willingly admitted to myself.

As Amanda and I continued to talk in the days and weeks ahead, without her ever saying a word, I began to realize why most of my black classmates refused to speak. It was a combination of fear and resentment. I represented something they had yet to experience, freedom, and I wore it on my sleeve as a badge of honor. Like New Jersey, I inadvertently offended the very people I so desperately wanted as friends.

I wore clothes that were in obvious good repair, in fact, they were new, while many wore clothing Goodwill would reject. The holes in their attire were not a fashion statement like today; this was poverty in full effect. I should have noticed sooner. Chalk it up to lack of maturity.

To make matters worse, I once again became a teacher's pet, often embarrassing them in class when I volunteered answers to questions. My hand shot up into the air like Arnold Horshack, from the hit TV series, *Welcome Back, Kotter*; ooh, ooh, ooh. The few friends I had to that point were all white, further alienating my black classmates. In the end, I was to blame for their not speaking.

Many of the black students didn't have enough money for lunch. The lunchroom staff would often slide food trays free of charge to those unable to afford lunch, or pay for student lunches out of their own pocket. Those less fortunate would sit near their friends and eat whatever a classmate left behind.

What kind of school system allowed kids to starve? This revelation angered me, something I discussed with Amanda during our more serious conversations. Life had dealt them a cruel blow. My classmates handled their predicament like business as usual. I hated it from the moment of my discovery. *Where was God in all of this?*

I took having three square meals a day for granted. Our refrigerator had no bounds. When I was younger, Dad worked his military job, and two others simultaneously just to make sure he could put clothes on our backs, and food on the table. At least he had options for part time employment thanks to the military.

My classmates, on the other hand, were literally begging for food. Many of the black parents did work, but the caste system of the South meant most blacks were stuck in menial, poor paying jobs that barely kept a roof over their heads, and one meal a day on the table. When Dad screamed at me about wasting food, it now resonated.

Some blacks in Panama City had become entrepreneurs, owning businesses that catered to the black community. Their kids were marginally better off than those blacks working for white-owned businesses. Unless blacks could work on the military base, or some entity where they were paid by the government; reports of equal opportunity and equal pay, was tantamount to committing perjury on the stand.

On the rare occasion they made eye contact with me, I could tell many classmates resigned themselves to a life of struggle, despair, and low expectations. They had already given up in the seventh grade; school a necessary evil mandated by law, otherwise, they might never have shown up.

For others, the determination to leave the South, even as young junior high school students, drove them to academic success. Education was their ticket out. Miraculously, the system hadn't beaten them down. They had hopes and dreams buttressed by progress in the Civil Rights Movement, and wonderful parents who pushed them to challenge themselves.

The black families I met weren't deluded into thinking the struggle had ended, they were well aware that this experiment called busing provided a step forward, a path out; nothing more, nothing less.

Many would end up in the military. Why not, they had a laboratory of possibilities sitting right under their nose in the form of us brats. It was relatable thanks to the busing.

College opportunities lie in wait for many of the more progressive black families. Amanda set her sights on the big colleges up north long before I arrived on the scene. She couldn't wait to escape the prison of poverty.

My discovery about poverty pushed me to seek a solution. I thought about talking to Coach, but feared offending him. I witnessed on numerous occasions Coach doling out his own money to feed a hungry student.

This was a nightmarish scene playing out before my eyes. One night, in a dream so vivid it stayed with me for weeks, I dreamt I'd been chained at the ankles; arms weighted down by cement blocks, dumped in the ocean, and told to swim. I began to imagine my own life living in fear, not being able to eat, forced to adhere to the wishes of people who wanted nothing more than to squash the life out of me.

I did have one thing to offer, hope. It required nothing more than friendship. I could provide optimism through example---sharing my life experiences, telling anyone who would listen; there is life outside Panama City and the Deep South. This thought emboldened me to act, but I had to act without the perception of arrogance, or condescension.

CHAPTER 8

A LOST LOVED ONE

After three months at Treasure Cove Cottage, the military finally gave us a move-in date to our new home---at long last, a bedroom to call my own. Our collective joy lasted less than twenty-four hours when tragedy struck. We would be moving into that home absent a family member.

Heidi was chained up outside around 9 p.m., a nightly ritual just before bedtime, to allow her to handle her business. She always barked when she finished. Since she didn't bark, we assumed she was fine, and kept watching television.

Dad went to retrieve her just before 10 p.m., no Heidi. Dad summoned me to help in the search. With flashlights in hand, we called her name, still nothing.

Mom joined us expanding our search grid. The loud scream we heard next on that cool night changed our lives forever. Mom found Heidi dead along the gutter of the highway. A vehicle had struck Heidi, no doubt traveling at a high rate of speed, since the speed limit on that portion of the highway was fifty-five miles per hour. Blood covered both westbound lanes.

Karen bolted through the front door. She knew before her foot hit the gravel Heidi was gone. Dad shielded Karen from the sight of our dog and its crushed body lying limp in the street. It took every once of energy Dad had to hold a ten-year-old from running into oncoming traffic. While Dad grabbed my sister, I held Mom tight, not wanting her to look at Heidi's broken body any longer. I eventually coaxed her back to the house. I'd gone into shock, too stunned at that moment to cry.

Dad borrowed a wheel barrel and shovel from the landlord. The two of us buried her that night about fifty feet from the water's edge, along East Bay, behind the landlord's house.

The bright moonlight that reflected off the water's surface, created a tranquil setting, perfect for such a somber occasion. We quietly went about the task of digging. Dad pounded that shovel into the ground, each blow harder than the previous one, masking his profound sadness through the act of moving earth.

Dad loved animals. Heidi was his idea for a Christmas gift in 1966 when we lived in Maine. Burying Heidi was the single most difficult act I'd ever performed. Death now had meaning, the finality of it all, haunting.

Our school bus drove right by Treasure Cove Cottage daily. That first day after Heidi's death, I choked back tears as our bus tracked through the bloodstained pavement.

A couple of kids noticed the blood, but I never mentioned our dog. The bloodstain remained visible for weeks. I said a silent prayer every time I passed that spot for four years. We owned two other dogs during our time in Florida, but none could replace Heidi.

Heidi's death brought me face-to-face with a reality I'd never considered before, tomorrow is not guaranteed. Amanda and I sat in our normal spot where I shared the macabre scene of the previous night. She kissed me on the cheek, wiping a single solitary tear from my face.

Losing Heidi created a sense of urgency. What could I do to get the black folks at my school to meet me half way? Amanda and I discussed my dilemma. Neither of us found a satisfactory answer. I decided to think about an approach over the weekend.

As if a prayer were being answered, the miracle of all miracles unfolded the Monday of Thanksgiving week. While Amanda and I were seated at our quiet lunch table in the corner, another student joined us, a black female, Rochelle, who I'd seen around school. The next day a few more girls joined our group. By Wednesday, there were eight of us, me the only male.

To this day, I have no idea why Rochelle, and the others decided to sit with us. The girls seemed captivated by my wacky New England accent. The jokes at my expense were the highlight of our thirty-minute lunch break, creating enough loud laughter to disrupt conversations at other tables.

We talked about Spain, Maine, and Atlantic City. I spoke broken Spanish, what little I could remember. It had been five years since I last conversed with anyone en

Español.

I took a Spanish class in eighth and ninth grade, never telling my teacher I'd lived in Spain for three years. My secret didn't last long. When students got stuck with pronunciation, or conjugating verbs, the Spanish instructor always called on me to lead the way. I'd gone out of my way to refrain from answering questions in any class for fear of alienating my classmates, now, I had a teacher putting me right back in the middle of controversy.

I compared the beaches of Atlantic City to Panama City. But the girls seemed particularly interested in the cultural aspects of life away from the Deep South, and how they would be treated in less hostile environments.

In my second honey that drew the bee moment in three months, a black male drifted into our group and quietly took a seat---too many pretty girls to ignore. By Friday, ten days after Rochelle joined our table for the first time, there were no fewer than twenty black kids, male and female, hanging out at the once lonely table in the corner.

The girls were comfortable in their own skin. They sang like a canary talking comfortably about any subject, the guys, a little more circumspect. Some sat quietly and listened, laughing when appropriate; others spoke sparingly, asking me a few questions about myself. I gladly answered every question thrown my way. I would have talked until laryngitis set in, if it meant the boys would be more receptive to my friendship.

At various points throughout our conversations, I turned the discussion to other people at our table. Whether they knew it, or not, they were my instructors.

The fellas had trouble articulating their plight, not because they couldn't speak properly; they were trying to mask their embarrassment and pain. They simply could not compete with my background, a fact, I made sure not to rub in their face.

Humor appeared to be the educational tool of choice. They joked about their own poverty, the Klan, or the white man down at the local convenience store who gladly took their money, then shouted pejoratives at them intended to strip these kids of their potential value to society.

I learned more about black life in the South, good and bad, in three weeks than anything I'd learned the previous twelve years. No history book could've provided such a valuable education. The best part, they didn't know I needed the education.

Coach, at his insistence, finally had that conversation with me that I'd put off weeks earlier for fear of offending him. He verified that the black males hated my guts, however, he noticed a thaw in their animosity. I asked him what I should do, he simply said, "be patient; they will come around." We discussed the lunchroom and that seemed to please him.

I had a quiet reverence for my black classmates, especially the boys. That could have easily been me, had earlier generations of my family stayed South. *There but for the grace of God go I.* I couldn't imagine how I would have handled their situation.

Coach managed to paint a bigger picture of life in, and around, Panama City. The portrait was stained with blood and tears. The message I took from our conversation: the never-ending legacy of Jim Crow had stripped away the dignity and self-esteem of the many young bright minds I now called my classmates.

But there were good stories, of good people, black and white, who pulled together for the betterment of our school and the local area. Rosenwald teachers were a case in point. Teacher desegregation preceded my arrival at Rosenwald. If there were a time at Rosenwald where bigotry trumped teaching and learning, that cancer, at least on the surface, had been eradicated.

Amanda helped me more than I ever let her know. Something so insignificant as sitting with me at lunch had a lasting and powerful impact on my life. My experience and relationship with black America, until now, had been superficial, more a circumstance of birth. Outside of family, that relationship lacked substance, value, and meaning.

I'd become so lost in my own suffering; I'd forgotten why Amanda and I developed our relationship in the first place. She had a huge crush on me. Our two-year age difference at a point in life where age matters; mattered little to her, if at all. She loved the idea that I was different. No stereotype existed at the time to truly define me, and Amanda found that appealing.

I had a crush on her too. In my eyes, she was the perfect girl. Even after she left for high school, we stayed in touch, talking often by phone. I wondered years later why I hadn't embraced her and responded to the obvious affection we had for one another more forcefully. I surmise my reticence was born out of fear. At the time, I was uncomfortable in my own black skin, and feared hers.

CHAPTER 9

ONE OF LIFE'S CRUEL LESSONS

The Mayflower truck pulled into our driveway the same day Rochelle joined our group at school. After eighteen months in storage, our furnishing looked dusty, dingy, and dated. But that didn't dampen our enthusiasm at seeing the familiar. I never had bedroom furniture. We'd always borrowed furniture on consignment from the military, so I took comfort in seeing our big brown sofa, and Dad's Archie Bunker-esque recliner. Most of my toys, except the telescope, would be headed to the Salvation Army, or the garbage, as would the old clothes, now several sizes too small.

As the movers continued to unload the truck, several kids gazed from afar curious about their new neighbors. The most brazen of the lot came over for a little introduction, first to Dad. That was the ultimate sign of respect, and one Dad appreciated. To my surprise, he allowed me to mingle, provided I stayed out of the way.

The questions were endless. The typical inquiries one

might expect from pre-teens; how old are you, what grade are you in, and what sports do you play? A couple of kids recognized me from the school bus, making the acclimation to my new surroundings easier than expected. Within a week I'd made friends with most of the kids in the neighborhood.

Our house was a single-story, fifteen hundred square-foot, three-bedroom, and one bath detached structure on a huge corner lot. The big tree in our front yard would become the gathering place for any kid who wanted to climb a tree, or just hang out.

The long meandering driveway on the left side of our house as you faced it from the street, led to a single car carport and a detached laundry room. My parents' had to rush off and buy a washer and dryer. We had never owned one.

A screened in patio called a Florida Room dominated the right front of 2545 Harding Street. That room was partially obscured by thick brush leaving it smothered in shade. As with most military houses, they all looked the same---ugly, perfectly square, and completely devoid of character. The only difference between houses; the address, the number of bedrooms and the shade of off white paint.

Across the street to the east sat a row of houses no more than ten feet from dense forest, intersected by small tributaries of East Bay. The forest crawled with creepy critters. Rattlesnakes delighted in leaving their normal habitat to sun themselves on the warm black pavement of the streets around our neighborhood. One snake managed to slip into our Florida Room terrifying Mom.

I heard her frantic call for help from a half-mile away.

I arrived on scene with one of the neighborhood kids and discovered a small coral snake, not a rattler, hugging the corner, as scared of Mom, as she was of it. We trapped the small critter in a box and carried it back to the woods, careful to avoid being bitten. Like rattlesnakes, coral snakes are also poisonous.

Needless to say Dad had that screen fixed immediately. Mom was a city girl. The only snake she'd ever seen close up resided in a zoo, behind walls of shatterproof glass.

The housing development sat on a bed of sand less than a mile from East Bay to the north, and a quarter mile from U.S. Highway 98 to the south.

I inherited the job of cutting a lawn that looked more sagebrush than grass. My first attempt nearly turned disastrous. I tried to get a head start on my chore before Dad provided instructions on how to operate the mower. How hard could it be? I poured oil in the gas tank and spent the next ten minutes yanking the cord waiting for ignition.

I ripped the cord with every once of energy I could muster, sweat pouring down my skinny frame---nothing. Dad emerged through the back door wondering why he hadn't heard the purr of a lawnmower engine. I pointed to the oil I'd just poured in the gas tank and quickly realized I screwed up. I expected Dad to launch into one of his animated temper tantrums.

We had a relationship that bordered on dysfunctional at times---the seesaw nature of Dad's personality since Vietnam often paralyzed me. One minute he would be the overbearing, hyper-competitive father-type; our family's Bull Meechum played by Robert Duvall, in the film, *The Great Santini.* The next minute, he would be a man of effusive praise, love, and affection: Gandhi-esque in nature and temperament.

Fortunately, I got Gandhi this time. He calmly explained the error of my ways, emptied the gas tank of oil, and refilled it with the proper propellant. Two rips of the cord, and the lawnmower sputtered to life, billowing light smoke, until the remaining oil I spilled burned off. Not another word was mentioned of my stupidity, at least not within earshot.

Dust, dirt, and sand shot out from the mower for thirty minutes covering me in a cloud like Linus, the cartoon character in the Charlie Brown series.

By 8 a.m. the whirl of lawn mower engines dominated the neighborhood. The reason for the early start was simple. By 11 a.m., the temperature would be a blistering ninety degrees and humid as hades. This lethal combination could easily lead to a bout of lightheadedness or heat stroke. I suffered blackouts and dizziness twice cutting grass for neighbors, both times lucky I made it home.

Cutting grass provided me with part time income. After I finished our yard, I cut the grass of several neighbors until nightfall, braving the Florida sun. This was the first of many jobs I held in Florida. I loved having my own money, $3 per yard, extra if I had to trim hedges.

The roar of fighter jets dominated our neighborhood on their way to another sortie over the Gulf of Mexico. Our home sat less than two miles from the runway. At 6 a.m. sharp, the first jets announced their arrival, rattling windows and drowning out the sound of the morning newscast on television, irritating Dad to no end. Those F-

106 Delta Darts were the best alarm clock our tax dollars could buy.

The kids in my neighborhood were a mixed lot. Across the street, on a corner lot like ours lived Captain Taylor and his family. They had a daughter, Alicia, a classmate of mine in the same grade.

Officers and enlisted personnel typically don't mix socially; in fact it was frowned upon in the military of the 1970s. The partially unwritten rule is used to maintain chain of command and discipline in the ranks.

That dynamic led to an extremely dysfunctional relationship between our two families, a potential friendship doomed to failure from the start. Today, many in the black community would call the Taylors bourgeois.

One thing we Bennett's didn't tolerate; someone thinking they were better than us. We were firm in our belief that we were the equals of anyone, black or white. Sadly, Alicia seldom left the confines of their house. She was a really nice kid, and very pretty.

Two doors down from the Taylor's resided another black family, the Jenkins. Miles, the oldest son was a high school sophomore when we met. He had the body of a middle linebacker, but didn't posses the temperament necessary to play football. He didn't have a mean bone in his body. Miles had a younger brother, a year my junior. The three of us started out thick as thieves.

Mr. Jenkins, up to that point, was the most physically imposing figure I'd ever seen. I have no idea how he managed to stay in the military with a body weight approaching three hundred pounds. But under that rolling mound of jelly, sat a muscular frame with bulging biceps and shoulder muscles to match. He would have made an excellent offensive or defensive lineman in the NFL.

Mr. Jenkins left no doubt he was the supreme commander of his castle. Their home was no democracy, rather a dictatorship. No opinion mattered but his. He presided over his sons daring them to disobey a command.

Most days, Miles and his brother couldn't leave the confines of their front yard. I found it repulsive and overbearing. I couldn't imagine a sixteen-year-old boy not being able to walk across the street to hang with his friend.

If Miles violated the old man's rules, Mr. Jenkins smacked, or beat him, often, right in front of me. I squirmed every time one of those blows rained down upon my friend's head. I would ride my bike past their house, and hear the anguish of another beating from the street. The old man essentially ruined my relationship with his sons.

The rest of my neighbors were white. One good friend, Joey Davidson was from Mississippi. The Davidson family treated me like a son. I spent several nights at their house; always welcome to eat whatever food they had in the refrigerator.

Wilson nearly fainted the first school day after we moved into our new home. He bolted from the bus almost forgetting to put on the brake and gave me a bear hug, lifting me off the ground. I'd known for two weeks our new house would leave me on his bus route. I took my usual seat right behind the driver and we chatted all the way to school.

I had an identity now, I belonged somewhere. I could play baseball with the kids in the neighborhood, listen to music, ride my bike to the store, or walk down to the shallow waters of East Bay. I could hang out and do things soon to be teenagers do. Life improved overnight.

School tensions eased somewhat. Although blacks and whites were still struggling to bond, the rift had begun to close. The students were communicating between classes, sharing lunch tables, and saying heartfelt hellos and goodbyes when our buses arrived or departed each day. This busing thing had taken root and started to sprout strong limbs.

Then, a racial disturbance at Rosenwald touched of a brief encounter with parents in the local neighborhood. Protestors made it to the school hallway near the front entrance. To this day, I have no idea what caused the demonstration, but the chants of protest were unmistakable. We students assumed it had something to do with busing white kids into this neighborhood. In a matter of minutes, most of the progress we students made had been eviscerated.

Teachers kept us in the same class for hours while the school administration and police negotiated a peaceful resolution. Even without violence, the damage proved a setback to race relations. Black students withdrew. The whites, fully aware of the tenuous situation became fearful.

The tension thickened. When school let out, I took my usual seat on the bus. Seconds later, a rock crashed through the window narrowly missing the back of my head. The rock hit no one, but startled everyone. I helped clean up the glass as Wilson quickly loaded the bus---time to go home.

No mention was made of the troubles that day on the local news. In the big scheme of things, the disturbance turned out to be nothing more than a minor nuisance. The rock thrower was a student not a protestor. I never told my parents' about that kerfuffle.

Thankfully, the holiday season arrived allowing things to simmer down naturally. That would be the only disturbance of my three-year stay at Rosenwald. Much of the credit for diffusing this potentially volatile situation goes to the faculty and staff. They kept their cool, stayed together, and put student safety first.

Academically, Rosenwald presented few challenges. I did learn, but the pace seemed slow and laborious. Was Rosenwald an inferior school given its recent past? I didn't have the answer to that question at the time. The courses all seemed age appropriate, Algebra, Civics, Chemistry, Spanish, English Literature, and U.S. History.

My rapid grasp of this new material led to a severe case of boredom like I'd experienced in Spain. I played little mind games with myself to pass the time. I took to memorizing whole sections of books word-for-word, just to see if I could do it.

I grabbed a dictionary randomly turning to a page and set about memorizing every word and meaning. I made it through seventh grade without doing homework. I usually completed assignments while listening to lectures in other classes.

Tyndall had a decent library, better than Rosenwald. I checked out books on my favorite subjects, baseball and World War II history. Most of the history books were written by academics using vocabulary beyond my years. Dad laughed when I showed him my initial collection. Undeterred, I set about studying my college-level history books in lieu of time I might have spent doing homework. These books prevented my mind from turning to mush.

My affinity for World War II history came from television and the many films of the era. I loved that ominous black and white setting. It added a sense of drama I couldn't explain. When the motion picture *Patton* debuted in 1970, I paid to see the film six times.

White America was depicted as singular war heroes in every film I saw. It was they, and they alone, who defeated the Nazis and the Japanese. Good storytelling aided and abetted this narrow interpretation of history reinforcing white superiority. I had never heard of the Tuskegee Airmen or the contribution women made. My grandfather served in Okinawa, but I didn't learn of his involvement until 2011 at his funeral, when the Army color guard paid tribute to his sacrifice. Like Dad, Grandpop never discussed the war, at least not with me.

School turned into more of a social affair than an academic setting. No longer relegated to the seat behind Wilson, I sat everywhere. One day I could be found chatting up a girl, the next debating sports and planning weekend pursuits.

One of those pursuits involved a birthday party at a classmate's house on a Friday night. Joey, ever the social butterfly, asked me if I'd been invited to Allison's home for her thirteenth birthday celebration. No, I hadn't received an invitation. Allison and I shared a few classes and spoke quite often, always about schoolwork. She had no reason to extend an invitation and I wasn't offended.

Somehow, Joey finagled an invite for me. I took the time to pick out a nice card and buy her a gift.

Joey's father drove us to the Allison's house, about six miles away on the other side of Tyndall. Mr. Davidson dropped us off at the curb and left. A warm feeling washed over me as Joey rang the doorbell.

Allison's father answered. His gaze told me I wasn't welcome, long before he blocked my path of entry that destroyed the warm feeling I had moments earlier. "You're not invited," he said. Code words for no blacks allowed. Joey explained that he already cleared the invitation with his daughter. Daddy didn't care. Access was not granted.

Several partygoers, all classmates, were gathered at the front door. A few shouted hello through the commotion. It took a minute before they realized I wouldn't be joining the celebration. Even after Allison protested, I remained persona non grata. Joey objected a little too loudly for my taste and left with me before I talked him into returning. It wasn't his fault I was black. I tossed the card and book I bought Allison in a nearby garbage can.

This white man had humiliated me in front of my friends. My sadness and tears, gave way to anger, and the need for retaliation. I thought about becoming a vandal, tempted to egg his car and house, but vandalism wasn't my style. Plus, I feared what Dad would do if he found out I broke the law.

The military's earnest pursuit of racial harmony obviously hadn't found a receptive audience at Allison's home. I'm not sure if being reared in Alabama during Jim Crow had anything to do with her father's reaction, but the rejection stung, the venomous bite finding its way into my psyche.

The beach sat about a half mile from Allison's home. In another of those bright moon lit nights, I could see boats trolling the waters just off shore. They appeared to be fishing vessels of some kind with nets cast over the side.

A sandbar known as Shell Island protected the harbor at Tyndall from the open Gulf of Mexico. Shell Island extended two miles east to west, no more than a quarter mile wide, with not a tree in sight. An opening several hundred yards wide allowed small boats to pass through to the Gulf. Shell Island helped minimize storm surge during a hurricane, but it also trapped fish inside during high tide.

I found a vending machine, bought a coke, and made my way to a small fishing pier. I stood quietly. I'd never seen anyone fish up close. The fishermen nodded in my direction without a word, probably so our voices wouldn't scare off their potential meal. Tonight would be a bad night; the fish simply weren't biting finding safe harbor away from nets and poles.

I noticed a few lovers holding hands walking barefoot along the sandy shore. I must have looked out of place all dressed up and nowhere to go. *Would this event be emblematic of my new life? Would my friends still be my friends on Monday, when I returned to school?*

I had three hours to contemplate, repeatedly asking myself; challenging myself to come up with answers. None were forthcoming.

Around 9:30 p.m. I walked back to Allison's house and sat on the curb waiting for my ride home. My classmates were exiting Allison's home. All stopped to apologize.

Allison saw me sitting on the curb and left her home to chat in an act of defiance. She extended an olive branch that I was in no mood to accept, the wound still too fresh.

I ran into her bigoted hypocritical father numerous times in the ensuing months. When other adults were around he acted like we were best friends. I wanted to slap the hell out of him.

Joey told his dad what happened not missing a single detail. Mr. Davidson almost turned the car around ready for a confrontation with Allison's father. He thought the better of it and started cursing---"sonofabitch, that f**king asshole"---as he drove us home. I remained quiet for the ten-minute trip.

Mr. Davidson dropped me off at home and expressed his sorrow. He wanted to speak with Dad, to explain the situation, but I convinced him that wouldn't be necessary. For all Dads' faults, being a coward wasn't one of them. Embarrassing his son would not have gone without confrontation, superior officer, or not. Dad's explosive temper could have easily earned him a night behind bars. We didn't have bail money.

Fortunately, my parents' were in their bedroom watching television when I arrived. I hollered hello through the partially open door and went straight to my bedroom avoiding any cross-examination.

Life after that party diminished my trust in white adult males. I emotionally withdrew for a few days, only talking to Joey, Amanda, and the handful of black friends I had at school. After a little thirteen-year-old introspection, I realized I wasn't being fair to white people, or my friends. I decided to live again, a little wiser than the previous week.

I received an invitation to a second birthday party just days after the incident at Allison's. At first I declined, but at the urging of several friends, I relented with a condition. Kelly would have to ask her parents' permission. It wasn't a request; it was a demand that sounded rather harsh upon reflection. Not only did Kelly ask permission, her mother called my house---access granted, please enter.

We became even better friends once I bonded with her parents. They were the coolest couple I'd ever met, like hippies dressed in military garb. Kelly and I challenged each other in school enjoying friendly competition for the best grades. A year later her father was transferred overseas and we lost all contact---life of a brat.

I attended a few more birthday parties, always insisting on parental approval. These gatherings became rather boring affairs requiring more energy than they were worth. Somewhere during the course of the evening, everyone paired off into couples.

Not knowing what to do to make the outlier feel welcomed, my friend's started to invite the one or two black girls who lived nearby. Good intentions, poor execution. Well aware of our circumstances, the girls and

I stopped attending. All we did was eat, listen to that acid rock music of the early seventies---not my preferred cup of tea; and watch the juvenile version of spin the bottle.

CHAPTER 10

THE INFAMOUS OUT

JUNE 1971

The school year ended quietly. The tension that greeted us back in September lingered in the atmosphere, more of a fine mist, than a heavy rain. I spent hours on the phone with my black classmates in anticipation of eighth grade, for better days loomed.

Summer is the time most military families get transferred. The Jenkins left that summer. A white family with an infant child moved into their former home, not exactly playmate material for a thirteen-year-old.

My best friend Joey left at the beginning of summer vacation. His father retired and moved their family back to Mississippi.

Only one black family remained besides ours, Alicia's from across the street. Tyndall Air Force Base had four neighborhoods; three of the four had no fewer than one hundred homes. We just happened to live in the one with just two black families.

The departure of my few close friends left a huge void that Dad quickly filled with a surprise announcement. He arrived home early from work and demanded I get in the car. Once in the car I asked where we were going. He didn't say a word until we pulled up in front of the baseball field about three miles from home, and removed my glove from the trunk of his car.

Dad signed me up for Pony League baseball, by far the best surprise of the summer, or at least it began that way. The league for thirteen to sixteen-year boys started two weeks earlier. I joined a Yankees team winless in five games. How ironic, playing baseball in the South for a team called the Yankees.

Dad introduced me to Coach Reader, who in turned gathered the players around to announce the arrival of their newest teammate. The team looked puzzled and none to friendly. Once again I found myself in a situation as the "only one," the only black face in a sea of white. The other seven teams had multiple black players.

Coach and I went over positions settling on my preferred location in the outfield. I was a great defensive player if I must say so myself. I had older boys hit me fly balls that I would track down in the soft sand around my house. Through that exercise, I learned how to anticipate, compensating for earth movement beneath my feet. This wasn't some predetermined practice routine. Our neighborhood had so much sand it just seemed a natural thing to do.

Most of the better players on our Yankees squad also played in the outfield. Jim, coach's son was not only our best outfielder; he was our best pitcher, and hitter. He excelled at everything

We spent an hour taking batting practice my first day, most of the time devoted to the new kid. The coaches didn't know if I could hit. I had a thirty-four-ounce bat, heavy even by major league standards. No way a six foot two inch, one hundred forty five pound thirteen-year-old should be swinging a bat that size. I was so comfortable the coaches left me alone after their laughter subsided.

I managed to spray the ball around pretty good, but something would have to give. I needed a faster, lighter bat. These kids were all older and physically stronger than my little league team of three years earlier. Even batting practice, where pitches are thrown at half-speed looked like ninety mile per hour fastballs. That speed would be ratcheted up a few notches in a real game.

With only ten players, the new guy started his first game on the bench. During our time in the field, the coaches sat with me discussing baseball strategy---the ins and outs of the game. Do this, don't do that, watch his fastball, check out his delivery---I had more fun on the bench than the players in the field.

We only played seven innings. In the top of the seventh, I took my place in centerfield. I felt important standing there adorned in Yankee pinstripes. I slept in my uniform that first night like a little kid hugging his security blanket.

We continued our losing ways. The next game, I subbed in late, this time in right field. I didn't get an at bat, but I didn't care.

The Ruth, Gehrig, Mantle, and Maris Yankees had nothing to fear from us, we were more like *The Bad News Bears*, without the humor, a pathetic lot were we.

Finally, after four games, I got my chance. Only nine players showed up for our game forcing them to play me, or forfeit. Coach started me in centerfield.

The opposing pitcher was a classmate of mine, a few years older, and highly competitive. Donald was one of those kids who would throw a hissy fit if things didn't go his way.

By the sixth inning, Donald had complete control of the game, ahead four to one. I walked and struck out my previous at bats. I couldn't figure out why we were unable to hit his fastball. His pitches moved in slow motion compared to other boys in the league. But Donald excelled at nibbling corners in the strike zone. He had an assortment of off speed pitches that complimented his slow fastball. For a fifteen-year-old, someone taught him well.

In the bottom of the seventh, the score now four to two, we had pretty much resigned ourselves to another loss. Then our first batter walked. The second batter hit a slow roller to third base; both runners were safe. Donald's coach walked to the mound. I expected him to get the hook, but he remained in the game. Our third batter walked loading the bases.

I took my sweet time walking to the batter's box, one of those mannerisms I picked up from studying major league players. Then I ran to the third base coach for instructions. I could either screw this up, or get us in the game.

The first pitch floated to the plate, Donald's version of a fastball. I stood watching as the ball sailed by, as if carried by a soft wind current. It barely made a sound when it struck the catcher's mitt---strike one. Donald served up a hitter's pitch on a silver platter and I stood there frozen in time. I stepped away and shook my head in disbelief. He'd been doing this the entire game and no one made him pay.

My instructions were to take the pitch to right field. Our coach noticed the right fielder had drifted in a few steps positioning his body shallow and almost directly behind the second baseman. The right fielder was close enough to speak to the second baseman without shouting.

I'd already decided after strike one, if I saw another slow motion fastball come my way, I was swinging, and I really didn't care where it landed.

I torqued my body and swung at the next pitch with all my might lifting a fly ball to straight away centerfield. It looked like a long out. I walked towards first base believing I would soon be sitting on the bench. The centerfielder started backpedalling, slowly at first, then in full gallop.

He reached the fence, but the ball still had some flight time remaining. It landed in a bush just beyond the barricade announcing the field of play. It was our team's first home run of the season, and our first win. The crowd erupted.

By the time my foot hit the second base bag, the only thing I heard was my own breathing. Despite the obvious jubilation of the crowd, my mind went silent. I rounded third base and headed home. My teammates and the home plate umpire waited. I took two steps inside the base line and touched the plate. A celebration ensued.

We went to the dugout, collected our belongings, and headed to the bleachers for the ritual snacks and refreshments brought by one of the parents after each game. The coaches didn't join us immediately. All three were locked in a heated conversation with the home plate umpire. I left the dugout when a coach stopped me. "Have a seat," he said. Unsure what to make of the moment at hand, I obliged, and took a seat in the dugout.

Coach Reader told me my run didn't count. Stunned, I asked why, in a tone that defied coach's authority. Thankfully, he didn't take it that way. When I stepped inside the third base line, just before touching home plate, I'd violated a rule of the game. I needed to stay outside the line that I couldn't see, because the umpire had allowed my teammates to block my path to the plate.

The three runs I knocked in counted. We still won the game. I shifted my gaze towards the umpire who was already looking into our dugout. He had a shit-eating grin on his face that told me all I needed to know. His act, while correctly called, had been a deliberate attempt to humiliate me, for reasons I couldn't fathom. *Why me?*

Parents and adults, who had nothing to do with our game, were furious once the announcement was made over the public address system. Adults I didn't even know berated the ump all the way to his car. "How can you do that to a thirteen-year-old," one shouted. I didn't know what to do but hide in shame.

A few days later, I ran into that ump in the restroom. He simply said, "Tough luck kid, I'll be watching you the rest of the year." *What had I done to him?*

Once Dad found out about the game he blew a gasket like I expected. He vowed not to miss another game the rest of the season. True to his word, Dad arrived for the next game shouting words of encouragement from the stands, with a steady gaze at the home plate umpire, looking for the slightest lapse in his judgment. Unfortunately, I returned to my previous role of late inning defensive replacement. Dad never saw me hit again, ever.

A week passed before our next game. We had a few practices, when Coach Reader announced one of our teammates would miss the rest of the year, his father had been transferred. I would be starting in centerfield. Elated, I let Dad know when I arrived home.

The prospect of our team qualifying for the playoffs had long since passed. We were officially playing for fun and pride. The next game was against the best team in our division.

My first time up, I hit a fly ball to deep left field for a long out. On the first pitch of my second at bat, a fastball off the arm of a sixteen-year-old buzzed my head knocking me to the ground. Thinking it nothing more than a wild pitch, I planted myself in the batter's box waiting for the next delivery. That pitch hit my helmet sending it flying towards the backstop. I took first base as Coach Reader complained vehemently to the umpire. The pitch at my head was intentional, a fact confirmed, at least in my mind, when no other player received as much as a brush back pitch from our opponent.

In the sixth inning, I stepped into the batter's box for my final at bat; we were way behind. That first pitch was thrown behind me; still no warning from the umpire. Coach Reader made a beeline for the other dugout in an attempt to protect me and call off the dogs. A heated discussion took place forcing the ump to quell the shouting before things turned violent.

The next pitch found its mark. A fastball slammed into my left forearm just above the wrist. I fell to the ground writing in pain. A fight broke out in the stands between parents that bled into the opposing team's dugout. Coach Reader and the pitcher who hit me came to my aid.

Like the pitcher I'd hit the home run off of, this kid also attended Rosenwald. He cried as he helped me to my feet. His teammates took their cue, all coming to my aid, even those players patrolling the outfield.

I made it to first base waiting for the game to resume. It took several minutes to restore order, us kids bewildered at the scene before us. I overheard one parent discuss with another whether it would be necessary to call the police for my safety.

While standing on the first base bag, my arm started to swell. By the end of the inning, it was so inflamed I couldn't get my glove on, and my fingers had gone numb. Coach wanted me out of the game, a command I steadfastly refused. Instead, a teammate helped force my glove onto my left hand out of view of the coaches. Then, I promptly took my place in centerfield.

The first hit, as luck would have it, was a towering high fly ball to center. I took one step to my right and waited for this piece of stitched cowhide to fall back to earth, neck craned skyward. The ball landed in my glove causing unbelievable agony all the way to my shoulder.

I knew my season had come to an end. Coach waited until Dad arrived to explain that evening's events. Dad had missed this, and all my other games, preferring instead to spend his time drinking at the club. Dad started suffering the affects of what is commonly known today as, Post Traumatic Stress Disorder (PTSD). Back then none of us knew about PTSD and how much he suffered. Alcohol had taken over his life.

In a fit of white-hot rage, Dad found the other coach, challenging him to a fight, while shouting a series of four-lettered words spewing phlegm from mouth and nostrils. Dad's Kryptonite had always been his temper, but in this case, he had reason to retaliate in my eyes. It took four people to hold him back, in the process, ripping his military uniform in several places.

Once calm, we were off to the emergency room where my fractured arm was reset, and placed in a cast for weeks.

Those rednecks not only cost me my season, I never played organized baseball again. My passion for the game simply vanished. No matter how hard Dad tried in the future to convince me to play again, I wouldn't budge. When it came to sports, Dad lived vicariously through me, because he never had the opportunity.

To this day, I have no idea why I became a target: a below average player, albeit one with lots of potential. Dad made the assumption my blackness was the culprit. I didn't want to jump that far out on a limb, but he had a point. I needed time to decompress and process my baseball experience.

I stayed away from the game the remainder of the summer, even refusing to watch on television. For the second time in less than six months, a bigoted white male flexed his perceived dominance over me. That bigotry ignited a rage that took months to extinguish. Dad wasn't the only one in our family with a temper; I just controlled mine better.

CHAPTER 11

CONTRADICTIONS

SEPTEMBER 1971

Riding a bus took on a whole new meaning for students who joined Rosenwald for my eighth grade school year. The idea of desegregation scared many new arrivals to the southern way of life. They approached our journey that first day with a great deal of trepidation, much like I had the previous year. Relaxation didn't come easy.

One ritual carried over from the previous year that seemed to alleviate some of those jitters, involved a spontaneous outburst of song. The songs chosen by one of the older students typically had something to do with hatred of the Vietnam War.

The songs were mostly ballads or folk music making it easy to understand and sing-along. By far the most popular song on our bus was a tune by Country Joe and the Fish, *I-Feel-Like-I'm-Fixin-to-Die.*

And it's one, two, three,
What are we fighting for?
Don't ask me, I don't give a damn,
Next stop is Vietnam;
And it's five, six, seven,
Open up the pearly gates,
Well there ain't no time to wonder why,
Whoopee! We're all gonna die.

That same year came the release of, *American Pie*, by Don McLean. That song, over eight minutes in length, while not a protest song, captured the imagination of a bus full of white kids. On occasion, someone brought a cassette or eight-track player better to create a more harmonic and cohesive sound.

So bye-bye, Miss America Pie
Drove My Chevy to the levee, but the levee was dry
And them good old boys were drinkin' whiskey and rye
Singin' "This'll be the day that I die
This'll be the day that I die"

The song itself made no sense. Even Don McLean, the songwriter, refused to provide interpretation, but that tune had a hypnotic effect that provided a welcome distraction.

Most of the white teens were saturated in hippie culture. The white guys wore shoulder length, or longer hair, psychedelic clothing, shower thongs and jeans with holes that looked liked they hadn't seen a washer in weeks---our version of Woodstock. For those who could grow something more than peach fuzz on their face, it remained largely unkempt.

Many of our parents had given up the fight for more traditional military style haircuts. The *Leave it To Beaver or GI Joe* days were a relic of the past. No self-respecting teenager would be caught wearing such a do. Show up in anything other than hippie gear and long hair, you were likely to be ridiculed unmercifully.

The girls often went braless, in halter-tops, with bare midriffs, and hip-hugger jeans. School officials summoned more than one young lady for a discussion about appropriate attire. You could always pick out the girls from conservative households; while dressed in counter-culture hippie fashion, their body parts were completely covered.

Everyone had a peace symbol adorned to his or her body. Some had peace symbol bracelets or earrings, others wore multiple rings on each hand, and still others had the symbol etched into their clothing.

Many of the white kids greeted one another with the two fingered peace sign, where the index and middle finger form a V-shape, the thumb holding the other two fingers down towards the palm of the hand.

Hippie culture never appealed to me other than the freedom and break from tradition it represented. I fell in love with the black style of the day, especially bell-bottoms to cover my massive feet---now a size thirteen and growing. I hadn't quite made the jump to the popular Angela Davis style Afro, but the transition was well underway. Black people called my hair "that good hair"---soft, thick, with very lose curls.

Dad tried countless times to straighten my curly locks, all for not. The most popular method he employed;

a stocking cap cut from Mom's nylons. Dad made me wear the cap while I slept in an attempt to flatten my unruly mane.

Black people throughout the 1940s and 1950s tried chemicals to straighten kinky hair, often causing burns, resulting in permanent skin and scalp damage. Fortunately, Dad didn't try that method on me. He experimented with countless creams. His favorite was Brylcreem. The creams made my hair even more unmanageable, further irritating him.

Dad then tried styling my hair by taking me to the military barbershop, but they only knew one way to cut hair, a fade with slick sidewalls, which drove Mom insane. She wanted to show off my "good hair."

Next, Dad tried to cut my hair. I looked like a cross between boxing promoter Don King and a little troll doll with curls. My sloppy Afro took root out of Dad's frustration.

Many of my black classmates took to wearing Afro picks as an accessory. My hair was simply too soft to hold a pick in place. The girls, black and white took, turns braiding my hair, but even the braids wouldn't hold.

As we sang these songs, and others that carried anti-war messages, I wondered if any of us truly understood the paradox that our defiance through song symbolized. Many of our father's had been to Vietnam, and all were still on active duty. It seemed peculiar, at least to me; or maybe this expression provided an outlet for our collective frustration that our father's were continually being put in harms way, for a war whose origins dated back before our birth.

War protests dominated the nightly news. By now,

most of us were fully aware of the massacre at Kent State University. Protesters and innocent bystanders were hit by a fusillade of bullets fired by members of the Ohio National Guard. It took just thirteen seconds for the guardsmen to kill four students, wound nine, and leave one paralyzed. The students were angered by President Richard Nixon's recent announcement of an incursion of U.S. forces into Cambodia.

In four years, many of us would be eligible for the draft, a fact not lost on any of us. But like most teenagers, we thought we were invincible, immune from harm. Dad worried. While I knew it was a possibility, I never gave conscription much thought.

Our arrival at school launched a massive family reunion style celebration. We sang, danced, told jokes, and hugged one another like we hadn't seen each other in years. The bell announcing the arrival of first period came and went. No one made a move towards class, including the teachers. They too appeared genuinely happy to participate in the reunion.

Rosenwald had traveled a long way in a year. Unlike the anxiety of the previous year, blacks and whites were fully engaged, jive talking and trying to one up each other in the cool department. The white girls, who previously refrained from getting too close to the black males, showed outward signs of love and respect. The black females, who previously kept a respectful distance from whites, were fully involved in deep and meaningful conversation one minute, and playful banter the next.

While busing had the primary purpose of equal education, the improving social dynamic proved to be more beneficial. No social scientist of the day could have predicted such a dramatic change in circumstances, at least not in our little part of the Deep South.

"Benneeeeeeet," Coach Collier bellowed as I arrived for gym class, hugging me hard enough to break a rib or two. Rosenwald had become a place of refuge and relative safety. My savior, Amanda had gone off to high school, but I no longer needed my heroine.

Poverty reappeared in my life with a vengeance. The dichotomy between the haves and have nots split along neighborhood lines. That meant many of my black friends weren't going to eat school lunch that first day, or any day. They simply couldn't afford the $1 lunch.

"Let me hold a dollar," many asked, looking for a way to stave off starvation. I let several "hold a dollar," fully aware my money would be gone forever.

I started bringing my allowance, plus money saved from my summer grass cutting gigs. Bennett National Bank opened for business. My terms for doling out lunch money, watching a hungry friend get fed.

Someone reported me to the principal's office. Administrators promptly ordered me to refrain from funding school lunches. I obeyed for a few weeks before reopening the bank faults. Until Rosenwald, I'd never experienced such a consistent, in your face level of poverty first hand. It was a visceral, blood-churning feeling that made me sick to my stomach.

A program existed to help the less fortunate, but for a variety of reasons my friends couldn't fully comprehend, they and their families fell through the cracks in a maze of bureaucratic nonsense. What an indictment on the richest country in the world.

Girls were beginning to change into young women. Something happened to them, or me, between seventh and eighth grade. Either they filled out, or I started to notice. Regardless of the reason, my loins started feeling urges I could no longer ignore, suppress yes, ignore no. Like most pubescent boys, I took great pains to hide my embarrassment.

These young ladies had become a lot more aggressive. For a shy kid like me, it made life easy. Our home phone no longer belonged to the family; it was my private line. I spent hours talking to the white females who called our house; often, well after bedtime, waking Dad from much needed sleep. Their parents didn't appear to be taking this interracial thing too seriously at Tyndall. They probably thought it nothing more than a passing fad, so it was tolerated; but you certainly couldn't tell by our behavior.

We were openly dating, holding hands, walking on the beach, going to the movies, sharing a few kisses, and anything experimenting teenagers considered a relationship, short of sex. I remained wary, but succumbed to the companionship. My dates and me were often targets of nasty, vile comments, mostly at the hands of white males, yet we continually flaunted our relationships like any good defiant teenager.

I always suffered the brunt of vitriol. I had the police called on me more often than I can count for walking with a white girl, although that's not the story the police were told. The po po responded so often, me and my dates were on a first name basis, sharing laughs---"oh, not you again." One of the military police officers frequently treated us to lunch.

White males threw lit matches and burning cigarettes at my face. Someone pulled out an awfully authentic looking toy gun in an attempt to scare us into submission. Parents of the young ladies often heard from nosy neighbors, complaining because their daughter held hands with a black boy. Many hated-filled whites called me "boy," fully aware of its negative connotation.

I worried these girls might be in danger for hanging out with me. But these young ladies, nor their parents, budged an inch, refusing to acquiesce to the demands of the great white southern social dynamics. I took my strength from their attitudes and behavior, although they never had to walk five feet in a black boy's shoes.

With no baseball, or other organized sporting activity to occupy my spare time, I started bowling again. When I wasn't league bowling, I spent hours practicing by myself on Saturday and Sunday afternoons. I averaged a whopping 135. The many adults, mostly white, who hung out at Tyndall Lanes became my guardians, in stark contrast to my experience with whites in the community at large.

It all started with Gladys, the adult who ran the kid's bowling program. Her daughter and I were the same age, both bowling fanatics notorious for our bad tempers. On our first day of league competition, I threw a ball so poorly; I slammed my fist into the ball return rack, easily drowning out all other sound emanating from a twelve-lane bowling center full of kids and balls crashing into pins.

Gladys calmly walked to where I was now seated, and whispered in my ear, "If I ever catch you hitting the equipment again, you can leave, and don't bother coming back." Still seething, I bit my lip and promised to comply. She made sure I complied, never leaving my side the remainder of the day, ignoring the other fifty-nine kids.

Gladys, a middle-aged, single white lady with two kids, and not very well off financially, treated me like her son. She started asking about home, my grades, my social life, and interests outside of bowling.

Our friendship blossomed to the point where I became her indispensible assistant. I took over the bookkeeping for the league, calculating averages, standings, and posting results. I collected monies, made bank deposits and coached the younger pre-teen group.

My relationship with Gladys started a trend that would continue through my high school years, the friendship of adults in lieu of strong connections with kids my own age.

By the end of that bowling season, my average climbed twenty more pins thanks to Gladys. I also learned to control my hyper-competitive temper. The phone calls to our house from the girls ceased, replaced by inquiries from adults, many volunteering to ferry me back and forth to the bowling alley. The more adult like conversation seemed, at the time, like such a natural fit.

Many of these adults had kids who were classmates of mine. These parents sought my counsel on numerous occasions about how to handle their unruly teenagers. I often knew more about what went on inside my classmates' homes, than they did. Their parents' confided in me and I always kept their confidence. When a parent needed an intervention, I often delivered the message--- strange indeed.

CHAPTER 12

THE UGLY STAGE

Like most adolescents, I'd reached a stage in life where my permanent teeth appeared huge in comparison to the size of my head. Someone I knew called it the "ugly stage."

My teeth were obscenely crooked. Some remained embedded in my gums, causing them to swell and my lips to protrude. Other teeth went off at angles that would make Freddy Krueger double over with laughter.

My parents' decided to do something about the "ugly stage." Dr. Johnson's office sat about two miles from Rosenwald, on Harrison Avenue, Panama City's main drag. The Sears store, the town's only McDonalds in those days, and the place where my parents' witnessed a Ku Klux Klan rally all took place on Harrison Avenue.

Dad arrived at Rosenwald mid-morning as we were changing classes. The intercom system on that particular day was inoperable forcing him to wait in the administrator's office until a student could track me down. Dad signed the early withdrawal slip and off we went to the orthodontist.

The following day turned into one that I just as soon forget. At gym class, my black classmates hit me with a barrage of questions and comments, some curious, others insulting. *Michael Bennett is your daddy white? Michael Bennett's daddy is a cracker. Honkie. White Boy. Uncle Tom.* The inquisition and insults lasted for the entire hour. I should have realized from the stares Dad received the previous day, his complexion and racial makeup would be completely misunderstood.

Most of my white classmates knew Dad, or knew of him, and didn't make a fuss. The revelation that Dad had features that could easily be mistaken for a white person exacerbated an already tenuous relationship with my black cohorts.

The flag football game that day turned violent. The target on my narrow back grew exponentially with evil intent, all under the guise of playing football. The pounding I took, even for a simple game with no tackling, left me bruised and battered for days---elbows to the head, fists to the stomach, and kicks aimed at my sore knees, which by now, were no secret at Rosenwald. I gave, as good as I got, but the number of misguided young men proved difficult to overcome.

After class, those black students who dared walk with me demanded an even more thorough explanation. They wanted to know why I'd hidden Dad's whiteness, thinking I was privileged because of his looks. In hindsight, I couldn't blame these kids for jumping to such false conclusions. The segregated South shaped these young mines, not allowing for the possibility that not every black person was dark-skinned.

I provided every detail I could, including a physical description of Dad's mother. I made it clear Dad didn't know the identity of his biological father. So they started speculating, like I had done several years earlier after meeting Grandma Jean.

The tenor of my relationship with the black student body hit a snag. My friends lost faith in me. I wasn't black enough. Certainly they'd seen light-skinned black people before. I realized for the first time, the shade of darkness mattered to some in the black community. *But what did my lighter skin mean to white America? Did it provide access or privilege?* I certainly didn't think so.

A month passed when both Mom and Dad checked me out of school for another appointment. The reaction this time was completely different. Everyone noted Mom's beauty, compelling me to smack a few boys upside the head for their sexual innuendo. The cold-shoulder treatment ceased immediately. *So this is what Dad went through in the 1940s and 50s---simultaneous acceptance and rejection.*

Never too far away from myriad forms of bigotry, that same day, our family exited a small store on Tyndall, called Tyndall Park. The store was a slightly larger version of a 7-Eleven. Dad spotted a dog just as it escaped through a car window sitting in the parking lot. Dad rescued the little pooch steps from U.S. Highway 98---the same road where Heidi was killed. Everyone in the parking lot saw that little dog bolt for the highway, but Dad was the only one who took action.

Dad handed the small animal to my sister and ran into the store to locate the owner. As Dad exits the store, he spots the owner, an older white lady. She had just snatched her dog, rather forcefully, from my sister's arms. He politely begins to tell the story of the dog's escape, when she blurts out "you nigger's were trying to steal my dog." She didn't have a problem figuring out Dad's identity.

Dad returned fire to the ungrateful bitch creating a scene. The woman just wouldn't relent, even when the other white people in the parking lot came to our defense. "Those niggers were trying to steal my dog," she said, over and over again. Who leaves a small dog in a car in ninety-degree heat?

Shortly after my fourteenth birthday, work on my mouth began in earnest. Before Dr. Johnson could begin, I had to have four teeth pulled, which the dental staff at Tyndall handled. I had all four pulled at once assuring the dentist I could handle the pain. That turned out to be a bad decision. I sucked food through a straw for a week.

Next, Dr. Johnson had to widen my upper jawbone to relieve overcrowding, using something called an expander. This device and the four pulled teeth would allow those pearly whites still buried in my gum line to find their proper place, or be pulled into position.

To accomplish this task, doc attached the expander to two molars on either side of my mouth. This metal device had a tiny hole in the center. Twice a day, I placed a wire-like key device about the size of a paperclip into the hole, and pushed twice. The expander would extend ever so slightly forcing the upper jawbone to widen.

At first the pain was negligible, but as time passed, it would be debilitating, causing severe headaches. Two months later, I had a two to three inch gap between my front teeth. When I smiled, my top front teeth were nowhere in sight---back to sucking food through a straw. Meat had to be cut small and swallowed whole.

My classmates measured the canyon between my teeth with rulers about once a week, taping the results to the inside of my locker. The gap had grown enough to fit half a roll of quarters.

Next came braces. In 1972, braces were cemented to teeth. It took four visits to get all the metal bands into their proper places. I looked like an alien, but in a matter of weeks, my four front teeth were back together straighter than ever.

Coach treated me with kid gloves during physical education. No one touched my mouth, or sore knees, which had taken a turn for the worse from too much activity.

Then, one bright morning, the normally mild-mannered Coach Collier became a tyrant, and for good reason. Someone stuff a rag into a sink in the boys' locker room and turned on the water. The flood eventually made its way to the newly resurfaced gym floor that cost the school thousands of dollars. For a school as poor as Rosenwald, one misappropriated penny was a big deal.

Since no one claimed responsibility for this brazen act of stupidity, Coach punished us all, me included. We ran a series of sprints and distance races for an hour, resting just long enough for him to blow the whistle beckoning us back to our feet.

My knee collapsed. Normally, a staunch protector of

my health, Coach had rightfully lost his mind. He ordered me to stand, I couldn't. He made a move in my direction, only to be stopped by one of the assistant coaches. Students carried me to a grassy area away from the track and gently placed me on the ground. Coach yelled at them, "get your ass back on the track," to continue the torture as I sat and watched.

Walking to second period, my left knee buckled once again, my body crumpling to the floor like an accordion. Two teachers carried me to the school nurse. She listened attentively while I explained Osgood and what the orthopedist recommended when I had an episode. She asked if I had done anything strenuous in first period to cause a flare up. I lied.

Coach was like a second father; I didn't want him in trouble. But word got back to him that I collapsed a second time. He pulled me out of another class and apologized profusely. His eyes welled ever so slightly when I put my hand on his shoulder assuring him I'd be fine. He couldn't single me out for special treatment.

Coach excused me from every gym activity for the next two weeks. In one of the bravest things anyone had ever done on my behalf, Coach called Dad, told him what happened and apologized. The apology wasn't necessary, Dad understood. Besides, Dad loved the idea of toughening me up.

Days went by before Coach worked up the courage to ask me to join his track team. What a question to ask a kid you just tortured. I knew I couldn't compete with any consistent hope of winning; my knees couldn't handle the constant pounding. But I was the best remaining athlete at school not affiliated with any Rosenwald sport.

Coach could be very persuasive. "If I give you the day off before a meet, would you consider it," he asked. I promised an answer in a few days. In the meantime, Coach went on the offensive. He approached several classmates, who in turned, hounded me to become a member of the team. I agreed just to get them off my back, uncertain what I was getting myself into.

I gave Coach my answer with an additional caveat. The five-mile jog before practice, I didn't participate. Instead, we created a series of exercises in consultation with my orthopedist. After a few weeks, the other athletes were doing my exercises.

Practice started a week later after the military brats convinced parents to share carpooling duties. We were stranded on occasion forcing Coach to make two forty-minute round trips in his personal vehicle to get us home. Coach was a good storyteller, regaling us with stuff like, "when I was your age blah blah blah." He always managed to lace his stories with humor and a few dirty words. We had a blast.

I became a miler and a quarter-miler. I tried the long jump, but I couldn't propel myself forward with the force necessary to explode off the block.

Something as benign as track shoes turned into a monumental problem. Rosenwald had no size thirteen track shoes. Mom worked in the Base Exchange (BX) shoe store and literally begged the supplier to include any size thirteens in stock. She paid for them sight unseen. As a result, I had a collection of some of the most grotesque and unsightly shoes known to man.

But finding track shoes fell to Coach. He searched high and low at every sporting goods story in Panama

City, nothing. Next, he called the two county high schools. They found an old pair of cleats from the early 1960s. They weren't track shoes; they were football cleats. I wore them anyway. My teammates had sleek, albeit, slightly worn track shoes. Mine were heavy cinder blocks. The jokes at my expense from friend or foe were endless.

The black sprinters on our team took to comparing themselves to Olympian Jesse Owens, the man who single-handedly destroyed Adolf Hitler's belief in German superiority at the 1936 Olympics, in Berlin. Owens won four gold medals. I'm not even sure how they heard of Owens, my parents' weren't alive in 1936, and neither were many of theirs. But the legend of Owens had obviously carried down a few generations, a testament to his greatness. I had to research Owens, I'd never heard of him.

The black athletes bragged about running so fast the wind parted their well-grown Afros. Of course our white athletes weren't about to let such claims go unchallenged. This started a series of "Yo mama" jokes during our bus rides to Tommy Oliver Stadium that left us in stitches.

He Joe, "Yo mama is so ugly her pillow cries when she sleeps." Well, "Yo mama is so ugly her shadow quit."

I never won a race. I finished second four times in the mile, collapsed once and was beaten so soundly one time, I counted that loss in minutes not seconds. For a mile, it's difficult to lose by that much. The fun and frivolity of the bus rides to our meets, more than made up for my anemic performances.

All Florida schools we competed against were desegregated. The lone Alabama school on the other hand was all black. I wondered at the time if they would ever desegregate?

I didn't realize the University of Alabama football team that I watched on local television, led by legendary coach Paul "Bear" Bryant was segregated when we moved to Florida. It was 1971 before the team had its first black player. LSU, Ole Miss, and Georgia didn't desegregate until the following year. Talk about ignorance when it came to race, I was ignorance personified. I just watched football, it never dawned on me the heads under those helmets were all white.

With the school year coming to a close my black classmates asked me to join the football team for my freshman year. At six foot four and one hundred forty five pounds, I had no business on a football field, except, maybe as a goal post. I should have been arrested and charged with a felony for impersonating a football player. "Kid Dynomite," Jimmie Walker from the hit sitcom *Good Times*, had more muscle on his frame.

I'd never played organized football, but I had such a good time with track, I pushed skepticism aside and agreed. Mom was none too pleased, giving me one of her disapproving looks at news of my playing football. She worried a two hundred fifty pound lineman would cripple me for life. I too feared a serious injury, but my need to belong pushed all common sense asunder.

Football was a big deal in Florida. The Miami Dolphins, the states only pro football team was about to embark on the National Football League's only undefeated season, following their Super Bowl loss in 1971. The teams in New Orleans and Atlanta were closer, but those teams were in other states.

We spent all our free time on Monday talking about

the Dolphins. They were the integrated championship team we wanted to emulate.

I wasn't looking forward to summer break. I'd already quit baseball and most of my good friends left that summer. I didn't want to spend another summer cutting grass, too hot, and the pay, horrendous.

Dad came up with an idea to help me pass the time. "Let me see if I can get you a job bagging groceries at the commissary. The tips are great." The response from his little entrepreneur shocked him. "No way am I working for tips." Angered, but still in sales mode, Dad said, "You could make $40 or $50 a day." That got my attention.

The commissary is the military grocery store. The heavily discounted prices are Uncle Sam's way of compensating soldiers, sailors, and airmen for horrendous pay.

Dad's base pay in 1971 sat at $550 a month. When added to other benefits and allowances, it jumped to just under $700. Even with free medical and housing, it proved tough to feed a family of five on that kind of money. A working spouse, while helpful, only slightly improved our economic lot in life. A person had to be terribly committed to our country's defense to risk life and limb for pay that left many qualified for food stamps.

The commissary is typically packed on the fifteenth and thirtieth of every month---military paydays. It's the best time to make a hundred dollars or more in a day. The work wasn't difficult, if you didn't mind standing on your feet for eight hours, and walking back and forth from an air-conditioned building into the Florida sun.

Dad went to the commissary in person to inquire about a position for me. The commissary had no formal application process for bagboys; just approval by the store manager, largely based on the word of a military member.

The commissary looks like a traditional grocery store with several aisles all emptying out in front of nine cash registers. Two bagboys were assigned to each register. We put grocery items into brown paper bags, escorted the owner to their car, stored the food away and collected a tip. Those tips were shared between the two assigned to each register. Minor physical labor and good customer service skills were all that was required.

Active duty personnel were always given priority for part time jobs. Many need extra income to support their families. During daytime hours however, active duty personnel were at their military jobs leaving openings for teenagers to make a little extra money.

Trouble brewed on day one of my new job. The two store managers, as part of their daily ritual, patrolled the aisle making sure shelves were stocked properly, and the store remained in general good repair. Like everything affiliated with the military, the commissary was subject to visits from the Inspector General.

Their last stop on this daily inspection usually took them to the front end, where customers entered or exited the premises. I recognized the two gentlemen immediately. Their photos were posted at the front entrance. One was the store manager, the other, the grocery manager.

When our eyes met, I expected a welcoming smile. None was forthcoming. Maybe they had something on their minds, so I just went back to work, determined to make a good first impression. The other guys thought I was some kind of idiot for working so hard.

The two managers had the same first name, Larry. As I soon discovered, the two Larry's didn't take kindly to me working in their store. While the two Larrys couldn't do much about the airmen working part time, they assumed I would be easy prey for dismissal.

Shortly after the two Larrys discovered my presence, my supervisor was given instructions to curtail my work hours. The bagboy system was based on first come first serve, with preference given to active duty military personnel. You simply showed up thirty minutes before store opening, put your name on a list, military on one, dependent on the other, then our supervisor would assign us registers to work.

My supervisor informed me of the edict handed down by one of the managers. When I asked why, we both assumed my skin color played a part. In defiance of a direct order, my boss agreed to cover for me provided I arrived forty-five minutes early, leaving no doubt the first person through the door. The GI's caught on to what the managers had directed and went out of their way to further shield me from harm. One gave up a lucrative position to me on a payday costing his family at least a hundred dollars, to protest my treatment.

Our solution worked for two weeks, until one of the Larrys had me relieved for the day without explanation. Rather than get into a verbal confrontation, I decided to save the battle for another day.

I waited a week before returning. Both managers saw me the first day and did nothing. I assumed they had better things to do. Well, I assumed wrong. They fired me a few days later in front of customers, with the command to "get out;" no reason given.

I went home and waited for Dad. He was furious and wanted answers. Whenever he sank his teeth into something, you could count on Sergeant Bennett seeing it through to its ultimate conclusion.

Dad went to the store for a face-to-face, which probably didn't go well for the two Larrys. Within days I was rehired and given an apology, something Dad told me later, he demanded.

By mid-August, I'd saved over a thousand dollars. I spent the remainder of my money on bowling. I bowled ten or more games daily, rarely, if ever stopping home for dinner. I missed that 10 p.m. curfew so often my parents' stopped checking.

The bowling alley was my home away from home, the people who frequented the place, extended family.

By the end of our second year at Tyndall, the greater Panama City area had undergone a slow, somewhat deliberate change for the better. Military retirees were buying homes in the area, improving both the social, and racial climate.

Even with that, I seldom ventured off base except to attend school, or visit my orthodontist. The abject poverty of the black community and the mosaic it painted remained deeply offensive. It stoked flames of intense rage one minute, doused by buckets of deep sadness and resentment the next, when I realized I couldn't do anything to help alleviate the suffering. I tried to ignore the obvious disparity between the black and white community, but reminders lay everywhere.

Many older generation blacks still steered clear of whites---a natural proclivity of mistrust decades in the making. When that generation encountered whites on the streets, it was yes ma'am and yes sir, often with heads bowed to avoid eye contact. I couldn't wrap my head around Jim Crow and what it had done to my people.

History classes I'd taken to date never got past the Civil War. It was as if American history beyond 1865 had been sanitized from the history books. I knew we had a profound and more meaningful history than slavery. *Where did Jim Crow come from? Who, or what the hell was Jim Crow?* My inquisitive nature and thirst for knowledge kept hitting one roadblock after another, frustrating me to no end.

In one of the many philosophical musings I had growing up, I began to contemplate the word success. *What does it mean? How do you measure it? Was it simply surviving until death, like what I observed from so many in the black community?*

I'd never previously succumbed to the notion I might fail, or have my dreams suffocated because I was black, but I definitely started thinking it possible.

I became acutely aware that the color of my skin came with baggage and negative assumptions. While my dreams as a young teenager lacked vision and cohesion, my long-term success, like those of most African Americans, would depend on my ability to shove low expectations aside. That realization was a bitter pill to swallow for a kid who never thought color mattered.

CHAPTER 13

IT'S A NEW DAY

AUGUST 1972

The bright star at the center of our solar system dipped below the horizon refracting a beautiful array of red, orange, and yellow that consumed the western sky. I stood motionless; watching, thinking, as the rest of my teammates meandered towards the locker room. Our first day of football practice had just ended. My mind wandered aimlessly from topic to topic, before settling on one overarching question. Could I handle the rigors of football? My body ached, and this was only day one.

For some strange reason, I also started thinking about the world in a broader context. Global society appeared on the verge of a cataclysmic explosion. By comparison, football seemed so trivial; yet, some of our players acted like their lives depended on this game. Maybe I just wasn't that into football.

The pent up anger of a generation had spilled over

into the 1970s. The arc of history, as I learned, is not experienced in neat decades, its fluid. The bloodshed of the 1960s and the assassinations of President John F. Kennedy, Malcolm X, Dr. Martin Luther King, Jr., Senator Robert Kennedy and countless others continued its journey through the rivers and valleys of Vietnam, Cambodia, Northern Ireland and the streets of cities and towns across the planet.

The continued global violence troubled me. Drawing the distinction between the gladiators on the football field and warriors on a battlefield seemed blurred to me, it was all rooted in a collision of forces that could leave someone maimed for life, or dead.

Earlier in the year, Alabama governor, George Wallace became yet another victim of an assassin's bullet, leaving him paralyzed for life. This segregationist governor, famous for uttering the phrase, "segregation now, segregation tomorrow, segregation forever," back in 1963, had to withdraw from the presidential race.

Speaking of races, America was in the midst of a high-stakes presidential campaign. The broadcast media wielded significant power that had been building since the Kennedy/Nixon campaign of 1960. I couldn't ignore this stuff. Dad remained the ultimate news junkie, discussing current events with any adult who indulged his rabid fascination with anything news and information.

President Richard Nixon and Vice President Spiro Agnew were reelected only to have both resign in shame in less than two years. One brought up on criminal charges, the other, facing impeachment over the Watergate break-in.

The Twenty-Sixth Amendment to the Constitution

became law on July 1, 1971 lowering the voting age to eighteen. In four years, I would cast a ballot for the first time. Yet, only a few of us standing on the football field that day had rudimentary knowledge of the issues at hand.

The death that permeated our televisions sets in the name of Vietnam and Cambodia now had a new rival, "Bloody Sunday"---Northern Ireland, January 30, 1972. While I didn't completely comprehend what led to twenty-six civil rights protestors being shot by British soldiers, it was eerily similar in some respects to what was happening in America.

Even the sacred 1972 Olympic games in Munich, Germany weren't immune to violence. The Palestinian group Black September took eleven Israeli's hostage. This was followed by an intense and dramatic standoff with police played out on live television. I can still see the face of ABC television sports anchor Jim McKay as he announced the deaths of six Israeli coaches, five Israeli athletes, five Black September members, and one West German police officer.

The world had indeed turned savage, devoid of compassion and understanding; at least that's what I thought as the sun bowed out for the day. It's easy to forget all the good when such carnage dominates the news cycle.

I walked back to the locker room, the mood decidedly more upbeat than my somber reflection a few minutes earlier. Not one to ruin the party, I joined in thinking I'd just walked into Utopia. I even got a "yo mama," joke in. "Yo mama is so old she took her drivers test on a dinosaur." Looking at all these black and white faces enjoying each others company gave me hope mankind would recover from its collective idiocy and penchant for violence.

My body, on the other hand felt like it might never recover. I couldn't lift my arms. I had to coax my legs into walking. My abdominals felt like they had just survived fifteen rounds with Muhammad Ali. The worst was yet to come, still a week away from hitting one another in full pads. By the end of the first week, I needed help getting my shoulder pads over my head.

Practice usually started with calisthenics, followed by one mile around the track in full pads. The heat and humidity made water a precious commodity worth fighting for, and often used as a reward by our coaches for stellar practice habits. Coaches handed out salt tablets to replace the sodium our bodies left on the field. Gatorade had only recently been invented and wasn't widely available to high school athletes.

After a week of running and calisthenics we finally got around to assigning positions. Coach Templeton started by assigning positions to the returning players. With thirty players and only a dozen with any organized football experience, Rosenwald, sorely lacked talent and depth, at almost every position. Kids like me were forced to learn on the fly or have our heads handed to us.

After shuffling a few papers, coach finally got to those of us who never played a down. He put the tallest, skinniest kid in all of Bay County at defensive end. I accepted my position without comment; unsure what duties a defensive end would be required to perform.

We returned to the locker room where the offense and defense were split into two squads. Next came the chalkboard with a bunch of Xs and Os. My eyes glazed over in a state of confusion. Twenty minutes later, we were on the practice field walking through our responsibilities.

Then came a light scrimmage. We were instructed not to tackle for the first week. No need to get anyone hurt when we barely had enough bodies to field a team. On the very first practice snap, I got hit so hard my braces slammed against my soft cheek tissue. I forgot my mouthpiece. The taste of blood would compel me not to make that mistake again.

The pounding continued unabated for several minutes when I realized I was the only one getting hit. So I did what anyone would do in my situation, I hit back. That put a halt to scrimmage. Coach Templeton sent me, and me alone, back to the track for more running, my punishment for self-defense.

Our uniforms were hand-me downs from previous teams except our jerseys, which each of us purchased. Despite the influx of more affluent military brats to the student body, Rosenwald still suffered from decades of separate and unequal.

Our helmets were made of thin plastic, but shaped more like the leather helmets phased out in the 1940s. The helmets were squared, with tiny ear holes, not the more rounded, modern variety the other teams had. The snaps where the faceguard attached to my helmet were broken. Several helmets, including mine had no padding inside. I taped rolled up socks into my helmet for a cushion. We ordered chinstraps only to discover they didn't fit our old school helmets. My helmet had the single bar faceguard for kickers, not a defensive lineman.

The shoulder pads were dated and practically useless, some missing parts of their plastic protective shield. The strings used to tie the pads in place were missing. A quick trip to the local shoe store took care of that problem.

I learned, after a few violent collisions at practice, linemen pads were supposed to be larger than a quarterback, receiver, or kicker. We didn't have enough of the right mix to go around. Our quarterback wore linemen pads the first game restricting his ability to throw the ball.

The pants were missing hip pad slots. The cutout slots meant to insert knee pads were completely ripped away from the fabric, not a good thing for a kid with chronic knee problems. The longest pair of pants didn't even reach my knees, rendering the kneepad issue a moot point.

Shoes were a mismatch of colors and styles. Everyone grabbed a single shoe from a huge box placed in the center of the room, then searched for a match. I was the only one who started with a pair of matching shoes. I repurposed the football shoes I'd been given to run track. The cleats were completely worn exposing their metal underpinnings---dangerous if I ever decided to play the game with malicious intent.

Despite the obvious lack of proper equipment, none of us made a fuss. We were happy just to be playing football.

The Rosenwald Bulldogs took the field that early September afternoon wearing our road uniforms, burgundy with white lettering. My number 85 with Bennett sown into the back looked larger than life. It made me feel like I could scale Mount Everest without the benefit of climbing gear.

We loaded up the bus, cheerleaders and all, and headed to our first road game across town at Everitt. The music rattled the bus windows, and the "Yo mama" jokes flew from the mouth of babes. "Yo mama is so stupid it took her an hour to cook minute rice."

The laughter from the Everitt fans was immediate. Our mismatched uniforms and old-school helmets made us the laughingstock of Bay County. Some teammates were upset at the ridicule. We were an odd looking bunch---thanks a lot Jim Crow.

Referees lined up both teams to perform a routine mouth guard check. No student could play without a mouthpiece. When the ref got to me, he howled loudly in a fit of uncontrollable laugher. One look at my braces and ill-fitting uniform sent him into an uproar. Even I laughed.

Everitt had a beautiful football field. The grandstands and press box painted with the Everitt logo, an Eagle, looked pristine. The field, with its lush green grass was immaculate.

Rosenwald didn't have a home field. Our home games were played at Tommy Oliver Stadium down the street where Bay High School is located. As a result, out stands were sparsely populated drawing no more than a dozen fans per contest.

We fumbled the ball away on the opening kickoff, a mistake that foreshadowed things to come.

The decision to put me at left defensive end quickly

proved our undoing. The first play, a sweep around left end, had me removing clumps of grass from my single bar helmet.

The next several plays were more of the same---ten yards and a clump of grass. No one told me about setting the edge. In fact, I'd never been taught a technique, other than getting down in a three-point stance. Everything I did that afternoon made me regret the decision to play football.

Our coaches were schoolteachers with an embryonic knowledge of football. Proper technique eluded them all.

After Everitt scored, the coaches spent the entire three minutes our offense had the ball, yelling and belittling their undersized, stupid defensive end. When Everitt's offense took the field, they decided to mix things up, temporarily saving me further embarrassment.

Then it was back to sweep around left end followed by a series of expletives hurled in my direction from our coaching staff. I had enough and yelled back. That earned me a seat on the bench for the remainder of that game, and the next.

I almost quit on the spot only to be stopped by a few teammates, who like me, were neophytes. I was the scapegoat that allowed them to fly under the radar. Watching the game from the sidelines provided perspective. My replacement fared no better becoming nothing more than road kill.

During a timeout, I shared a solution with Donald and it worked. Line up wider than the offensive tackle and stay wide no matter what. At least you could slow them down long enough to get help.

That left end sweep disappeared from the Everitt

arsenal. They simply ran that same play to the right with moderate success. We lost and lost big, coaches openly blaming me for the defeat.

The next practice started with more ridicule. The coaches appeared determined to strip me bare of any pride I had in myself to cover their deficiencies.

After sitting out the following game as punishment for my insubordination and poor play, I was inserted into the game at linebacker with moderate success. It allowed me to read things better and use my speed to the ball. I loved the position. It beat the constant pounding at the line of scrimmage.

Still not in Coach T's good graces, game three would most likely have found me back on the bench, if not for the intervention of my number one fan. Coach Collier stopped by practice. He asked what position I played, "defensive end and sometime linebacker." The quizzical expression gave way to a shaking of the head back and forth in disbelief. He thought, like I did, that defensive end was no place for a kid with legs as slender and as fragile as fraying toothpicks.

After observing a few practice plays at defensive end, he helped me grasp the position, sharing techniques that paid immediate dividends.

Coach Collier, never one to hide his feelings walked up to Coach T, and asked, "Why is Bennett playing defensive end?" Templeton didn't have a good answer. Collier went on to explain that I might be one of the fastest kids in the county.

My blend of size and speed made me an ideal receiver. The two coaches openly feuded. Collier walked off in disgust, looking over his shoulder at me, giving me the, "oh well I tried," look.

The next day I was handed a slim playbook with no more than ten pages. I didn't even know we had a playbook. Whatever Collier said hit its mark. Just like that I was practicing as a receiver, or split end as Coach T called it.

A quick eight-yard slant pattern found me open over the middle. The ball arrived on target. I outran our defenders chewing up real estate all the way to the end zone. In the distance I could see Coach Collier smiling.

The next play, the same thing, with the exact same result. Then coach wanted the cornerback to bump me at the line of scrimmage, to no avail. In three plays, I'd scored three touchdowns.

We tried a few other plays, some requiring me to block, others were fly patterns, and some down and out to the sideline plays. Then Coach T called another slant pattern.

This time, when the ball arrived, so did two defenders. The simultaneous explosion into my chest and back forced a rush of air from my lungs. I gasped hard searching for precious oxygen. Teammates gathered around, some laughing, others certain I was dead.

Once on my feet, I walked back to the sidelines, sore, but walking without a cane. Thinking I'd get a brief respite, I grabbed a cup of water, only to hear Coach T yell for me to get my ass back on the field.

The same play was called again. This time the collision occurred near my head. Someone wanted to teach me a lesson through intimidation, willing to risk injury, if necessary. A suspicion confirmed minutes later by one of my white teammates who overheard a coaches' conversation.

Coach "T" called the play a third time. Like the previous plays, the ball arrived on target, but this time I didn't extend my arms to corral the throw. I withdrew my hands, elbows extended, landing two perfectly timed blows to the throat of one defender, and the nose of the other. I couldn't have executed that any better had I been a karate master. Both defenders collapsed. One suffered a broken nose.

I slammed my helmet on the ground and quit. No need risking life and limb for a game, no matter how much I wanted to belong.

Coach Collier was in a full gallop, having witnessed the shenanigans on the practice field. The scene turned ugly as two grown men shouted at one another.

I woke the following morning covered in bruises, breathing short and labored. I lifted my t-shirt revealing a darkened painful hue around my rib cage that the warm shower water did little to alleviate.

I hobbled to the kitchen to make my normal breakfast---waffles and juice, all while attempting to hide my discomfort from Mom. Our eyes met, her warm smile reassuring. She observed my behavior in passing at first. I grimaced opening the refrigerator door, letting out a loud moan that startled her.

Forced into a confession, I lifted my shirt. She placed a phone call to Dad, who hadn't arrived at work yet. She left a message. He called back before the school bus arrived. Mom implored him to get me to a doctor, then handed me the phone. I managed to convince him Mom overreacted. I told him I quit football, which made Mom smile, but Dad didn't seem too pleased I figured by the tone of his voice. If my decision stood, it would be the second sport I'd quit in two years.

Off to school I went, unable to make it up the bus steps without help. I gingerly walked from class to class not allowing a student to get within arms length. An accidental bump would be devastating. This was my prearranged day off from gym class, but Collier wanted to look at my ribs. Lifting my shirt almost brought him to his knees. We walked to the locker room where he applied some sort of soothing gel meant to numb the pain. The ointment smelled like Vicks Vapo Rub. The warm tingling sensation penetrated the soft tissue providing temporary relief.

At home, Dad took a look; he too, shocked at what he saw. An x-ray that evening revealed nothing broken, just deep bruising. Another ointment was applied to my rib cage then they were wrapped in an ace bandage.

Dad and I talked about football on the drive home. I really didn't want to quit, I told him; I had to for my own safety. Dad agreed, but in one of the few sermons he ever gave me growing up, he challenged my manhood. Dad invoked Jackie Robinson, who, in a huge coincidence, actually died that same week.

Most of us only got to hear about Robinson the hero, the man who desegregated major league baseball. The often-harrowing journey was glossed over in history books. Dad admirably filled in the details. He told me about the racial epithets, the intentional slide with cleats face up in an attempt to injure. He mentioned how Robinson wasn't allowed to stay with teammates during his minor league days, and how some teams, especially down South, refused to take the field when he played.

Dad's recollection of Robinson lasted long past our arrival home. "If I quit" he said, "you would be giving someone else the power to control and manipulate you. Don't give anyone the satisfaction of knowing they got the better of you. The decision to play, or not, is yours." With that he was off to bed, leaving me in the living room by myself watching the *Tonight Show with Johnny Carson*.

I stayed home from school the next two days. My perfect attendance record of nine years had come to an unceremonious end. I thought about Dad's words and realized I'd reached a crossroads. My body and brain were in the midst of a game of tug of war. My common sense said stay off the football field. The emotional quadrants of my brain fought back, imploring me not to give anyone the satisfaction of seeing me quit.

Reaching no conclusion, I returned to school on a Thursday feeling marginally better, physically. Breathing still required effort. Several football players asked if I'd really quit. "Yes" was my rapid, emphatic reply.

Coach Collier grabbed me in the hallway between classes and gave me a different version of the same speech Dad had given me a few days earlier, only his was a little more emotional. I listened out of respect and admiration I had for this man.

At 3:15, while walking to the bus for home, my legs made a detour towards the locker room. I put on my practice uniform and made my way to the field. No words were exchanged with the coaching staff, just smiles of approval, and a nod of the head acknowledging my arrival.

I sat and watched, still unable to run. We had a bye-week. One of the assistant coaches sat on the grass next to me. We talked about everything but football. He tried valiantly to hide his emotions. I took it as a sign he was apologizing without a formal apology. When practice ended, he helped me to my feet and patted me on the back, as if to say, everything will be okay.

I sat out the next game, my rib cage still not ready to take a hit.

With two games left on our schedule, I needed to get back on the field. Practice turned festive my first full day back. We still hadn't won a game, but the fellas were having fun. No one touched me, whiffing on plays to avoid further injury to their skinny receiver. The day before the game, I told someone to hit me. I needed a pain tolerance test. I took the hit and smiled as I bounced back to my feet---all good.

Our next game took place in Port St. Joe, a lazy Florida panhandle beach town of about three thousand residents an hour east of Panama City, and a mere thirty minutes from Tyndall Air Force Base, in Gulf County. Port St. Joe sits just east of the eastern and central time zone divide. The salt-colored sandy beaches were largely unspoiled, protected from the open Gulf of Mexico by a small spit of a peninsula attached on the eastern end.

The early evening game was the first, and only football game my parents' would ever attend. We had roughly fifty to seventy-five supporters in the stands, by far our largest of the season. The evening game and close proximity to Tyndall allowed parents to attend for the first time.

With warm-ups, marching bands, and cheerleading over, we took the field for the opening kickoff. I watched

187

from the sidelines as we gain our first, first down.

First and ten on our own thirty-five, I entered the game split right. Our quarterback barked the signals. At the snap, I bolted down the sidelines. I faked inside and turned towards the sidelines rather nonchalantly. I got my head around just in time to feel the ball hit my left hand; only them did I realize my defender had fallen. With nothing in front of me for thirty yards, it was game on.

The roar of the crowd alerted me that someone was closing in, but the only voice I could understand was Dad's. He must have hollered "that's my boy" a hundred times as my legs churned down the sidelines nearest the stands. Then his voice disappeared replaced by my own heavy breathing and sense of satisfaction swirling in my head.

Fifteen yards before the end zone, a deep safety entered my peripheral vision. He had the angle that would have prevented me from reaching the end zone without some sort of fake, or change in direction. I moved inside a step eluding him, but he slowed me down enough for another defender to tackle me from behind five yards short of the goal line.

I lay breathless slamming the ball into the turf. That sixty-yard play was by far the longest of our season. Teammates, coaches, and cheerleaders mobbed me while I made my way back to the bench. A couple of people ran onto the field as if the game were over. They had to be ushered back to the stands.

We settle for a field goal, but more importantly, I had a moment to cherish for life soaking up the adulation for all it was worth.

After that play, I was doubled the remainder of the

game, catching a few more balls, one leading to a touchdown by a teammate. The Rosenwald Bulldogs were finally victorious.

The emotional high lasted a week. I'd gone from goat to hero in thirty seconds. If I accomplished nothing else, this changed forever my relationship with my black classmates.

A week later we played the final game of my short-lived football career. I fought double coverage the entire game catching a few balls for modest gains. I had not quit, but football and me were not compatible. My slender frame simply wasn't built for repeated violent collisions. I walked away proud I hung in to the end.

CHAPTER 14

TIME FOR A NEW SPORT

With my football career relegated to the mothballs of history, I decided to try a sport my lean body was better suited for, basketball. Tryouts were a formality. The team had been handpicked to include me, a kid who'd never played organized basketball in his life. There's one thing you can't coach; height, and I had plenty to go around compared to everyone else at Rosenwald.

Our team had a good mix of black and white players. Other than me, these really were the best twelve players at Rosenwald.

I went on a quest to learn more about basketball. I started in the library looking for books. I found a few about the game's inventor, Dr. James Naismith. Another couple of books preached basic basketball fundamentals.

Several newspaper articles featured stories about the Boston Celtics, a team I remembered from Maine. The Celtics had just completed the greatest run of championships in professional sports history. I knew a little about Bill Russell, the legendary center, coach, and outspoken supporter of the Civil Rights Movement.

But by far the biggest influence on my young basketball mind was the great UCLA teams of the 1960s and 70s, and one person in particular; Lew Alcindor, better known today as Kareem Abdul Jabbar. This man intrigued me like no other.

Rosenwald had a huge picture of Alcindor in our locker room shooting the famous sky-hook. I read about his time at Power Memorial in New York City. Like me, education was important to him. By the time I learned about Alcindor, he'd already graduated from UCLA, and played for the Milwaukee Bucks in the National Basketball Association (NBA). After three successful championship seasons at UCLA, Alcindor led the Bucks to the 1971 NBA title.

I became equally enamored with the man who followed Alcindor to UCLA, Bill Walton. I never missed what few UCLA games we received on television in the southeast. During the Final Four that year, (1973), Walton played the single best game I'd ever seen, and arguably the best in college basketball history. He scored forty-four points, making twenty-one of twenty-two shots, and pulled down thirteen rebounds in UCLA's win over Memphis.

Both Alcindor and Walton played center, the same position I would play for Rosenwald. Each had a slightly different skill set that made them equally effective in a team first concept. It was more than scoring for these two; they excelled at passing to the open player when double-teamed, and setting up teammates for easy baskets, rebounding, and playing defense.

They learned at the feet of legendary coach John Wooden. Later in life, I read everything I could about Wooden. I regretted never meeting him, despite living in Los Angeles for twenty-three years. The effusive praise his former players heaped upon him, made Wooden, and what he stood for, must read literature for education about life, not just basketball.

None of this newfound knowledge made me a better basketball player, but at least I knew something about the game that I could talk about with teammates. I practiced Alcindor's skyhook for hours on my own. Although I wasn't seven feet two inches tall, that shot helped me score over taller opponents without getting the ball slammed back into my face. The grace and beauty of the skyhook was something to behold when executed properly.

I also became a darn good shooter from distance, picking up techniques from books and television. If I'd had a true mentor, no telling how far I could have gone with basketball, assuming my knees held up, which they didn't.

Our first practice took place just before the Christmas holiday. Like football, it was more running, this time with suicide drills. Then we ran layup drills careful to finish with the proper hand depending on what side of the basket we shot from. Next it was free throws, followed by dribbling around cones placed strategically around the court. Then back to suicide drills and more free throws. At the time, I didn't understand the purpose of suicide drills. I thought it was punishment for poor play, or not following instructions.

Coaches spent hours teaching me things other students took for granted. Coach Townsend worked one-on-one with me on rebounding and positioning, footwork and floor spacing, and the difference between high post and low post. He thought about refining my jump shot, but when I made ten in a row from distance, he left it alone. Coach Townsend was a six foot four inch former college guard. He knew the game well and delighted in sharing his knowledge.

Prior to our first game, Coach Townsend named me team captain. It definitely wasn't for basketball skill, rather, as a reward for hard work. I fell in love with basketball because someone took the time to teach me.

Our first game arrived mid-week in late January, a road game at one of the other junior high schools in the area. Like football, the team and cheerleaders rode on the same bus. By now, the cheerleading squad, predominantly African American when I arrived three years earlier, was mostly white. Their whiteness wasn't a problem for any of us; it seemed like such a natural fit; no one noticed, or cared.

With less than a minute left in the first quarter, I rose from the bench and made my way to the scorer's table. Another ten seconds evaporated before the buzzer blew announcing my arrival on the court.

The first play was a pass into the high post; from there I had the option to pass to a cutter, or, pivot and shoot. I pivoted, and shot the ball from just outside the free throw line. It didn't feel like a shot, more of an adrenalin push. Next thing I know, the ball caromed off the backboard, and fell softly into the basket.

I played the first five minutes of the second quarter,

and got whistled for three-seconds at least a half-dozen times before someone explained the rule. In all the rush to teach me basketball fundamentals, no one bothered to mention the three-second violation. My teammates' laughed at my inexperience.

The second half, with little help from me, we lost in a close one. Despite the loss, and my terrible play, we were all upbeat. This wasn't like football, we figured out we could play and win consistently. Our record stayed above .500 after that opening game loss.

One Saturday, I found myself on campus for something unrelated to sports, when I noticed several cars parked near the gym. I walked into the gym and was greeted by the tallest human being I'd ever seen, practically bumping into him as he headed to the water fountain.

He was a giant of a man at seven feet two, with a goatee, and Afro that made him look at foot taller---his name, Artis Gilmore. Gilmore, a native of the Northwest Florida/South Alabama region, would go on to have a stellar career in the now defunct American Basketball Association and the NBA. He was playing a pickup game with a group of really talented athletes. I watched in awe as this powerful man moved effortlessly around the court, toying with his opponent. My encounter lasted less than five minutes, but made a lasting impression.

The alarm clock started singing its tune, awakening me from a deep slumber. I swatted the clock, knocking it to the floor. The clock read 6 a.m. I stretched my muscles under the bed linen and glanced out the window looking for signs of life. The sun hadn't quite made it over the horizon. I had an hour before the bus arrived.

Dad was still in the shower, so I waited in bed. We had a pecking order in our house, Dad first, then me, Mom, Karen and Amanda. By the time Mom woke Karen and Amanda, Dad would be out the door on his way to work.

With the radio now playing, I swung my feet around, planted them on the floor and sprung to life before collapsing on my cold tiled bedroom floor. My right knee buckled sending shockwaves from hip to shin.

I stayed put trying to decide whether to call Mom, or wait a minute and try again. I opted for the latter. Using all the strength my skinny arms could muster, I placed my hands palms down on the bed frame and pushed off lifting myself onto the bed.

I tried to stand again. I stood slowly, the pain increasing in intensity as my waist and knee joints unfolded into a straight line. Both knees were throbbing alerting me to impending danger. I stood erect for less than thirty seconds before slumping back to my bed.

Six straight months of sports without a break had taken its toll. My body exacted revenge for the abuse I put it through. I'd completely ignored the doctor's admonition to rest, too caught up in the excitement of the moment. To make matters worse, I had a game that night; the first time my parents' would ever see me play basketball.

Realizing I hadn't come out of my room yet, Mom knocked on the door. I told her I would be out in a moment while I tried to rub life back into my knees, kneading them with the palms of my hands. The softball-sized knot just below my kneecaps responded ever so slowly to the love and care I provided.

I got it together long enough to fool Mom and get on the bus. Deep down, I knew trouble loomed. Taking leave of my senses again, I convinced myself, if I could just get through this game, I would take a week off. My game had improved immeasurably these past few months, not hard when you start from zero. I needed to show Dad I could really play.

I snuck over to a cooler Coach Collier kept loaded with cokes about an hour before game time. I was one of only three people who had a key to the locked room. I unlocked the door, removed a huge chunk of ice from the cooler, and sat on the floor applying the ice to the soft tissue under my kneecaps. Relief was immediate. I sat there for forty-five minutes alternating knees with this chunk of ice until it melted away.

I rose from the cold cement floor and led the team onto the court as team captain. I shot several layups from the left and right side of the basket. Next, I practiced jump shots and free throws. I made eye contact with my parents' delighted they were in attendance. Dad knew very little about basketball; calling him a novice would be a disservice to other novices. His sport was baseball, which explained his disappointment, when I decided to walk away from the game.

The horn blew. I took my seat with the coaches on the bench. The starters made their way to the center of this ninety-four by fifty-foot hunk of wood. Center court featured a menacing looking burgundy bulldog painted on the floor, with a spiked collar, and sharp fanged teeth.

The game was underway. Play goes back and forth for a few minutes; no team more than two points ahead. As usual, I entered the game with about a minute to play in the first quarter. In the ten or so minutes I sat on the bench, my knees stiffened. Without warming them up, I slowly jogged onto the court, exchanged hand slaps with our starting center, and took my place along the free throw line.

The free throw bounced off the rim and landed in my hands without me jumping. I made a quick pivot to pass the ball when my knee screamed its displeasure, "don't do that again." I willed my legs down the court leaving everyone none the wiser. I rebounded our missed shot, put it back up, and missed an uncontested layup from a foot. Not only did I miss the layup, I missed the rim and backboard. I couldn't jump.

Still I played on, knowing I needed to sit. Dad looked disapprovingly. I expected words of encourage from him, but none were forthcoming.

Dad's temperament had slowly gotten worse since Vietnam. Simple things that never bothered him before now required federal court intervention. But the worst part of all continued to be his drinking. Never one to refuse a scotch on the rocks, Dad had become a full-fledged alcoholic. He'd become hyper sensitive and hyper critical of his entire family, but the brunt of that harsh criticism was usually reserved for me.

Dad hollered from the stands, his diatribe laced with several four-letter words, invoking his inner Bull Meechum. Once back to the bench, Coach Townsend asked if I still wanted to play, he knew about my knees. I gave him a thumb up. In the third quarter, I was back in the game, but the pain became too much to bear. I removed myself, earning another round of criticism from Bull.

I buried my head in a smelly gym towel, as Dad continued to pile on the insults. Mom screamed, telling him to shut up. That rebuke froze him in his tracks momentarily. Coach Collier stepped in, summoning Dad from the stands. Coach told him about my knees and the cooler.

Dad had a few drinks before the game and brushed Coach's comments aside. The alcohol had fully lubricated his tongue and dulled his common sense. After the game, Dad dropped us off at home, and drove straight to the NCO Club. Mom had to fetch him later. For the first time in my life, I wanted to punch the daylights out of my own father.

My black classmates resented Dad for his outburst. The apologies over the next few days were heartfelt making me feel like I'd joined a new family. They were warm, thoughtful, and very much appreciated.

I took a week off from all physical activity, short of walking to class. All of my teachers provided an empty desk or chair to rest my legs, like they'd done years earlier when I sported my cast.

We were scheduled to play a road game in Alabama my first game back. On the schedule it simply said Carver. Carver Junior High is located in Dothan, about two hours north, straight up U.S. Highway 231. The school was named after the famous African American scientist, botanist, inventor, and educator George Washington Carver.

Carver came up with techniques to help farmers

recover from soil depletion after decades of cotton farming. Continuous cotton farming stripped the ground of vital nutrients necessary for it to remain a viable crop. Carver's crop rotation system, urging farmers to plant sweet potatoes and legumes, helped restore nitrogen, a necessary element for cotton growth.

Arguably, Carver's greatest contribution was a legume we know as peanuts. Farmers grew so many peanuts that the laws of supply and demand tipped sharply towards too much supply. Farmer profits plummeted.

To combat that problem, Carver invented alternate uses for peanuts creating an entire industry. He jotted down more than three hundred uses of peanuts, some he had to invent. There were so many peanut farmers by 1921; the United Peanut Association of America was formed.

Carver testified before the United States Congress much to the chagrin of southern farmers, not wanting to put their total faith in a black man; despite the fact he singlehandedly saved their hide. His testimony fascinated congressional members as they continually extended his time. Carver became known as the "Peanut Man."

Approximately one-quarter of the U.S. peanut crop is produced near Dothan, with much of it being processed in the city, earning the town the title of "Peanut Capital of the World." Dothan's population in 1970 was just over thirty-five thousand, a third of whom were black.

We piled into a greyhound type bus, without the restroom, for the journey north. Upon our arrival, the bus was pelted with eggs, tomatoes, rocks, and any other hard object that could be used to inflict damage.

We departed the bus passing through a gauntlet of

students yelling "Uncle Tom," "Whitey," "cracker", "bitch" and "honkie," and those were the nice names. I had become so desensitized since moving South, I simply ignored the taunts, quickly making my way to the gym. I can't speak for my teammates, coaches, or cheerleaders, but they looked shocked.

The gym floor was barely visible, like walking into a partially lit movie theater. At least half the lights were missing. The stands, other than the first few rows, were covered in darkness.

Carver, like Rosenwald looked like it suffered the vestiges of Jim Crow. I assumed, but wasn't certain at the time, that Carver was still segregated. Every student, parent, adult, opponent, and the referees were all black. The only whiteness in the entire building came courtesy of our bus.

During layup drills, boos and objects rained down from the stands in a feeble attempt at intimidation. The start of the game was delayed as officials, and eventually the police, along with school administrators seized control.

Inserted into the starting lineup to help combat Carver's decided height advantage, I was shoved by the biggest man-child I'd ever played against. No way this kid could be fifteen-years-old, I thought. He was a few inches taller than my six foot four frame with arms like Arnold Schwarzenegger. The rest of the team looked much the same.

A Carver player shoved me while walking onto the court. He noticed my braces and promised I would need a replacement set by the end of the game. I took that threat seriously. Carver jumped out to a huge lead; double digits, by the end of the first quarter. I escaped the first quarter with all my teeth still intact.

The second quarter saw Rosenwald chip away at Carver's sizeable lead when a well-timed and well-placed elbow found its way to my mouth, dislodging my mouthpiece. Blood spurted to the gym floor. My mouth and skull throbbed. I could feel both pulsating as my heart push blood to the affected area. My face swelled slightly as man-child attacker stood, grinning from ear-to-ear. Coach Townsend expected a technical foul, or at least a referee time out, neither happened forcing us to use our own timeout. I even had to clean up my blood from the floor.

Rather than succumb to fear, I became enraged, vowing revenge, when the opportunity presented itself. Coach sat me for a few minutes. In this environment, I was my own dentist. It took several minutes, a bag of ice from someone in the stands, and little wax balls I always carried to cover the sharp edges of my bands, to staunch the bleeding.

The black lady who handed me the ice stayed behind our bench for the remainder of the game, chatting with me briefly throughout. At least not everyone in attendance wanted to cause us harm.

Reentering the game a few minutes before halftime, I made a beeline to Mr. Man-Child and told him what was about to happen. True to my word, he took a vicious elbow to the Adams Apple as the clock expired.

Left searching for his faculties, Rosenwald, and the cheerleaders walked off the floor to our shared locker room. The cheerleaders were too fearful to leave our side. No one talked at halftime, not even the coaches. We all thought trouble loomed and it showed on our faces.

The third quarter saw us continue to whittle away at their lead. Carver's coach had had enough and called a timeout. He belittled his team like nothing I'd ever heard. Expletives laced with threats of severe punishment flew from his mouth. But the worst offense of all, he played the race card, wondering for all to hear, "how is that team with a bunch of white boys kicking your ass?"

Only then did I begin to realize the pressure heaped upon Carver players by their fans and coaches. Their players were in a no win situation. Even my nemesis, Mr. Man-Child's demeanor had changed. Sadness swept over him, the fun ripped away, replaced by a more business like attitude. Carver had to win, or suffer some unknown consequences for their failure.

Carver regained their mojo and gave us the worst beating of the year. The rowdy crowd made it impossible for the time-honored tradition of shaking hands. We were escorted from the gym to our waiting bus, which by now was under police guard.

With Dothan in our rearview mirror, we stopped at a fast-food restaurant for a bite to eat. All of us freely shared our meals and expenses. Rather than tear us apart, the horrific events of Carver reinforced our bond, acting more like a catharsis for evil.

All of us congregated at the rear of the bus, the long bench seat jammed tighter than a can of sardines. I sat in the middle seat, my legs extended down the aisle, a courtesy my teammates' afforded me on every journey. Two blond-haired blue-eye cheerleaders were on either side, one, with her head on my shoulder fast asleep. On the other side of both cheerleaders were two black teammates, followed by two more cheerleaders, one black, one white, talking softly so as not to disturb those who dosed off.

The tree of desegregation had taken root at Rosenwald through sport, and extended its branches throughout the student body. A few of us talked on the way home, wondering how much, if any information we would divulge to our parents' about Carver.

I never mentioned Carver to my parents'. I was far too happy, other than the obvious swelling of my face, to let anything diminish the memories of the bus ride home. I'd spent three years looking for a time like this never thinking it would be brought about by adversity.

Carver journeyed south to Rosenwald the following week, where we beat them soundly. Half the Carver team didn't make the trip leaving them shorthanded. It left me to speculate if it had anything to do with our experience in their gym.

CHAPTER 15

THE END IS NEAR

Basketball season ended a week later, after a road trip to Defuniak Springs, a rural town about an hour northwest of Panama City. This predominantly white school, with a total student body of fewer than five hundred treated us like rock stars, in sharp contrast to Carver. Sitting on the bench, it finally dawned on me basketball was over. Young minds just never think things end. The cavernous hole left in my heart was palpable.

I returned to the track where once again I ran the mile and quarter mile. The discus was added as a placeholder to make sure Rosenwald got full credit for fielding a team. No one expected me to win, and I didn't disappoint.

That bus ride home following our final track meet proved to be more heart wrenching than the end of basketball season. We were having the time of our lives. My time at Rosenwald was on a collision course with finality, and with it, the most rewarding experience of my life.

Rosenwald altered my often-sketchy perception of black America. It taught me to never look down upon another individual because of my exalted station in life. Life can be fickle, as I would soon learn. Tomorrow that person doing without would be me.

Before the end of the year, I performed in a school play, first in front of the students, followed by a Friday evening performance for parents. My thoughts weren't on the play, rather the composition of the audience. Would the parents of my black classmates attend? Most had never appeared at any school function in support of their children.

Unfortunately, this evening would be no different. An audience of one hundred fifty white parents made the forty-minute drive from Tyndall. Even my parents didn't show, but I was okay with that. The play didn't mean so much to me.

One couldn't help but feel a sense of melancholy witnessing my black classmates. They observed all these white parents rallying around their kids. Much to the credit of the white parents, when the play ended, they embraced all kids, not just their own. It brightened the day for a group of young people who wanted nothing more than to be loved and recognized.

Rosenwald still practiced corporal punishment. While walking to class, after a visit to the nurse's office for a minor scrape, I witnessed a classmate shimming up a rusted old pipe, to retrieve a ball, he inadvertently kicked on the roof. He couldn't get down, so I offered a helping hand.

Next thing I know, both of us were sitting in the principal's office, having been escorted there by Mr. Edison, the teacher who found us and assumed we were vandalizing school property. No explanation worked on Edison; swift punishment was required.

Mr. Spicer, our principal, a totally bald man, in his mid-40s, short in stature compared to me, and slightly rotund, seemed equally pleased at the thought of smacking to fifteen-year-olds with a paddle. I had a great rapport with him, until that day. Sentencing had been swift. Our punishment, three licks with a long wooden paddle. Thoughts of being struck by a slave master flooded my conscious. Here are two black boys about to be whipped by a white man. The symbolism pissed me off.

Tim went first. His eyes moistened, but he stopped short of crying. I revolted. No way was I pulling down my pants for anyone. I would start swinging if necessary to prevent a spanking: not to my behind. The last time Dad hit me I was eight. Spicer and Edison grabbed my arms. I pushed them away, both stumbling backwards landing on a sofa in the corner.

I could have easily taken my paddling and gone on about my business, but there was a greater point at play here, and a practice that needed to be halted. Spicer threatened to call Dad. In an act of defiance, I told him to call, and they obliged.

Bull Meechum arrived with a serious bad attitude for having his day interrupted. He walked into the principal's office, slammed the door shut and glared at me, daggers in his eyes. The principal explained what he thought happened, embellished with a few exaggerations. Right then, I expected Dad to slap me right out of the chair, but he didn't.

Instead he turned his wrath towards the principal. Dad got the inference of slavery and said as much. He further admonished the principal that any punishment administered to his son, would be at his own hand. With that, Dad looked at me and said, "lets go," storming out of the office. I was done with school for the day.

Dad was seething as he drove through traffic at an accelerated speed, screaming out the window at anyone who dare get in his way. The powerful V8, 429 engine of our Ford Thunderbird was being put to the test.

Finally, a calm settled over him, when he asked, what really happened. Dad excelled at ferreting out fact from fiction. He contemplated my responses then apologized. I asked, "what for?" Dad certainly didn't owe me an apology. Without fully explaining, he said, "don't you ever let another man put his hands on you, ever, or I will beat you myself."

What happened at Rosenwald that afternoon struck a nerve with Dad. The nuns at the Catholic school he attended as a child beat him mercilessly. In a rare moment of humility, Dad shared the shame and anguish he felt. This painful glimpse into his past conjured up memories he buried long ago. While all of Richard Bennett's kids were spanked, whipping us pained him deeply. It was discipline, nothing more, nothing less, only meant to correct behavior.

I returned to school the following morning and not another word was said about the incident.

That same week, it was time for a trip to Dr. Johnson.

No way would Dad make two trips to Rosenwald in the same week. He told me to walk the two miles to the orthodontist office. I panicked. I'd never walked that neighborhood without an escort, and knew of the areas high crime rate, relative to the rest of Panama City. Convincing myself it would be okay during daylight hours; I willed my legs deeper and deeper into Panama City's small black community.

Suddenly, two knife-wielding assailants appeared demanding money. Both men wore tattered white t-shirts, shorts, and some sort of gym shoe. The smell of alcohol laced with marijuana violated my airspace. Their eyes were bloodshot.

Frozen in fear, I complied with their demand a little to slowly for their liking. That earned me a quick trip to the ground with a knife closing in on my throat. I pulled the $5 bill and a check Mom gave me for Dr. Johnson out of my pocket. They snatched the money and tossed the check to the ground, disappearing, just as fast as they had appeared. Witnesses just walked by, looking at me like a discarded piece of trash.

Shaken, I ran the remaining mile to the doctor's office. The nurse, another of my surrogate mothers, came to my aid, noticing my torn shirt and blood stain pants from a scratch on my arm. I never even felt the scratch. Unable to summon Dad, the nurse found Mom, who scrambled her work schedule, making it to Dr. Johnson's office in record time.

Mom lit in to Dad something fierce that evening for demanding I walk. Nothing short of imprisonment or death could save poor Dad that night. Through her shouts and screams, Mom was sending a message---"teach your son, help him" she demanded, "you made him fight this place alone."

After all this time, Mom recognized and acknowledged, life in Panama City had been difficult for me. The premonition she had, fearing for my safety when we left Spain eight years earlier, manifested itself in Panama City. She wanted Dad to stop turning a blind eye to my troubles---too little, too late. I'd learned to fend for myself, even if I didn't always have the right answers, or an outcome to my liking. No one applauded our eventual departure from Panama City more than Mom.

Rosenwald's year-end awards ceremony took place at the Four Winds Restaurant, located at the marina, in Panama City. The ceremony, for most, was nothing more than a big party to celebrate moving on to high school. For me, it served as a coronation, a crowning achievement of perseverance.

The podium and head table sat on risers, about two feet higher than the tables below. The head table was draped in white tablecloths embellished with flowers. Perfectly placed silverware and china adorned each place setting, with a triangle-shaped white cloth napkin lying in the center of each salad plate.

The head table featured Principal Spicer and all the coaches, nametags announcing who would sit where. The podium was decorated in Rosenwald colors, burgundy and white, with a picture of our school mascot, that menacing bulldog prominently displayed on the facade facing the audience.

There were several rows of round tables leading away from the podium towards the back of the room, enough seating for approximately two hundred people. All the students, dressed in our Sunday best, made a beeline for the back of the room, while our parents sat in those first few rows. This turned into a wonderful opportunity for parents to get to know one another. My parents' sat in the first row, stage right from the podium.

Us kids were having a great time. For many, me included, this was the first time any of us had attended a formal dinner. Being served and waited on made us feel like kings and queens.

Awards were handed out for best football player, best basketball player, most outstanding golfer, team captain, sportsmanship, and more. By the end of the evening all the elite athletes, and some not so elite, were recognized.

The final award for the evening combined academic achievement and athletic excellence. Coach Collier and Principal Spicer took turns extolling the virtues of this particular award. For the first time that evening, the room fell silent.

Next came the description of the winner, without mentioning names. About two sentences in, the realization that I was about to make a long trek to the podium struck. They talked about my three-point-nine grade point average and how I lettered in three sports despite my bad knees. The pats on the back started before my name was announced.

I rose slowly as the room stood in applause. I temporarily lost sight of my parents' in the commotion. I exchanged handshakes with Spicer as if the incident in his office a week earlier never occurred. Coach dispensed with handshakes, lifting me off the floor with a full body hug.

I began shaking uncontrollably. A fact not lost on a young lady sitting in the front row, who commented to her parents about my severe case of the nerves. On cue, I looked for comfort spotting Mom balling like a baby while holding Dad's arm so tight, blood ceased to flow. Dad had tears streaming down his face onto a beautiful suit.

My parents' served on the committee that organized this event, but were left in the dark about the evening's final award. Hollywood couldn't script a better ending to life as a Rosenwald student. I'm not sure this could have happened three years earlier; blacks, whites, parents, students, and teachers standing in unison to honor a kid who suffered many a sleepless night just trying to adapt and identify who he was.

We were the first class to graduate Rosenwald that completed all three years of court-mandated busing. I'd been put there for reasons only God knows. *Could I have learned about black life in another setting? Would I have recognized what is possible in another school?*

I didn't completely grasp my blackness, segregation, or how others perceived me; but no amount of formal education could ever provide a more valuable series of life lessons than those I received at Rosenwald. The experience shaped my outlook towards the future in profound ways.

The ride home that evening was a joyous one. Dad had the window down, screaming and hollering at anyone who would listen, gushing with pride. He took my huge trophy and held it from the car window while stopped at red lights. The trophy was big enough that it required both hands to hold. A few people honked acknowledging Dad's exuberance.

Monday, sadness replaced the euphoria of Friday night. We began the process of turning in our books and cleaning out lockers. Final exams had all been completed. In two days school would be over.

Teachers hugged students one last time. More tears flowed. Coach Collier stood by my bus waiting for me as I waded through the crowd. We embraced before he gave me his home phone number. He exacted a promised from me that I vowed to fulfill. He wanted me in college and promised to do everything in his power to make sure I got there. College seemed a little too far off to me at the time, but the seed had been planted.

College was the ultimate prize for the African American community and military brats of enlisted personnel. It was seen as the singular ticket to a brighter future. To some, it might have been equally as important as attending church.

For many of us brats with enlisted fathers, we would become first generation college graduates. We were acutely aware of the career arc of an enlisted person, versus that of an officer and the benefits therein.

I sat behind Wilson for the ride home. We talked, avoiding the obvious. The extraneous noise of students celebrating the last day of school disappeared.

If Coach was like a father, Wilson was that uncle who always stopped by bringing goodies. In times of trouble, I could count on him to provide words of wisdom. We joked about the shy kid he met at the motor pool three years earlier.

For the first time he discussed race with me, in terms a soon-to-be high school sophomore could understand.

Wilson let me know I had great survival instincts and offered some sage advice. "Life was tough," he said, "and might get tougher going forward. The age of childhood innocence is over my friend. White people will see you differently. Some will see you for the person you are, others, simply won't care, seeing only skin color. You can't make everyone happy, be yourself, God will watch over you." I'd never known him to be overtly religious or sentimental, but his message resonated.

He also talked about the struggle. "The history of civil rights is still being written," he went on. Wilson was old enough to know that for every step forward, there would be some backpedalling, wiping out previous gains. "Fight through it," he admonished, "you're smarter and better equipped than most kids your age. You understand what's at stake." I'd inadvertently become part of the "struggle" and accepted my role as inevitable.

I remember Wilson's words like he said them yesterday, the message so profound and unexpected.

Wilson finished on cue as the bus doors swung open. He put on the parking brake and escorted me outside irritating the remaining students on the bus. We embraced one final time. With that, I turned my back and walked off, turning one last time to wave goodbye. Wilson was gone and so was Rosenwald.

CHAPTER 16

THE CROWNING OF A CHAMPION

The Florida State Bowling Championships were held in Pensacola the summer after my freshman year. Pensacola, at that time, had a population of sixty thousand. The town is located one hundred miles west of Panama City at the juncture of the Gulf of Mexico and the Alabama state line. One of Pensacola's most cherished entities is the Pensacola Naval Air Station with its myriad destroyers and cruisers docked in its protected harbors.

Several teams from Tyndall participated in the tournament spread out over four weekends. Since we were so close, most of the older kids hitched a ride with a teenaged friend with a driver's license and a car.

And like most teenagers away from home, with little adult supervision, we provided a lesson in bad behavior. Once at our hotel, we partied long after the 10 p.m. curfew imposed by the property. When management finally ran us out of the pool, we ordered pizza and continued to whoop it up until the wee hours of the morning.

Several eighteen-year-olds took advantage of Florida's liberal drinking laws at the time (legal drinking age eighteen), and snuck off to a local liquor store. They shared those libations with anyone willing to experiment with drunkenness regardless of age.

For some reason, I didn't drink that night, but certainly enjoyed the company, and the appearance that I had indulged; nursing a coke that I told everyone was mixed with rum. Watching Dad the previous three years squashed any thoughts I might have had at inebriation. The use of alcohol actually scared me.

Around 3 a.m., I fell asleep, fully clothed, diagonally across my bed. The party spilled over to the adjoining room. I woke five hours later to observe a room full of white kids, male and female, in various stages of undress, littered across my room. Some kids slept on the floor, others on the extra queen size bed.

Fearful Gladys would rupture a blood vessel at the scene before me, I rousted everyone from my room, and ushered them down a long outdoor corridor to their own rooms. It took fifteen minutes to move everyone and clean up the liquor bottles strewn across the floor, in the bathroom, and on my second-floor balcony.

Satisfied I'd destroyed all evidence of our transgression, I quickly showered and hopped a ride to the bowling alley with a black family with a ten-year-old daughter who adored me.

Hours later, Gladys bounded through the glass doors of the bowling center with several teenagers sporting hangovers. Anger doesn't begin to describe her gait.

She pivoted in my direction and sat down beside me.

"Just be quiet and listen," she commanded. She began to share the story of a hotel proprietor. It started as a tall tale; then devolved into some semblance of non-fiction about events from the previous evening's festivities.

The only kid the proprietor singled-out for verbal assault in absentia, "the nigger." Gladys was too classy a lady to use the "N" word, but the inference made it clear the manager did. I was the only sober one in the bunch, but the proprietor only remembered the nigger.

Gladys finished her narrative never once asking of my involvement. Her account was more a cautionary tale, a warning to remain vigilant of my surroundings. I recognized her admonition, as a threat from the proprietor of physical harm or police arrest, just as she had intended. I still had another night at that hotel.

Gladys rose from her seat and strolled off to check on the younger kids. Several of my fellow teenaged bowlers filled me on the details of an encounter with hotel management. They confirmed the nigger comment. My color trumped all, just like Wilson warned me it would: how prescient of him.

Now on notice, we decided as a group, to have our evening fun on a beach, far away from the hotel. I made it a point to never find myself alone, even for something as mundane as using the restroom.

Of the six games I bowled that day, two, were well over 200. Not bad for a kid with a 150 average. Spectators of all sizes, shapes, and colors congregated behind my lanes to watch. I had far and away the best scores in the room that day.

On Sunday it was more of the same---good bowling, even for me. While our team suffered, as an individual, I excelled.

The ride home that Sunday afternoon turned into a festive, slow moving, parade. Rather than take the bypass route allowing for quick travel, we cruised the beaches, enjoying life in Destin and Panama City Beach.

Several girls in our group, all white, had previously changed into their swim attire. These scantily clad young ladies played the role of tease to the growing cadre of young men patrolling the beaches looking for easy prey.

I, like the other boys in our caravan, were in a testosterone-induced coma, staring intently at the girls and their partially naked bodies. They rubbed their bodies next to mine without a care in the world. Why had any self-respecting parent allowed their daughters to ride with a bunch of boys out of town?

We stopped numerous times to enjoy the warm surf. The only black person on the beaches we stopped at stayed on red alert for the slightest sign of trouble. I could never predict who would be offended by me hanging with white kids, especially pretty girls.

Once home, I started working at the commissary like the previous summer. The two Larrys did everything to make my life miserable, denying me workdays or putting me in places where I would have little customer contact. But I showed up everyday like clock work, a full forty-five minutes early.

Unable to consistently earn any money, Ryan, who had taken over as supervisor for all the front-end bagging and customer assistance operations, came up with a solution. Ryan had an extra job representing several of the vendors whose products adorned the commissary shelves. He worked for Birdseye, Minute Maid, a cereal company, and one of the milk companies.

He hired me at four dollars an hour to price and stock the foods of his vendors. Ryan showed me how to read the cost and inventory reports, and how to work the stamping machine, providing me one of my own to keep. The two Larrys tried to intervene, but were quickly slapped into submission by one of the vendors who loved my work ethic.

I usually arrived at 5 a.m. and waited for the suppliers to show. Since I was too young to drive, I often left home at 4:15 a.m. and walked or jogged the three miles to work. Many of the other vendors took a personal interest in my wellbeing. On the days when their stock boys didn't report for work, they requested me by name, and paid in cash out of their own pocket.

Ryan made it his mission in life to protect his prize employee, always assigning me to high traffic counters to increase my tip potential when bagging groceries.

I treated bagging groceries like an art. I kept the food items within the symmetry of the bags. I studied the customers. If they were a retiree, or an elderly lady, I took precautions not to make the bags too heavy. I asked customers how they wanted their items handled. I worked those tips, and they came in hot and heavy. Customers knew me by name and waited in long lines just to reach my counter, often ignoring smaller lines.

Between the two jobs, I was easily earning upwards of $400 a week. Not bad for a fifteen-year-old kid, in 1973. One month, I earned more than Dad's military paycheck.

I saved thousands that summer, opening my first ever bank account at Bay National Bank.

I rushed to the bank everyday after work to deposit that days earnings, and inquire about interest on my money. I proved to be a persistent pain in the ass once I entered the bank. I wanted to know precisely how interest was calculated and when it was paid. How did compounding work? What did the bank do with my money while it sat in their vaults? I didn't realize at the time, money doesn't sit, its always working.

It was work and bowling all summer to the exclusion of all else, short of bathing. I didn't even make time to gawk at the girls unless they were part of my bowling environment.

One afternoon, Gladys sent word through a friend at the commissary to have me stop by after work. At 5 p.m., I sauntered through the doors of Tyndall Lanes and noticed several friends had congregated in a corner at the far end of the concourse.

Gladys emerged from the group, grabbed my hand, and pulled me in their direction. The group parted, revealing a huge cake, with white icing, a plastic bowling statue in the middle and the words, "Congratulations, Michael Bennett, State Bowling Champion."

This little impromptu party lasted for an hour before I excused myself and ran across the parking lot to the Base Exchange where Mom worked. I shared my triumphant news with her.

Mom went back to an office and called Dad. For the second time in three months, I'd given my parents' a gift, a reason to be proud of me. Nothing made me happier than putting a smile on their faces.

Unbeknown to me at the time, my sister Karen had also placed high enough to take home several trophies, but I was the state champion. My accomplishments overshadowed her moment in the sun.

Once I discovered my sister had earned several awards, I tried, in vain, to divert attention towards her, perfectly willing to share the spotlight. Dad made it a point to praise her success. Unfortunately, Karen didn't stand a chance, everyone reminding her, that her brother is the state champ. Surprisingly, she never turned bitter or resentful of my success, a testament to the wonderful person she had become.

My winning was a big deal in a region with a total population of less than thirty-five thousand. I sat down for a television interview, followed by a radio interview, and a third interview with one of the local newspaper reporters. Dad listened to the radio interview and lauded my performance. Dad, always the stickler for proper English, would have skewered me alive had I bastardized the language, or comported myself inappropriately.

My sophomore year was rapidly approaching when I befriended a kid in my bowling league named Gabe. Gabe was a loud-mouthed, ultra confident, boisterous white kid, slightly overweight and very opinionated. He was entering his senior year of high school and owned a Kelly green Volkswagen Beetle. His inflated self-worth, and mister-know-it-all personality, alienated all the bowlers in my inner-circle.

But Gabe and I had one thing in common---a love for

basketball. His dad, a Lt. Colonel, installed a hoop along their winding driveway, perfectly position under a street light for evening play. With bowling now on summer hiatus, we played one-on-one until dinnertime, which I usually ate with Gabe's family. Then we returned to our makeshift court for some serious trash talking and intense play.

My height advantage made life miserable for him. Gabe loved a challenge and detested losing. If he didn't win the last game, we would compete until dawn, if his parents allowed. His mom and dad had to yank him off that court, often threatening him with the loss of his precious car, if he didn't comply.

Gabe's family, and how they comported themselves, reminded me of *Leave it to Beaver*. Gabe had a precocious little brother, a younger sister, about Karen's age, and a sweet, but demanding mother. Gabe's father was the strong, silent type, who challenged my friend to succeed, willing to impart a few painful lessons if necessary.

While my family struggled on two incomes, Gabe's family lived the good life; the difference in pay between a mid-level military officer and a mid-level enlisted person. Gabe had a stay-at-home mother. My mom became part of the labor force before my little sister hit kindergarten. At least now Dad didn't shoulder the burden of two part time jobs.

Gabe's family took great comfort in life's simplest pleasures. I learned to make ice cream at Gabe's house, often taking turns churning the delicious vanilla treat with his family. For Gabe, that ice cream had to be perfect. No one ate until it passed his test. Their familial bond left an indelible impression.

Gabe was a highly intelligent, straight-A student who would go off to college through the ROTC program, and become a military officer. His dad planted that seed early on and I got to watch it germinate. I wanted to be an Air Force officer because of Gabe.

I envied Gabe's station in life often wishing Dad and I talked more about career choices. Dad deemed my future success to be a great high school student, who would go on to be an enlisted man in the military. Dad's common refrain, "if it's good enough for me, it's good enough for you." I grew to hate that phrase. Dad worked so hard to provide me a good life, only to lack vision of a brighter future for his own son.

It took me decades to convince Dad I could accomplish more than his narrow-minded dream of success. Dad's military career and the advancement in civil rights opened my eyes to the possible. Butting heads with Dad over my potential was exhausting and demoralizing

Gabe, on the other hand, had no such mental restrictions. He shot for the stars. If he missed and hit the moon, he would still be wildly successful. I had no doubt in my mind Gabe would be an outstanding military officer.

While my other friends refused to hang with Gabe, he remained a loyal friend and confidant for years after we both left Tyndall.

CHAPTER 17

THE SOPHOMORE CHALLENGE

SEPTEMBER 1973

Rutherford High School opened its doors in 1961 as Bay County's second high school. Compared to Rosenwald, Rutherford looked like the penthouse suite at a fancy hotel. Rutherford's clean, well-manicured lawns represented white middle class suburbia in all its glory. The books were relatively new, the campus, graffiti free, the floors polished to a fine sheen, even the lunchroom food was edible.

Rosenwald and Rutherford sit just two miles apart, but the stark contrast in appearance and quality felt like I'd been transported from the ghetto to Beverly Hills--- *The Fresh Prince of Bel-Air* 1970s version. Just over one thousand students attended Rutherford, seventy-five to eighty percent, white. The student parking lot featured vintage 1960s and early 70s vehicles, most in good repair.

No need for "forced busing" at Rutherford. Its natural

boundaries and the presence of Tyndall left the school naturally desegregated.

After three years, I still lived in a predominantly white Tyndall neighborhood, and remained the only black male on my new school bus. The military doesn't assign housing based on race, that's just the way things worked out.

By now, the Bennett family had become the neighborhood's senior resident. I'd become the "it" kid thanks to that longevity and my state championship.

Gabe and I shared the same bus. Our thirty-minute ride gave us ample time to chat with our fellow high school students. The conversations took on a more mature tone than the Rosenwald bus. We often discussed the war winding down in Vietnam, our future plans, or sports. The political climate was a hotbed of discussion. We never discussed race, it seemed unimportant in the big scheme of things.

The male/female dynamic took center stage. All of us testosterone driven boys could be found frequently chatting up our female classmates. No one appeared disturbed by a busload of white females showing more than a passing interest in the black kid. The fellas encouraged me to start dating again.

We usually arrived at school thirty minutes early and gathered in the lunchroom to play hearts or spades. Gabe, myself, and two classmates who rode our bus drew large crowds, delighted in our boisterous bravado and trash-talk. Even the girls, who typically shunned such nonsense gathered around.

Football was out of the question. Rutherford fielded a decent team with several players earning college scholarships, but that field was no place for me. I hadn't added one once of muscle to my narrow frame in a year.

My grades dictated that I register for honors classes. My elective was marine biology; no reason for that particular class, it just looked fun. Physical education class lacked the importance of Rosenwald. I had nothing to prove.

A fine southern lady, Mrs. Brady taught geometry, my second period class. She spoke with a southern drawl, speech slow, and deliberate. Five words would take her five minutes to deliver. Her monotonous drone often put students into a deep coma.

For the first time, I actually met a teacher I thought didn't belong in a classroom. Her rules were harsh, punitive measures, swift. Arriving in class without two sharpened pencils led to an hour of detention after school. That proved a huge issue for military kids who depended on that bus to get home.

She openly challenged parents and students who defied her authority or questioned her teaching methods. This woman had no sense of humor. Not once did we witness her provide counsel to a student outside normal class hours.

Candy and I had been friends for two years. She sat behind me in geometry class. We often studied together, or talked on the phone at night going over class notes.

We were both well prepared for our first geometry exam. Candy earned an "A." Despite my finishing several minutes before everyone else, confident in my grasp of early geometry, my test paper had a big red "D" underlined at the top of the page. My black skin went pale.

Candy grabbed my shoulder massaging my hurt feelings. I gave her my test to review. We talked after class as I cowered in embarrassment, wrestling with my putrid performance. Thinking I'd just gone through the exam too fast, I resolved to slow down and thoroughly review each and every answer, multiple times if necessary.

Two weeks later came the next exam. The results were even worse, a bright red capital "F" etched across my paper, with a sad face drawn for added insult. I'd never failed in my academic life. Candy again offered condolences treating me as if someone had passed. My somber mood turned to one of confusion. For the first time in my life, I questioned my cognitive abilities.

With Mom and Dad out for the evening, I took my geometry book and both exams home, shut my bedroom door affixing a handwritten "Do Not Disturb" sign to the door exterior to keep my sisters' away.

I started with the first test. I took it over without looking at my corrected paper. Satisfied, I compared my self-exam to Mrs. Brady's corrected version---perfect score. I did the same with the second exam; the results were the same---perfect score.

I finished just as the air conditioner kicked on scattering my paper's across the room. I scrambled to put everything back in proper order, when I noticed a slight anomaly on my first test. I studied the exam for a minute like I expected the markings to animate and walk off the page.

My eyes glanced down to every incorrect answer on

the original exam. I set it aside and looked at the second exam. Then I sat back contemplating. I was about to accuse a teacher of sabotaging my grades. I needed to be sure.

Every wrong answer had an erasure smudge next to it. I never erased anything on Mrs. Brady's test. We were instructed to use scratch paper and transfer our work to the exam. It made for slower test taking, but it also allowed for cleaner papers, easier to grade.

I ran to the phone, called Candy, and shared my discovery. We spoke for an hour trying to devise a battle plan. It was a restless night of sleep. I thought long and hard about how to approach my dilemma. Do I accuse the teacher, or bite the bullet?

I found a risky middle ground. Rather than take the next test in pencil, a Brady rule violation, I would use a pen. This time I earned a "B" with a note scribbled across the top "Use Pencil Next Time." I still wasn't satisfied.

Candy studied my exam while Mrs. Brady began her lecture on a new chapter. Candy sent me a quick note alerting me to more shenanigans. Instead of erasure marks, some of my numbers had been altered. The number three, rounded to look like an eight. The number five became six. It still wasn't definitive proof.

Do I take it to Dad? I decided no. In matters of academics, he always sided with the teacher. Do I take it to the principal? No, he probably wouldn't take too kindly to a student accusing a faculty member of academic malfeasance.

The only course of action would be direct confrontation. I figured out a way to soften my accusatory tone, by asking if she needed a student aid. I knew she had several student assistants; maybe I could be one.

Set for battle, I walked up after class and pitched my proposal. Her terse reply, "I don't need help, and if I did, it certainly wouldn't be you. What makes you think you could help me?"

I tutored half of Mrs. Brady's class on the Pythagorean theorem, axioms, postulates, tangents, angles, and anything geometry. I knew the material better than almost every student in my class. Even after my poor performance on the first three exams, those students came to me for explanations and answers. Most of my class owed part of their success to my tutoring skills.

I was more than qualified to be Mrs. Brady's assistant, but my grades weren't reflective of my knowledge. She was the only one unaware that I tutored a majority of her students.

After being rejected, I pulled out the three previous exams and blatantly accused her of academic fraud, showing her erasure marks and alterations. I explained to her why I'd taken the third exam in pen. Our conversation quickly devolved into a shouting match. She had been caught in my opinion, but wasn't going down without a fight.

I marched to the counselor's office and demanded I be put in another geometry class. My request was refused, the school year too far gone to make that a viable option.

The rest of the school year became a battle of wills between teacher and student. I refused to take a test in pencil drawing countless warnings. I figured getting a "B" or "C" looked better than an "F."

The first semester ended just days after my sixteenth birthday. I celebrated that birthday by passing my driver's exam. My reward was using the family car to drive myself to all my bowling and after school functions; freeing my parents' from a chore they'd both grown tired of performing.

My freedom slammed to a halt when report cards were issued just days after I received my license. Thinking I'd earned a "C" in geometry, I ripped open the envelope with zeal. My grades, "A," "A," "A," "B," "F," and "A." I started to tremble. Brady failed me. I had some explaining to do when I got home. An apology to Mrs. Brady, I already decided, was out of the question even if Dad demanded I do so.

I spent several evenings looking for a way to stay off Richard Bennett's version of death row. A day before the signed report cards were due back in school, I worked up the courage to show Mom. She went back and forth between the report card and my face without saying a word.

"What happen," she asked in a soft, understanding voice. I shrugged my shoulders in one of those stupid teenage moves that drew a quick rebuke, "that's not an answer young man." I thought about telling her everything, but I couldn't. Any explanation I rationalized would look like I was making excuses. I'd let my battle with Mrs. Brady go on too long without asking for help.

Mom admitted she wasn't a good math student and admonished me to try harder next time. She grounded me for a week, which I thought was a lite sentence. Then, she said, "You have to tell your father."

The dreaded Richard Bennett confrontation arrived earlier than I planned. For some reason, Sergeant Bennett came home from work early that day, before I could steel myself for what would surely be one angry father. I opted to tell him just before the evening newscast. My rationale, I could minimize the almost certain damage to my psyche and mitigate the punishment, since he would be in a hurry to get back to his precious news.

Dad's booming voice penetrated the low flying F-106 fighter jets over our house; his anger audible several blocks away. He wanted to slap the hell out of me, but in a moment of monumental restrain, and because Mom stood a foot away, he held back. But that didn't stop the venom spewing from his mouth.

Punishment was swift. He tacked on an additional three weeks to Mom's restriction and ripped the driver's license from my wallet, tearing the leather. I stood their speechless, which infuriated Dad even more. He wanted the fight. There was nothing to be gained from arguing with him, so I remained quiet.

After being ordered to my room, Mom and Dad had a heated discussion about their "F" student. "How dare any son of mine come home with a grade like that," he said repeatedly. He slammed a glass of scotch on the kitchen table breaking it in his hand.

"Do you really think your son is that bad a student," Mom asked? At first he said yes, but Mom screamed at him, "Look at the rest of that report card." I heard silence through the door as he snatched the card from her hand. After some reflection, he admitted I'd actually done pretty good, other than the outlier grade, and began to wonder out loud what happened. He dismissed it and sat down to watch what was left of the nightly news.

I'd survived Hurricane Richard, but I had another semester of Mrs. Brady. After speaking with my black friends she taught at different times throughout the day, they reported similar experiences, although none as egregious as mine. They thought she was a bigot, a leap I wasn't willing to make just yet, despite the mounting evidence to the contrary. This would end badly for me. It turned out to be the only grade lower than "C" I ever received, and one of the few less than a B in all of K-12.

I confronted Dad a few weeks after my grounding about my driver's license. I yelled at him for the first time in my life demanding that license back. "You didn't pay for it, I did," I shouted. Looking at me like I was half crazy, Dad relented, but got in a good parting shot, "that damn car is mine," translation, you can't drive my car. That lasted about week. He asked me to drive him to the Bay County Jail, to assist with bailing out an airman arrested for DUI.

Dad was too inebriated to drive, having spent the afternoon and early evening at the NCO Club tossing down a few. Dad's a natural comedian when he drinks. The exchange between Dad and the desk sergeant on duty sounded like that famous Abbott and Costello baseball skit.

> Abbott: ...*Well let's see, we have on the bags, Who's on first, What's on second, I Don't Know is on third base...*"
>
> Costello: ...*That's what I want to find out.*
> Abbott: ...*I say Who is on first, What is on second, I Don't Know is on third.*

The desk sergeant laughed so hard at Dad's antics, I had

to remind them we were there to pickup someone in holding. After the officer checked my sobriety and driver's license, we were on our way back to Tyndall, Dad joking with this junior enlisted man in our back seat.

The next day wasn't so kind to either man. Dad had to administer some form of punishment as the squadron First Sergeant. Then he had to endure the wrath of Mom for involving me. Not a pleasant few days in our house.

Rutherford conducted its junior varsity basketball tryouts back in December. I'd waited three months for this opportunity. My knees, while sore, were well rested. We started a series of hardcore basketball drills intended to separate the men from the boys. We worked on rebounding, dribbling, footwork, shooting, free throws, and reaction drills to the sound of a whistle, followed by intense five-on-five scrimmages. When all was said and done, I'd made the team by the skin of my teeth.

At our second practice, I decided to attempt something I'd never done before; dunk. I had little doubt I could make it; I had hops and long arms. The only reason I hadn't attempted a dunk previously, I feared the jarring pain the landing would have on my knees.

My opportunity came on a fast break. I raced down the court by myself, pushed off on my left leg like I saw on television, and palmed the ball in my huge right hand. As I reached the rim, a player came out of nowhere and took my legs out from under me. My wrist slammed into the rim. The ball caromed off the backboard and disappeared from view.

The loud sound of my crash landing on the wooden floor was erased by a thundering scream emanating deep from within. I landed arm first, my right wrist bearing the brunt. Coaches and players streamed down to my end of the court, but before they could reach me, I was on my feet giving chase.

That assault on my body had nothing to do with basketball. This kid and me had words a few minutes earlier after he elbowed me in the mouth. Dragging my right arm, which I knew was broken; I caught my assailant in seconds only to be dragged away by coaches and teammates before I could take a swing.

This young black kid had been a rival of mine at Rosenwald. He once struck me in the face with the hardened heel of a dress shoe over a foul called by a coach in gym class.

X-rays revealed a broken wrist and radial bone. One was a clean break that needed resetting. Next came the cast and months of inactivity.

It also meant bowling took a backseat while I mended. I turned the bookkeeping over to Gladys. I coached the younger kids when I thought I could help. My part-time job at the commissary on weekends: gone.

Four months later, cast still in place from just below my elbow to my hand, I started to get a little antsy. State bowling championships in Miami were less than two months away. I wanted a shot at winning again. I'd actually moved up one division thanks to an improving game.

In a brazen attempt to resuscitate by bowling career, I walked into the bowling alley restroom with scissors in hand. I applied water to the portion of the cast that covered my hand and cut away just enough to get my fingers in a ball. I walked out, grabbed a ball, and bowled like I'd never been away.

Someone called Mom fearful I would reinjure myself. She arrived as I started my third game, watched for five minutes, and left like she'd entered, quiet and fast.

With my sophomore year winding to a close, Dad summoned me home for a quick chat. I thought it odd, Dad didn't chat, at least not with us kids, and we were rarely home alone.

Dad sat in his favorite recliner. He asked me to take a seat in a soft concerned parent voice. He was about to deliver news I'd feared for awhile. I'd done the math; we lived at Tyndall for four fears---time for a new duty assignment following his recent promotion to master sergeant.

He went into this long labored discussion about the military. "Are we being transferred," I blurted out. He got up, put his hand on my shoulder and said, "yes." I turned numb. It was easier to move when I was younger, now I had deep roots in the community. Panama City had gotten into my blood, warts and all.

"Where are we going," I asked. "The Air Force Academy in Colorado Springs," he replied. And like a real estate agent, he started selling me on the Academy, Pikes Peak, and skiing. He did his best to console me and offer hope for a brighter future.

"When are we leaving?" "Early August." He got up, walked into the kitchen, poured an alcoholic beverage of some kind, two fingers, in a glass with ice cubes, and rejoined me in the living room.

I had about three months to say my goodbyes. We talked about life in general for several minutes when both sisters arrived home from school. He hadn't told either one of them yet, that would wait until Mom came home.

I gained a newfound respect for Dad. He didn't have to single me out, or express his sorrow. He thought enough of me to have this one-on-one. That was special; I wished we had more of these moments. I rose from the sofa and headed towards my bedroom, when Dad rose and gave me the longest embrace he had given me in years.

I borrowed Dad's car and made a beeline for Gabe's house. He would be the easiest to tell. With his high school graduation the following evening, he would be leaving for Bradley University in the fall on an ROTC scholarship.

Gabe informed me his Dad just received orders for Peterson Air Force Base, in Colorado Springs. We laughed briefly, before I went in and spoke to his father. Having been there earlier in his career, he assured me I would fall in love with The Springs, as he called it. Gabe would be home for holidays and summer breaks. Sure enough, we picked up our friendship right where it left off.

With the end of school just days away, I had to make some quick farewell speeches. I started with those African Americans who'd come over from Rosenwald with me. Of all the goodbyes, these turned out to be the most difficult. I felt like I was abandoning them for greener pastures.

They asked lots of questions. I had few answers. I didn't know the name of my new school or have an address. Other than our yearbook photo, I didn't have a picture to remind me of our shared sacrifice. I knew I'd never see them again.

On my final day of school, the bus dropped me in front of my home. I waited twenty minutes before a second blue Air Force bus stopped at my feet. Wilson opened the door allowing the Rosenwald kids to exit the bus. I boarded the bus to say goodbye. He applied the parking brake and led me outside. He stammered for a minute before asking "why goodbye?" I'd see him occasionally over the past year, because the Rosenwald bus stop sat directly across the street from our home.

He burst into tears. I wrapped my arms around his shoulder, while the remaining kids on the bus watched, thinking I'd just delivered some terrifying news, like a death in the family. He regained his composure, turned his back, and like that he was gone.

Next came Gladys and the bowling alley staff. When I told Gladys, she hollered "no" and ran to the ladies room. She stayed away while sixty teenagers started their league session.

Gladys emerged from the ladies room calm and composed, walked over and grabbed the PA microphone. She had us all stop bowling and announced I would be leaving in August. The stunned expressions on the faces of kids, adults, parents, and bowling alley staff gave away to a standing ovation.

I spent the next hour between frames answering questions and exchanging pleasantries. Dana, a girl I'd just started dating, pushed through the crowd sobbing uncontrollably, the combination of makeup and tears staining her shirt.

The profound sadness of others at news of my departure left me little time to grieve outwardly. I'd bottled up my emotions trying to console everyone else.

Before I knew it, school ended and we were carpooling to Miami, some six hundred miles away, for the Florida State Bowling Tournament. We took turns driving, laughing, and enjoying our time. Like the kids at Rosenwald and Rutherford, I would never see most of my fellow bowlers again. Many of my friends in that car would eventually be transferred to new bases and make new friends. That's the life of a brat.

The only downer during our journey, gas lines along the Florida Turnpike. They snaked around for miles blocking exits off the roadway. Arab states introduced the world to an oil embargo that year. The embargo inflated global prices and caused massive gas shortages. Few places felt that pinch more than the United States. The embargo came about thanks to the Yom Kippur War.

Gas prices almost doubled between 1973 and 1974. Some states dealt with shortages by rationing gas. Those license plates ending in even numbers filled up on even days, odd numbers, on odd days. The all to common, "Sorry Out of Gas" signs appeared everywhere.

We planned our trip around the days we could fill up the tank. Despite the gas lines, nothing spoiled our mood. This was my last hurrah.

The bright lights of Miami sparkled against the night sky from my third floor hotel window. Those lights lured us to explore the city and its nightlife. None of us had ever been to Miami.

We took a cab to North Miami looking for a restaurant someone recommended. Why not South Beach, I have no idea? Two black guys and six whites exited the cab on some major thoroughfare in what looked like a deserted neighborhood. We looked around and started to walk. It took seconds for us to attract a crowd of police officers thinking we were a local mob.

The white guys in our group spoke up, explaining our situation, and where we came from. An officer got on his radio and hailed two cabs. Half dozen police officers waited, hovering around in a protective posture. When the cabs arrived the officers had us gather around. One officer spoke for the group, "get in the cabs, go back to your hotel, and don't come back." It wasn't a threat; the officers were trying to protect us from our naïve selves.

After watching a kid throw a Molotov cocktail through a store window, we got the message. The police escorted both cabs all the way to our hotel.

The tournament itself proved uneventful. None of us did any good. We treated our journey more like a vacation. Just as quickly as we'd arrived, it was back on the road for the ten-hour journey home.

Before I knew it, movers had descended on 2545 Harding Street, packed our furniture onto the Mayflower truck and took off.

Dana and I had a tearful goodbye with all the typical teenage promises of staying in touch, loving one another, and promises to visit; like that was really going to happen.

August 14, 1974 we crossed DuPont Bridge one last time, heading west in our green Ford Torino station wagon, destination, the United States Air Force Academy.

ACT 3

FULL CIRCLE

CHAPTER 18

AMERICA THE BEAUTIFUL

AUGUST 1974

The incandescent glow of the morning sun brightened my otherwise gloomy disposition as we reached Destin. Temperatures hovered in the upper 70s with a strong breeze, a breeze aided by a speeding automobile blowing air through our open car windows.

Dad slowed our car waiting for beachgoers to cross U.S. Highway 98, all headed towards the beach. After crossing a bridge onto Santa Rosa Island, traffic remained at a complete standstill for thirty-minutes. This temporary delay in our travels played like a cruel joke.

The two-foot swells lapping the shoreline ever so gently looked as if they were waving goodbye. My eyes moistened as I sat in total disbelief that we were leaving all of this behind.

Our journey continued through Fort Walton Beach, Mary Esther and Hurlburt Field, part of the Eglin Air

Force Base reservation, and geographically, America's largest air force base.

Dad eventually reached fifty-five miles per hour, only to slow once again in Gulf Breeze, where U.S. Highway 98 takes a sharp turn north across Pensacola Bay. The Gulf of Mexico disappeared from view not to be seen again.

Thirty-minutes later we drove through a tunnel under Mobile Bay emerging near downtown. Mobile is the birthplace of baseball legend Hank Aaron, who had broken Babe Ruth's homerun record earlier in the year. A few signs were in place commemorating his achievement.

Just outside of Mobile, Dad veered northwest towards Hattiesburg, Mississippi, then onto Jackson. The natural breeze disappeared shortly after we left the Gulf Coast, flags hanging limp, heat and humidity suffocating.

We passed through several sleepy southern towns, crossing over small streams, swamps, and patches of dense forest. Rusted cars and trailer park communities were scattered about on either side of the road, laying testament to the fact everyone here was poor, not just black people.

Mississippi looked just like Alabama. Were it not for the sign marking the border, you couldn't tell the difference. They should have combined the two states and called them Alaissippi or Misabama.

Dad learned his lesson about driving down South from our experience four years earlier. We had enough food and beverage stored in our station wagon to feed a small army.

Gas stops were short and sweet so as not to draw attention. We stopped in Jackson drawing the ire of locals, piercing blue and green eyes ripping Dad to shreds, but they kept their physical distance. Dad didn't believe in guns. Protecting ourselves meant keeping our wits about us.

Finally, after three hundred seventy five miles of back roads, we merged onto a completed interstate highway. Dad was ecstatic, no more stop-and-go traffic through rural southern towns fraught with danger.

In response to rising gas prices created by the Arab oil embargo, President Nixon lowered the national speed limit to fifty-five earlier in the year. Dad, like most drivers, basically gave the middle finger to the lower speed limit. He accelerated to a smooth sixty-five miles per hour on this freshly paved segment of I-20 westbound.

Next stop, Vicksburg and a collision with the mighty Mississippi River. For once, a southern town I knew a little something about. The Siege of Vicksburg turned into one of the defining moments of the Civil War. Sitting high atop a bluff, Vicksburg proved impenetrable to Union attack. The forty-seven day siege starved the city compelling Confederate forces to surrender. When the siege ended, Union troops controlled the entire Mississippi River, and with it, the flow of supplies and weapons.

The Mississippi River looked massive from the bridge. Barges heading in opposite directions had ample room to maneuver in a display of American commerce at its finest. The muddy banks on either side appeared steep. A clear line marked the former height of the river, the northern snowmelt long gone by mid-August.

Once in Louisiana, Dad made quick work of the distance between Vicksburg and Shreveport, where we spent the night at a motel just off I-20.

The following morning we pushed farther westward, crossing the Texas border in a matter of minutes. I saw signs for Marshall, Longview, Kilgore, and Tyler.

Just before reaching the outskirts of Dallas, Dad turned in a northwesterly direction to bypass much of the heavy traffic in the Dallas/Fort Worth metropolis. By noon we were sitting at a Denny's in Denton.

The place was deserted except for the two women making out in the corner. This was the first gay couple I'd ever seen. My gaze fixated on them for what seemed like an eternity, sneaking peeks, trying to avoid being too obvious. I didn't know how to process this outward display of affection between two women. The couple stopped fondling one another long enough to take a bite of food and look in my direction. The ladies smiled. I nodded and smiled back. Satisfied, they went back to groping one another, tenderly at first, then decidedly more passionate.

By 1 p.m., we were back on the road headed for U.S. Highway 287 and Wichita Falls. Dad entertained the idea of spending the night at Shepard Air Force Base, just outside Wichita Falls, but quickly dismissed the thought--too much daylight to waste.

So we soldiered on when Dad started to tire. After prodding from Mom, he reluctantly relinquished control of the command module.

I assumed the wheel and drove two-thirds of the way to Amarillo, one hundred seventy five miles. I incurred Dad's wrath only once. I'd become trapped between two eighteen-wheelers barreling down a three-lane portion of the highway. I wasn't sure whether to speed up and pass, or fall behind one of the trucks and stay under the speed limit. "Get your ass moving," Dad shouted, startling everyone in the car.

Driving helped clear my mind. I needed a distraction from my broken heart. Every song that came on the radio reminded me of Panama City. The ballads struck a particular chord. The number one song on the R&B charts that summer, *Sideshow* by the group Blue Magic. It must have played ten times a day, each and every time eliciting some emotional response from me.

The lyrics reminded me of Dana when we embraced on a moon lit beach my last evening in Panama City. For a kid with little understanding of true romance, I could be romantic at times.

See the man with the broken heart
You'll see that he is sad, he hurts so bad
(So bad, so bad)
See the girl who has lost the only love she ever had
There's got to be no sadder show to see

Those lyrics kept replaying in my head. Forty years later that song still elicits a visceral pull on my psyche.

It's often said smell is the most powerful of the five senses. For me, it's the sound of great music. I equate many of life's experiences to music, and *Sideshow* was my aphrodisiac.

Dad resumed command of the ship just before nightfall. During my drive, the landscape changed to dirt, sagebrush, and tumbleweed. The temperature in the Texas high plains hit one hundred. A strong wind blew dust and dirt obscuring the road ahead, at times reducing visibility to near zero. Much of that dirt and debris accumulated on our windshield. Light pebbles pelted our fenders and door panels. Bugs stuck to the windshield that no amount of cleaning solvent could remove at such high speeds. The riverbeds were parched and cracked under the intense heat.

We planned to bed down in Amarillo, the quintessential west Texas town of cowboy boots, cowboy hats, large belt buckles, cattle, and billboards challenging those who dared, to a beef-eating contest.

Dad looked for one of those easy on, easy off, motels. In less than five minutes, Dad looked in the rearview mirror to find nothing but open road. Amarillo had disappeared creating a temporary panic. The rolling hills of west Texas swallowed towns whole in seconds, giving the appearance a massive sinkhole sucked everything underground. We doubled back finally finding an exit to Dad's liking.

Those signs coming in about steak whetted Dad's appetite for a steak dinner. As he was fond of saying, when in Rome, do as the Romans do. The smell of cooked beef permeated every once of oxygen in the vicinity. We found a restaurant attached to a country and western bar. If our blackness was an issue, it never manifested itself. The people were wonderful and we were richer for the experience.

At one point in Amarillo's not to distant past, Amarillo Air Force Base, among its many functions had been the basic training center for newly enlisted airmen. Seeing African Americans didn't strike those we met as odd or out of place.

Dad continued north on U.S. Highway 287 to Dumas, before veering northwest once again merging onto U.S. Highway 87, for Dalhart. The Springs lay three hundred fifty miles away. The terrain looked much the same as the previous day: sagebrush, dirt, tumbleweed, rolling hills, and dry riverbeds.

The Land of Enchantment marked our entry into Mountain Standard Time, gaining us an hour. We joined I-25 heading north at Raton, New Mexico where I caught my first glimpse of the southern Rockies. Even at a distance they looked impressive, dwarfing the Appalachians.

The volcanic mesas looking west were equally extraordinary and set the stage for the Sangre de Cristo Mountains. Few journeys are as suggestive of awe and beauty as a car ride along this stretch of I-25 at the Colorado/New Mexico border.

Our car started a slow twenty-mile ascent when my ears popped for the first time, the change in air pressure wreaking havoc on my hearing. The farther north we drove, the closer the canyon walls appeared. Signs alerted us to possible dangers ahead.

The first sign read, "Raton Pass Summit 5 Miles." The second sign read, "Beware of Falling Rock." Another sign illuminated with bright yellow flashing lights read, "Dangerous Crosswinds Ahead."

The canyon walls featured a reddish clay-like hue. They were slick and shinny from years of wind erosion and likely glacial activity from millions of years earlier. You could hear a pin drop if it weren't for Dad repeatedly telling Mom, "Nita look at this," as if Mom didn't posses her own set of eyes.

We spotted numerous unusual rock shapes and formations. Large boulders teetered on smaller boulders looking like they'd fall over with a slight nudge or strong gust of wind. The colorful cactus and flowers of the lower elevation had given way to tall pines, some atop rock formations, others wedged between. During winter months, this road, at times, would be impassable, but not on this mid-August afternoon.

Raton Pass was part of the old Santa Fe Trail and Santa Fe Railroad. For over a century, Raton Pass had been the primary direct land route between the Arkansas River Valley to the north, and the upper valley of the Canadian River towards Santa Fe to the south. Raton Pass allowed for easier passage around the Rocky Mountains.

We reached the summit, 7,834 above sea level, before beginning our descent. Next came a sign, "Welcome to Colorful Colorado," followed by more warning signs. The canyon walls slowly receded as Dad navigated a series of twists and turns down the pass. The winds buffeted our car requiring his utmost concentration.

Once down the pass, we started another climb, not as steep as Raton Pass, before reaching the town of Trinidad. We stopped for gas even though we still had three-quarters of a tank. None of us objected to the delay.

The architecture of Trinidad was a splendid mix of Spanish, Native American adobes, and Victorian. The canvas is an artistic wonderland full of amazing vistas.

Back in the car, we continued our downward trek for miles approaching Walsenburg. To the east were rolling hills and dry grassy plains all the way to Kansas. The eastern landscape took on the color of wheat. To the west, peaks and plateaus as far as the eye could see. This is the place where east shakes hands with the west. It was the most distinct change in land formation I'd ever laid eyes on.

Dad blew through Pueblo, Colorado's third largest city in minutes, now just thirty-five miles from our final destination. Panama City became a distant memory.

The approach to Colorado Springs from the south was rather nondescript, more rolling hills and dry brush to the east, mountains to the west.

Without warning, it appeared. The mountain of all mountains moved into place by the movement of our car. Pikes Peak towered over the western sky casting a shadow on Colorado Springs so enormous it made everything else seem insignificant by comparison. The tree line disappeared around the 11,000-foot mark leaving a naked summit.

Pikes Peak rises 14,115 feet above sea level and 8,000 feet above The Springs. It is one of Colorado's fifty-three "fourteeners;" mountains that rise above fourteen thousand feet. Named after explorer Zebulon Pike, Pikes Peak is the tallest mountain in the United States east of its longitude.

Colorado Springs, at 6,035 feet above sea level is nearly one thousand feet higher in elevation than the Mile High city of Denver, fifty miles to the north. The city population of one hundred fifty thousand in 1974; made The Springs the largest city outside Madrid I would live in to date, yet it seemed small and quaint.

The city had no skyscrapers or tall buildings to speak of and traffic appeared manageable. Moments after Pikes Peak exploded into view, Dad exited I-25 at Academy

Boulevard, heading west towards the south gate of the United States Air Force Academy.

The first thing I noticed, the grassy center median on the Academy gave new meaning to the words thick and green. This Kentucky bluegrass could swallow footprints whole. Dad found his new office, walked in, introduced himself and the family before departing for a hotel on Nevada Avenue, one of the city's main thoroughfares heading downtown.

After dinner, Karen and I decided to release pent up energy at the hotel swimming pool located right outside our door. The sun had just set relieving us of a ninety-five degree day. I opened the door when a blast of cold air slammed into my shirtless body. The bitter wind said, not now, not on this evening. Karen and I beat a hasty retreat to the warm comfort of our room and turned to Dad for answers. He had none. This was our first experience at six thousand feet after nightfall.

Welcome to Colorado, where ninety-five degrees by day, turns into fifty degrees or lower on a summer night. The breeze dropped the wind chill several degrees lower. Temperatures in Northwest Florida by contrast would be eighty-five by day, seventy-five at night. Auntie Em, we're not in Florida anymore.

Over the next few days, Florida remerged in my mind with a vengeance. It was just too soon to begin the process of letting go. *When could I go back? Would I go back? What were my friends doing? Was Dana still in tears?* Being stuck in a hotel for two weeks left plenty of time to do the one thing I needed to avoid, ponder my circumstances.

Colorado Springs is home to several military installations. The Air Force Academy sits in the northwest corner of The Springs. East of town is Petersen Air Force Base, or Pete Field as it was known back then. This is where Gabe's dad would be stationed. In the middle of downtown, sat the soon to be closed Ent Air Force Base. South of town, Fort Carson, one of largest army posts in the country with over ten thousand soldiers.

Cheyenne Mountain was home to NORAD, the North American Aerospace Defense Command. This triple-peaked mountain, just southwest of Colorado Springs hosted an underground operations center to monitor North American airspace, and any potential missile strikes from the Soviet Union. Built during the Cold War, this underground facility was designed to withstand a nuclear bomb and the resulting fallout.

Thousands of military retirees called Colorado Springs home. Its African American population was less than five percent, with no true inner city, or ghetto. Some people were poor, but not impoverished like Panama City. At first blush, the people of Colorado Springs seemed friendly and inviting.

Weather, like we discovered in our attempt at an early evening swim, dictated a different form of dress. T-shirts, shorts, and sandals were replaced with jeans, waterproof hiking boats with thick socks, jackets, coats, sweaters, denim shirts, and gloves.

Certain foods came with pressure-cooking instructions to compensate for the high altitude. That was a lesson Mom learned the hard way when she baked a cake that didn't rise.

I suffered a brief bout of altitude sickness waiting for my body to adjust to the lower air pressure.

Snow tires, ice scrappers, and electric dipsticks became a driver's best friend in the winter, along with warming a car engine for several minutes before shifting to "D." No more popping the car in drive immediately after ignition, lest you had a few thousand dollars to spare to replace a cracked engine block.

CHAPTER 19

OUR NEW FRONTIER

The United States Air Force Academy sits at the base of the Rampart Range. With elevations ranging from 6,200 to 9,000 feet above sea level, the views from Academy grounds are spectacular. On a clear day, one could look east for twenty miles with the naked eye before being interrupted by the earth's curvature.

The mountainous terrain is equal parts tantalizing in its majesty and challenging gateways during winter snows.

Dad worked at the Department of Defense, Medical Examination Review Board, or DODMERB, one of the many military acronyms we memorized over the years. This was a prestigious assignment bestowed upon the best in their field---an honor Dad more than deserved.

DODMERB processed the medical components of applicants who would go on to become students at all of America's service academies---West Point, the Naval Academy, Air Force Academy, U.S. Coast Guard Academy, and the U.S. Merchant Marine Academy.

Cadets, who otherwise passed muster with grades and proper endorsements from congressional leaders, and other high-ranking officials, had to handle the physical rigors of being a military officer. One negative mark on a medical record could stall a career in the starting gates.

Dad relished the responsibility, and like the rest of his distinguished career, tackled his new job with gusto often bringing home manuals to become familiar with a new set of regulations.

Approximately three miles from the south gate entrance to the Academy, a fork in the road at the base of a mountain forces traffic north or south. Heading north on Stadium Boulevard takes visitors past Falcon Stadium, home of the Air Force Academy's college football team. I was a hotdog vendor for one season during high school. The money was awful.

A couple of roads heading west from Stadium Boulevard leads to the training grounds for four thousand cadets. The most iconic structure at the Academy, and arguably in all of Colorado except Pikes Peak, is the Cadet Chapel. Completed in 1962, the Chapel features seventeen spires reaching skyward one hundred fifty feet. Perched atop an elevated plain in the cadet area, the chapel can be seen for miles by anyone looking from the east, and visible as a lone beacon of light at night silhouetted against a darkened sky.

Graduates of the Air Force Academy earn a Bachelor of Science degree and commissioned as second lieutenants in the Air Force. The Academy is also Colorado Spring's most popular tourist attraction bringing in over one million guests a year. These tourists were euphemistically called "gnats" for all the obvious reasons. They disrupted the otherwise orderly flow of Air Force life, especially during the summer, but we took great pleasure in sharing our surroundings.

Heading south from the fork in the road, the street changed names to Pine Drive. It looped around a mountain before continuing its westward journey. Two miles later, just off Pine Drive to the south sits Air Academy High School.

Air Academy is the only high school on the grounds of a military academy. It consistently ranks as one of the top high schools in the country. The school's mascot is a Kadet---a fictional bird of mythical proportions. Kadet is a play on words and seen as the younger sibling of the Cadets attending the Air Force Academy. The school colors were blue and silver mimicking those of the Air Force.

The school grounds and the interior corridors were immaculate, just like Rutherford. The floors were spotless; the lockers that adorned the walls were pristine, light fixtures in good repair, everything in its proper place. It said school but lacked character.

When I arrived for registration, the receptionist greeted me like a long lost family member, cupping my right hand in a violent motion thrusting my shoulder up and down almost jerking it from its socket.

My new counselor, Mr. Bookman overheard the commotion and sprinted in my direction to offer a hearty handshake of his own. He whisked me away to an office cluttered with books and papers---the sure sign of a man with too much on his plate, or a slob. He called it organized chaos.

We exchanged pleasantries before I handed over my

transcripts. He looked approvingly at first, then paused, "What happened," he asked, referring to my "F" in geometry. I gave him the condensed version knowing full well I'd be taking geometry again. Not sure if he believed me, but its all I had.

Air Academy had become a victim of overcrowding. To compensate, juniors and seniors started class at 7 a.m. and were home by 12:30 p.m., sophomores would arrive around 11:30 a.m. and stay until 5 p.m.

Air Academy didn't have a lunch hour. They had staggered twenty-minute breaks starting after third period to allow students the option of purchasing snacks from vending machines, or bring their own treats from home. Nothing in those machines spoke nutrition. It's amazing we all didn't suffer from hyperglycemia.

After registration came something I hadn't antici-pated. Mr. Bookman and I engaged in one of the strangest conversations I'd ever had with a school official. He warned me about Air Academy's social structure in language so cryptic, I didn't truly comprehend the mes-sage, or his intent. I nodded in agreement just to end the discussion.

He quickly pivoted to a conversation about President Nixon. Nixon resigned on August 9, 1974, just days before we left Florida. Since our belongings were on a Mayflower truck, I didn't get a chance to watch news, or hear all the political banter.

Being a military brat and someone eligible to join the armed forces in less than two years, Bookman asking my opinion wasn't surprising. The president is the commander-in-chief so it made sense to talk. My fear wasn't Nixon's transgressions in office; that had been dealt with; it was the appearance of a rudderless ship. We'd lost a president and vice president in less than forty-eight months. "America and the military needed stability," I told him, "and a strong leader."

We discussed the pros and cons of Gerald Ford while he gave me a tour of school grounds---an extraordinary setting that belied the school's true state of ordinariness. Bookman escorted me to the football field and waxed poetic about the Air Academy team. By the time I arrived the school had won multiple conference titles.

He asked if I played. I shrugged my shoulder, turning my head back and forth without explaining my knees. I'd put on ten pounds during my sophomore year, definitely not enough to sustain the punishment my body would take if I decided to play.

Dad arrived after my registration to give us a tour of our new home. In Academy parlance, we lived in a cluster: a group of five or six duplexes connected by a circular driveway, each with a single car carport. In the center circle of the cluster are extra parking spots for those two or three car families.

Ours was the first duplex on the left after entering the cluster in an area known as Upper Pine Valley. The house looked perfectly square from the exterior. It was a rather nondescript off yellow edifice on a slight hill, the grass thick, like that at the South Gate. The Rampart Mountain Range jutted skyward less than a quarter-mile away.

The front door opened onto a living room to the right, approximately twelve by fifteen feet. To the left, a short hallway led to a kitchen and small eat-in dining area that would barely hold our family.

Farther down the same hall sat three bedrooms and

one full bathroom. As usual, I got the smallest bedroom since I didn't have to share with anyone. My room barely fit my new full-sized bed, dresser, and desk.

Back through the kitchen, a door led outside to the backyard. Opposite the backdoor, a flight of stairs led down to a full basement. The stairs bisected the basement. The larger side was barren other than washer and dryer connections. It featured cement flooring, with a couple of steel pilings to support the weight of the house. At the top were two small windows. The other side we converted into a family room, complete with sofa, carpet, and a television set.

The tour lasted ten minutes before heading to Black Forest. The community of Black Forest sits off Academy grounds in a thicket of trees and high timber that gave credence to its name. Large properties with horses and farm animals were mixed in with smaller, but equally impressive homes. Karen would be attending middle school here before joining me at Air Academy for her sophomore year. Like Air Academy, the school grounds were pristine and somewhat sterile.

School started on a cool, crisp morning in early September, the same week we moved into our house. The temperature that first morning hovered around fifty, the air pure, as I started my mile-and-a-half walk. I dressed like a Florida kid, no t-shirt or sweater. I didn't own a sweater. To my body, fifty degrees may as well have been thirty below zero; I couldn't stop shivering. I found very few kids walking to school. Most had cars, or were dropped off by parents.

I entered the hallway and stood quietly off to one side near my locker. Teenagers scurried about renewing old acquaintances and sharing summer experiences.

At six foot four and an Afro bigger than basketball great Julius "Dr. J" Erving, I was an imposing figure, difficult to miss, much less ignore; but these kids did just that, providing just enough space for me to walk by. It was typical self-absorbed teenager behavior; I took no offense.

First period physical education came and went. Second period typing and third period English passed without incident. Forth-period geometry had me a little nervous, but the teacher gave off the vibe of a professional educator, not someone with a vendetta against black people.

The morning had been quiet; no one spoke to me except a teacher. My only words, "here" in response to roll call. I bought a juice and donut during my snack break and sat at the end of a large picnic bench in a corner. The strategic location I'd chosen positioned me perfectly to take in my surroundings. The loud chitchat among students continued unabated for a full thirty minutes.

I scanned the crowd looking for a friendly face. A few girls made eye contact, smiled, and went back to their conversation. I took it upon myself to make small talk with those sitting at my table; my overtures were largely ignored. Most gave me that "whatever" look without exchanging names, and went back to their business. I felt foolish.

It took twenty minutes to realize what should have

been obvious from the start. I brought the only color to sea of white. *Was it an aberration? Was I hallucinating?* I hearkened back to my conversation with Bookman from the previous week. Our cryptic discussion resonated in my subconscious. Now the warning shot over the bow made sense.

History and science class brought more of the same--- a lone black face. It took two full days before I spotted another person of color; a female, I later learned was a cheerleader who lived in Lower Pine, a lot closer to school than my home. Then a black male appeared. This obnoxious kid seemed to relish the attention heaped upon him by those young white kids in his click. To me, he gave off the appearance of the class clown.

That was it, three blacks out of a student body of nearly eight hundred. By my senior year, I'd be the only black male at Air Academy in my graduating class. After Rosenwald, and to a lesser extent Rutherford, I'd grown to expect a diverse student body. Here I'd been thrust back into a world of total white dominion. Not even an African American teacher.

Desegregating Air Academy under some court man-date would have required an airplane, not a bus. Colorado Springs simply didn't have enough blacks to make desegregation a viable option.

The only thing whiter than Air Academy was the snow-capped summit of Pikes Peak, the occasional jagged rocks breaking through the snow providing its only change in color.

It took weeks before I made my first friend, a neighbor named Kent, who happened to live in my cluster. Kent and I were the new kids on the block, his family having recently arrived from Hickam Air Force Base, Hawaii.

We made Oscar and Felix from the original television series *The Odd Couple* look tame. Our friendship was borne out of necessity and convenience. By Air Academy standards we were both social misfits: me because of my pigmentation, Kent was just socially awkward. His conversation didn't blend with teenagers. Like me, he bonded better with adults.

Both of us were bowlers. For the first year at the Academy, we spent almost every afternoon on the lanes or working part time jobs at the commissary. Despite the wealthier Academy clientele the tips here were lousy compared to Tyndall.

Kent eventually dropped bowling, in large measure because I was better and drew a lot of attention. He hated playing second fiddle. Kent had three brothers, and while they were tightknit, they competed over trivial matters, often resulting in shouting matches and fistfights.

Kent's family adopted me as their fifth son. I ate dinners at their house, played pinochle until all hours of the morning, and dabbled in a little three-on-three football with his family that included his father.

Kent was a grease monkey in the most flattering sense of the term. He loved vehicle engines. He took cars, trucks, and motorcycles apart and put them back together like a seasoned pro. He built a solid reputation around the Academy that allowed him to pick up work repairing vehicles, either from home, or the Academy's Auto Shop, a building set aside for self-maintenance.

School for Kent proved to be an inconvenience of the highest order. His career path had been set the second he picked up his first wrench.

Unfortunately, I didn't pickup the mechanic gene, but Kent taught me enough to do minor maintenance on the station wagon, and Dad's new car, a red and white 1960s Volkswagen Van. That van looked like one of the hippie vehicles used at Woodstock.

Kent owned a Suzuki motorcycle with enough room to carry two passengers relieving me of walking to school. Mom hated the sight of me on the back of a motorcycle fearing injury on the icy roads during winter.

Her worst fears almost materialized following a January snowstorm. Kent lost control of the bike on an ice patch coming out of the school parking lot. We'd slowly pulled away from a stop sign, fully aware of the conditions on the ground, when the tires lost traction. I managed to plant my feet firmly on the ice-covered pavement and lift the back wheel off the ground just long enough for Kent to grip the handle bar, and pull us upright. I don't know how we stayed vertical. We couldn't execute that maneuver again if our lives depended on it.

Air Academy High School reeked of elitism. A vast majority of kids were the offspring of military officers. Their fathers made more money than both my parents' combined, even with Dad working an extra job. Many of their mother's didn't work, but were deeply entrenched in the social strata of one of the military's most prestigious destinations.

If the wives of these officers accomplished anything worthy of public attention, it typically received a little ink in the local newspaper written as, *"Mrs. Joe Smith, wife of Colonel Joe Smith,"* as if their contribution and success were always tied to their husbands'. They accepted their station in life as second fiddle without complaint.

As a result, many of my well-heeled classmates had a parent at home. Those parents expected their offspring to attend college, a subject Dad completely dissuaded me from discussing, much less try to pursue.

Many kids drove better cars than my parents'. Very few of my classmates' worked. They had no need for extra money. They were already being provided for with cars and a healthy stipend.

I didn't fit in at Air Academy, a fact I recognized from the start. While my race was a factor, it wasn't the sole reason. Everything, for some inexplicable reason felt off, like being trapped in a matrix of doors, each leading nowhere.

CHAPTER 20

VICTIM

I had great philosophical debates with self, asking a series of hypothetical questions. *How would we be today if slavery had never happened, yet black people still found themselves in America? If we couldn't go back and change slavery, how about a court with the guts to reject Plessy v. Ferguson?* One minute I played the learned professor, the next, an eager, but naive student.

I debated man's voracious appetite for subjugation and need to dominate others. I thought about the misguided fear some Caucasians retained about blacks. I thought about the large numbers of whites who participated in the Civil Rights Movement. I thought about how slave owners hid behind the Bible to justify their actions and brainwash their servants. I thought about the white and black people who guided me and brought such joy to my life. I thought about how lies and innuendo were passed down from generation to generation; that while lacking in veracity had gained some semblance of acceptance as truth. It was a series of contradictions.

The Constitution was certainly a forward thinking document, but did our forefathers, many slave owners themselves, ever think slavery would become illegal? I know some had an outright contempt for human property, but for it to be abolished, I think not. I loved having my internal deliberations. It provided a challenge and kept my brain occupied; better not to think about my current circumstances.

The older I became, the more I couldn't escape my blackness, even if I wanted to, which I most certainly did not. What happened to the young kids who played together as preteens? As we aged, many divided along racial lines, forgetting we were a mixed race group of playmates at one time---my thoughts appeared to be an apt description of life at Air Academy High School.

What I discovered during my debates was the state of victimhood, my own. I'd been victimized and willing played victim at times. Playing and accepting victimhood only fed the beast encouraging more self-doubt and self-pity. To find my true self, I had to lose the victim mentality.

Days after meeting Kent, I befriended a female in my typing class. Each student sat at a typing well attached to the next in a horizontal line. There were six desks to a row. Janice sat next to me, but for the first month of school, I could have easily been sitting in China. Maybe she envied my typing prowess. I typed faster on a manual with fewer mistakes than she did on an electric typewriter.

Janice was a beautiful brunette about five foot six, very shapely with a little bit of a pug nose, that in its own way looked cute. She carried herself as the highly intelligent student I knew her to be, well dressed, but not overly so. Her skin was flawless requiring little makeup.

I'd already been in my seat when Janice introduced herself. I looked up, responded in kind, and quickly returned to preparing for class. Janice kept the conversation going long after the teacher called the class to order, first by whispering, then writing quick one sentence notes joking about her own typing. Next thing I know we were giggling like two little kids who had just been treated to a bowl of ice cream.

I looked forward to our in class rendezvous. It broke the monotony of an otherwise boring day, and my growing contempt for everything Air Academy.

Janice and her friend Joan, who sat to her left in our typing class, began walking the halls with me between classes. Our blossoming friendship didn't go unnoticed. Janice had the courage of her convictions and invited stares of the Air Academy student body. She almost dared anyone to speak ill of us.

We started meeting during our snack break. Then we stayed after school until she caught her ride to Douglass Valley, her home on the other side of the Academy about five miles away. We attended home football games together.

We elevated to holding hands acting as if we had an amorous relationship. It all happened so seamlessly; it never occurred to me we offended anyone. She kissed me for the first time walking to third period, about a month after we met. Several students smiled, others looked in disgust, mainly the males.

Three weeks into our relationship came the invitation of a lifetime. She asked me to be her date for the homecoming dance. Without hesitation, I said yes, followed by more kissing.

Dad bought me a brand new suit. Mom helped me pick out a corsage and provided money for dinner. I would be dressed to the nines sporting a freshly cut and well-manicured Afro. Janice's mother had gone out of her way to make sure her daughter looked the part of a young, classy woman.

Two days before the big night, Janice was unusually quiet, lost in thought. The next day she didn't show. Joan delivered a handwritten message on her behalf.

"Dear Michael, I have to cancel our homecoming date.
My Dad won't let me go with you,
Love Janice."

Word spread quickly that my dated bailed, earning me insult after insult from white males; angry I would dare think of dating a white girl. The word nigger shouted in the school corridors landed one young man in the principal's office, followed by a three-day suspension.

On homecoming night, I sat at Air Academy Bowling Lanes watching the adults. By now, I'd become friends with the entire staff. There was Chuck, Ed, Art, Gordie, Stoney, Bernie, Dick, Jim, and Pam. All, except Pam, were active duty or retired military working part time for extra income.

They seemed bewildered by my appearance at the

bowling alley on homecoming night. Several made jokes using humor as the ultimate shock absorber to assuage my hurt feelings. "Don't send a boy out to do a man's job," one bellowed. By the time they were through I had tears of laughter streaming down my face.

Chuck noticed, after the jokes subsided, my smile and sense of humor waned. He poured a beer into a plastic cup, slid it across the counter, and told me to keep my mouth shut. I was still a minor.

After the doors closed for the evening I practiced while the staff cleaned up. Chuck sat down to ask why I hadn't attended the dance. Chuck, a very good-looking, straight talking African American, and father of three, sat patiently while I provided all the gory details.

By now, the others on duty sat listening, a mixture of black and white staff. Next came another cup of beer. That cemented my relationship with the bowling staff.

Chuck gave me a ride home that night. I thanked him, and turned to exit his truck when he grabbed my arm in a vice grip. He looked me in the eye and said, "if you need anything, anything at all, no matter the hour, call." He wrote down his home and work phone numbers on a sheet of paper. His act of kindness began a relationship that lasted fifteen years. Physically, we actually looked like father and son, and that's how he introduced me.

In the three months we'd been at the Academy, Dad's reputation for the sauce had already become legendary. I found myself on numerous occasions awakened in the wee hours of the morning to drive him, and his two buddies home from the NCO Club.

Chuck saw something in me I'd yet to figure out for

myself, I was a survivor on a rudderless ship. My life had no direction. I lived minute to minute. No future plans, and no one to offer guidance. This late in my high school life, I needed to think about a future.

Dad loved me, of that, I have no doubt, and I loved him too. But alcohol controlled his every waking move. The warm, loving, determined man I knew before Vietnam was buried under an avalanche of inner demons that none of us understood at the time. I needed a father figure; someone to kick my butt and Chuck filled that roll admirably.

When I screwed up, Chuck was direct and to the point, not afraid to get his hands dirty providing guidance and a moral compass without being preachy or religious.

When it came to issues of race, we didn't talk much. No need, I just watched Chuck and learned. He extracted the name of Janice's father from me, a Lt. Colonel. While he outranked Chuck by a country mile, I have little doubt he placed a phone call on my behalf. He'd hurt me and Chuck just wasn't going to stand for it.

Chuck checked on my grades demanding report cards as proof. He was the only person, besides Coach Collier, to mention college and me in the same sentence.

In later years, Dad had lot of latent guilt at not supporting my college aspirations, often sharing that guilt in phone conversations while sloshed---alcohol, the ultimate truth serum and elixir.

At Chuck's suggestion, I mended my friendship with Janice, but kept my distance. Chuck told me to take the high road. She was obviously torn between a bigoted father and me, but her dad would always win out. "Don't put yourself in the middle of their family issues," he said.

Determined to be part of something, and hopefully make a few more friends, I decided basketball would be my version of Custer's Last Stand. I hadn't played since breaking my arm at Rutherford. Chuck and I both thought sports would provide a platform of commonality and shared sacrifice. My Osgood flared frequently thanks to the cold weather, but the year away from sports made the pain manageable.

I bought a basketball and put myself through drills at a court near home. I practiced alone for hours bundled in a coat when necessary. I stayed outdoors long after nightfall dribbling, shooting, pivoting, and rebounding in the dark. I practiced on a thin sheet of ice; that in hindsight was really dangerous.

Tryouts took several days. The really good players were easy to spot and had secured positions on the team before tryouts began. The rest of us fought for three or four openings.

In a preemptive move, I told the coaches and trainers about my Osgoods disease, figuring honesty would minimize reaction to my bad play while I knocked off the rust of inactivity. The trainer wrapped both knees so tight that first day of practice my legs felt like they were strapped to two-by-fours. I walked like Lurch from *The Addams Family*.

Sport usually brings out the best in people, especially if you might be a future teammate. For a solid week, no one, except a coach uttered a word in my direction. I reached out, tried to exchange high-fives, acknowledged good play---all overtures greeted with an icy silence. I didn't think deafening silence could get any louder, but it did. They even froze me out in five-on-five scrimmages.

The writing I feared was on the wall. Even the head coach subtlety stopped offering advice. Down to the final thirteen on a twelve-man roster, someone had to go. My knees had taken a turn for the worse, yet I still outperformed all but a handful of players, even the returning starters.

The extra player quit on his own, leaving me on the team, but no coach confirmed my position. I attended practice and started learning the system. Coach knew basketball; it showed in how he ran practice, a lesson in precision. During a drill, my knee buckled. I collided with the cement wall just behind the basket before crashing to the floor. Pain shot down from both knees, through the shin, to my ankles and feet.

After a minute, I limped to the stands and watched the remaining ten minutes of practice. The next day I showed up, determined to impress, but something still bothered me. I hadn't been cut, nor told I'd become part of the team. I finally asked. Coach started practice without answering.

The next morning a memo circulated revealing the team. My name wasn't on the roster. The kid who quit somehow made the final cut. Why hadn't I been told? Why had I been allowed to practice for nearly two weeks with the first team?

My head ruptured in fits of anger and rage to the point of being rendered speechless. I shared my story with Chuck that evening, my words full of venom and hatred. I didn't need advice; I needed an ear to vent. I picked the wrong ear. Chuck exploded, telling me to stop feeling sorry for myself. I dropped an "F" bomb and walked out. We didn't speak for weeks. I even avoided the bowling alley during his shift.

Few people stood up to Chuck, regardless of station in life. He was gruff around the edges, frightening off anyone who dare cross him, except his wonderful wife. I'd gotten away with something I've never seen anyone attempt before, or since. After a few heart-to-heart conversations, and intervention of others, we mended our unique father/son relationship.

No other Air Academy sport truly interested me except basketball. I asked Dad to transfer me to another school so I could play. That request fell on deaf ears. I refused to attend an Air Academy game in our own gym. I went to our opponent's gym, and watched my school team from the opponent's stands, with my identity hidden in their school colors so I wouldn't be discovered. I'd become friends with many of the players at other schools by participating in pickup games around Colorado Springs.

My high school career ended that late December day in my junior year. I wasn't going to play at Air Academy team even if I were the next coming of Kareem Abdul Jabbar.

Once my anger subsided, a sense of calm washed over me. I stopped caring. I simply didn't have the strength to take on another battle. The environment proved too caustic and not worth the effort.

CHAPTER 21

FREE AT LAST

Basketball was a microcosm of my aggregate experiences at Air Academy those first four months. I'd been slapped away at every turn with little positive reinforcement. At a time when academics and college preparation should have provided all the motivation necessary to excel, I was two seconds away from leaving Air Academy behind. The only thing that stopped me, I didn't want to become a negative black statistic.

Dad and I continued to lock horns over my attending college in the ultimate Battle Royale. Dad always shut down my argument for higher education, at times loudly, frightening everyone within earshot---he definitely had the bigger horns. He remained resolute in his opinion that I would be an Air Force enlisted man, period: end of discussion.

It never dawned on me at the time that in eighteen months, I could make my own decisions. While I over-heard my classmates' talk about life beyond high school, and all the support they received from school and parents, my focus was stuck on simply making it to graduation.

While my blackness played a role in Air Academy's low expectations of me, it was Dad's opinion of me that mattered most, always seeking his approval for the most trivial of pursuits. Mom's love and support I knew to be unconditional. She would support me even if I decided to run through a brick wall. Dad proved the tougher nut to crack. I relished the challenge of meeting his, heretofore rigid expectations, especially academically. Now I'd met those challenges with no payoff.

Of the six courses I took my junior year, only three were academically challenging, and even they didn't stimulate me much.

My grades suffered. I went from an "A" to a "B" student overnight. The final report card of my junior year, six "Bs," all accomplished without ever taking a book home.

In a peculiar way, my detachment from all things Air Academy proved liberating. I found myself dreaming, smiling, and enjoying life once again. The constant strain carved into my face disappeared. No one, except Chuck, had any expectations of me. My bad attitude and lack of support made me complicit in my own demise.

Bowling, already an important factor in my life, now took over the dominant position. Not only did I compete in junior leagues, I coached the younger kids, and took part in planning and executing our annual Special Olympics. Working with a group of handicapped kids taught me a great deal about myself---I had the capacity to show unconditional love and selflessness without asking for anything in return. The joy we provided those courageous boys and girls left an indelible impression.

Failure never fazed these kids. No matter how many times they missed hitting a single pin, they never quit. They were just happy to have the experience. Hitting one pin turned into a victory celebration. If only I'd paid better attention, I could have learned a great deal from those Olympians. Instead I was drowning in my own little pity party, contrary to what I promised myself I wouldn't do.

I'd become a decent bowler, average in the mid to upper 160s, but I wanted more. There was no better place to learn the art of bowling than the Academy, and the greater Colorado Springs area. The manager of the Academy Lanes was a professional bowler, as were many around The Springs.

God must have read my thoughts. A coach materialized from the most unlikely of sources. Pam worked at the bowling alley during daytime hours. On days I didn't work; I scurried on all fours up a dirt path that rose two hundred feet, to reach the bowling center, which sat high atop a hill.

Pam offered to teach me, all I had to do: listen and learn. She was the white version of my mother---stunning, calm, witty, and compassionate. Her husband Greg, and their nine and six-year-old daughters, Nicole and Carrie became another member of my extended family.

Days after my seventeenth birthday Pam and I started daily lessons. First we fixed my ridiculous approach. She held my left hand and wrist, slowly guiding me into a comfortable five-step cadence.

Next we worked on my delivery. I stood at the foul line rolling ball after ball, positioning my wrist just right; bending my knee and waist properly. Another week goes by before she turned me loose. Within a week, her lessons started paying dividends. My average jumped twenty pins in thirty days. I'd gone from mediocrity to the best junior bowler at the Academy in a month.

Then I turned to the professionals to learn how to read lane conditions and proper usage of equipment depending on oil pattern. I soaked up this knowledge like a sponge.

My exploits started making the local papers. *Could I do this professionally one day?* My newfound ambition proved more than a fleeting thought, heightened by watching the top pros on television. During our Saturday morning junior leagues, the Professional Bowlers Tour aired on ABC. Between frames I sat glued to the television set.

Earl Anthony was easily the best bowler of his generation. We took to calling him "Big Earl." The world's premiere bowler, with a military style crew cut, had the smoothest delivery any of us had ever scene. Consistency was the name of his game. Chuck often worked that Saturday morning shift, providing me deep insight into "Big Earl's" technique. Anthony earned $107,000 in 1975, big money in my book.

I read books by Dick Weber and Don Johnson, the two kings of the sport. When they were interviewed on television, I listened attentively.

I kept at it day and night. By now, I'd quit the commissary and started working nights at NCO Club as a dishwasher for $1.65 an hour. I had the same job at Tyndall in 1974, when minimum wage sat at $1.10 an hour, before being raised to $1.30. I always thought Dad helped me get the job so he'd have a ride home.

Next came my first car, a 1964 baby blue Ford Fairlane. I bought it from one of Dad's co-workers for five hundred dollars. My payments were seventy dollars a month, financed through the local credit union.

With a car, I started travelling to the "big boy" leagues to watch the professionals. I positioned myself close enough to overhear conversations about lane conditions and oil patterns. Were the lanes wet or dry? Were the best bowlers using soft plastic or a hard rubber balls? I tried to blend into the background as best I could. Given my youth, size, and humongous Afro in a totally white environment, this proved difficult at times. But the bowlers always treated me with the utmost respect.

That summer, a team of junior bowlers put together a team to participate in the Colorado State Bowling Championships in Greeley.

Greeley, a town of forty thousand is located about sixty miles northeast of Denver in the middle of cattle country. The town is home to Northern Colorado University and a large meat packing company. The stench that greeted our arrival thanks to the plant almost choked the life out of us.

By the time we left Greeley, our team had won the Colorado State Championship. Not bad, I'd managed to win two state titles, in two different states, in three years.

The weakest link on our team, Allison was a classmate of mine at Air Academy, who had just graduated. Allison was pale white, about five feet one with a bust so large she couldn't see her tiny feet. She and I often laughed about her body proportions, comfortable in her own skin. Everyone noticed when Allison entered the room.

We became fast friends. She had a smile that could melt butter. Wary of another Air Academy dating failure, I resisted Allison's overtures for months. She finally tired of my indecisiveness and confronted me in front of the entire bowling alley staff. They too noticed the obvious attraction and secretly conspired to get me off my ass and ask her out.

I picked up Allison at her house where I met both parents---truly wonderful people. She was the spitting image of her mother in every way, shape, and form.

Driving away, she slid next to me on my long bench seat, placing my right arm around her shoulders. When we arrived at the movie theater, I removed my arm from her shoulder, and went to bundle myself to combat the single digit temperatures outdoors, when I inadvertently elbowed her in the left eye.

The swelling and discoloration was immediate. I couldn't find a rock to crawl under fast enough, but true to form, she started laughing. We entered the movie theater arm-in-arm when I made an off-handed joke at the popcorn stand that I'd punched her for misbehaving. Bad joke. Next thing I know, the manager rushed to call the police, before Allison stopped him. I could see the newspaper headlines now, "Big Black Kid Arrested for Punching Little White Girl in the Face."

We arrived at her home well after midnight. Her

mom made hot chocolate and together we watched television until her father arrived at 3 a.m. from a gig as a musician.

For the next year, Allison and I dated in one of those on again, off again romances. I was so scared of committing I ruined our relationship. Even after we broke up for good, her mother continued to call my house wondering when I'd come over to play cards, or watch television. I often found myself sitting in Allison's living room with her mother, as Allison walked in with her new white boyfriend. Any awkwardness I felt, Allison's mother quickly dismissed.

My junior year ended without much fanfare weeks before Allison and I had our first date. When I presented Chuck with my straight "B" report card, he was none to pleased, and said as much, in that stern voice, uniquely Chuck's. He kept urging, pushing, and prodding me towards college, admonishing me to ignore Dad.

While it wasn't his place, he'd taken parenting me seriously. Chuck avoided confrontation with Dad in deference to me, not wanting to exacerbate our already deteriorating relationship. On the rare occasion he would stop by the NCO Club for a drink, Chuck would sit and look at Dad in disgust. It placed me in an awkward situation.

Dad's drinking forced Mom to contemplate divorce. Her body language all but said so. She had talked herself out of it several times for the sake of us kids. Besides, she still loved him, trying desperately at times to save him from himself.

I hung with my adult friends all summer, often going to work with them to learn about their jobs. Bart was a staff sergeant at the motor pool. One of his duties was to drive cadets on field trips away from the Academy. I accompanied him on more than one occasion, getting an up close and personal look at the life of an Air Force Academy cadet, and future leader.

I knew the Academy was off limits to me. "B" students need not apply. Besides, my bad knees all but guaranteed I would never make it through the front door. Even with a father whose job it was to approve medical clearances for the service academies, Dad couldn't hide my problem.

But talking with those cadets on our longer journeys reinvigorated my pursuit of academic excellence. I learned about routine, discipline, the types of courses they took, and the demands involved in the pursuit of excellence.

I asked several cadets what motivated them to become Air Force officers. Almost all answers took the form of service to our great country, not surprising, since I too had that gene. They wanted to belong to something bigger than themselves. I, admittedly, envied all of them, and told them so during our frequent trips around the state. The younger cadets were only a year removed from high school, leaving them just a year older than me.

Many cadets I spoke with had fathers who served, or recently retired. Most came from really good nuclear families, with a strong father figure as head of household. Some were politically connected, which came in handy for the necessary congressional recommendations. Several cadets came from poverty, and beat odds significantly more difficult than mine.

From the northeast corridor to the Deep South, from Alaska to California and everything in between, these cadets had an unshakable bond and strength of character I rarely observed in young people at this stage of their lives.

Pam continued her bowling lessons over the summer, even when I no longer needed her help. Her friendship meant so much I didn't want the teacher student relationship to end. I'd become a big brother to her daughters.

Pam and Greg trusted me with their children. These two little white girls often rode in my car with me, alone. If I had a bowling tournament downtown during daylight hours, they were usually with me. If I had errands to run, they were in the car. Nicole, the nine-year-old was quiet and reserved around most people, except me.

Carrie was fun loving and silly in a good way; she enjoyed life and could often be found sitting on my lap, with my long arms wrapped around her in a protective posture. I loved those two little white girls like I did my two sisters.

Gabe, my friend from Florida came home for the summer. I introduced him to Kent and the three of us roamed the streets of The Springs. For once I got to be a teenager.

They would pick me up after work at the NCO Club,

and we'd go cruise Nevada Avenue, like a scene out of the movie *American Graffiti.* More often than not, a carload of girls would flag us down for conversation. The three of us became so well known, the girls asked for us by name and tried to ply us with alcohol. We weren't into drinking much to their dismay.

Gabe and I spent many a night reminiscing about Panama City. I loved all my adult friends and their families at the Academy, but I had no relationship with the Air Academy student body. I missed Florida. I spent four years cultivating and nurturing relationships at Rosenwald and Rutherford, that I knew, I could never get back. The timing of our move to The Springs couldn't have happened at a worse time.

Having the support of my extended Panama City family could have easily kept me on solid academic footing. We worked together and challenged one another. A group of us openly discussed future plans that included college. I'm certain many of us would have wound up at the same universities. Nothing like peer pressure to keep one motivated. My profound sadness at moving during high school, especially to a place so culturally bereft of diversity, took years to overcome.

Gabe hated Florida, reminding me at every opportunity about some of the racial troubles I'd endured. He would draw out the word redneck in a harsh guttural tone that sounded almost German. He could be obnoxious, arrogant and downright rude at times, but this white boy made protecting me from harm his mission.

But what Gabe never understood was that all that racial animus actually strengthened me, it made me a better person. It made the friendships I cultivated black or white meaningful.

I stayed in touch with Florida, calling, or writing often. Gabe dismissed the place like it never existed even though he graduated from Rutherford.

CHAPTER 22

MY SENIOR YEAR

SEPTEMBER 1975

I started my senior year reinvigorated thanks to my conversations over the summer with Air Force Academy cadets. These young men were going places, and while I couldn't join their team, I was determined more than ever, to find my path to upward mobility through education.

After years of political strife, war protests, and civil rights battles, the close of the Vietnam War fell silently at the Academy. Even my adult friends, many who'd served in Vietnam, let the moment pass without comment.

At school, Armed Forces recruiting posters were prominently displayed in the counselor's offices, challenging young people to accept the call to duty. Most were the ultimate soft sell about potential high achievement, playing on tradition and patriotism, very little about education.

The recruiting posters of the mid 1970s era gave little credence to the seriousness of the mission at hand. They played up military service like a fraternity, which in some respects I guess it is. Those posters completely ignored the serious nature of military service. They needed the soft sell approach given the country's collective hatred of Vietnam.

Despite my misgivings about the message, students were taking a serious look at serving. I already decided if I served, I wanted to be an officer, which required a college degree.

Chuck began his campaign to convince me college led to a brighter future. I didn't need convincing, the cadets had rerouted my priorities. After one of those really good father/son talks over a beer, I decided my senior year course load had to change.

I'd already met all of Air Academy High School's, required courses, save for one science class, before I started my senior year. Because I wanted out of Air Academy, I'd made a huge mistake at the end of my junior year, and registered for the minimum four classes. Only a biology course truly represented something a college recruiter would respect.

On the first day of school, I made a beeline to the counseling office to inquire about adding more rigorous classes to my schedule, even if it meant returning to the more traditional six-class course load.

Due to overcrowding, my request was denied leaving me with physical education, biology, library science, and some elective I've long forgotten. By 11 a.m., I sat home eating a loaf of peanut butter and jelly sandwiches, suffering from brain atrophy.

Halfway through my junior year, Mr. Bookman called me into his office for mandatory career counseling. Instead of providing career options and college advice, we talked about sports. The "Thrilla in Manila," the third and final boxing match between Muhammad Ali and Joe Frazier slated for that fall.

When I forced him back on track, he changed the conversation to the Pittsburg Steelers, my favorite team, and their recent Super Bowl win. We never discussed college.

I lagged behind every college bound student at Air Academy by the time I arrived for my senior year. I hadn't filled out applications, or taken an SAT or ACT exam. I mentioned it to Dad once again igniting another nasty argument that resulted in me walking out, slamming and shattering a glass door in frustration. I guess I never learned.

I scheduled another appointment with Bookman the second week of my senior year. Bookman ducked, dodged, and deflect better than Muhammad Ali. Maybe this is where Ali learned the rope-a-dope. If I made it to a college campus, it would be of my own doing.

I spent two hours a day for two weeks in the library researching universities. I had no idea how people got into college. Deciding a major was easy. I always wanted to be a play-by-play announcer, if not a military officer. I'd never seen a black announcer. Maybe I could be the first I thought.

I rummaged through one book after another looking

for journalism programs. I found the University of Southern California, University of Illinois, Columbia, and Arizona State. All, I determined were great schools, each requiring an SAT or ACT exam. So that's where I decided to start.

One Saturday in late October, I snuck off to a school across town and sat for the ACT exam. I paid for the exam only telling Mom of my intentions. Unfortunately, I didn't perform so well. I didn't know they offered preparatory classes for both the SAT and ACT. What was the big deal anyway? I'd taken standardized test before and always performed in the top ninety percentile. My ignorance taught me a lesson in preparedness.

At first, I thought maybe Dad was right; I didn't belong in college. Then my competitive juices kicked in and I started all over again, setting up an SAT exam for February. This time I studied and performed exceedingly well restoring my faith in self.

Due to my late start, I missed the fall semester application deadline for every college I wanted to attend, a set back I hadn't figured into the equation. I also didn't understand the competitive nature of the top universities.

I returned to the library for more study, when I realized I had no idea how to pay for college. Out of state tuition rates were daunting. Financial aid, grant money, and scholarships were a foreign concept in the Bennett household.

Tuition costs might have contributed to Dad's reticence about my attending college. We certainly didn't have that type of cash on hand. Dad might have been trying to mask his disappointment at our family finances all this time, something I hadn't considered. Whatever it was, something scared him off when it came to my attending a university.

I decided the best course of action might be a junior college. It would buy me time, and it was affordable. I took two courses over the summer after high school. Mom paid my tuition and books without telling Dad. I earned an "A" in both classes. I loved the college class-room challenge. Listening to such learned individuals share their knowledge convinced me I belonged at a university. I jumped in with both feet studying often, even after I mastered the subject matter. To say I was stimulated would be an understatement.

Bowling picked up right where it left off, only better. My average, now in the 190s was the talk of the youth bowling circuit throughout The Springs. "18-Year-Old Rolls Top 695 Series," was the headline of the Gazette Telegraph on January 18, 1976, ten days after my eighteenth birthday. At the time it was the second highest series in the history of the American Junior Bowling Congress Pikes Peak region: with games of 229-211-255.

I considered professional bowling as an alternative to college. I'd never seen a black on the televised portion of the PBA tour, just like I'd never observed a black sports play-by-play announcer. I thought I could change all of that, the bowlers in The Springs certainly accepted me as an equal competitor.

It would be years before I learned of Fuller Gordy. Gordy was the older brother of Motown Records founder Berry Gordy. He bowled professionally in the early

1960s. After further investigation, I dismissed the thought of a professional career. I needed a sponsor and didn't have time to figure it out. Besides, the paydays weren't all that great. Only the top five percent of all bowlers earned enough to sustain a basic quality of life.

I kept bowling anyway despite my discovery. After consuming my peanut butter and jelly sandwiches, I made the five-minute trek to Academy Lanes and bowled until I started work at five o'clock.

My devotion to the sport made it easy to locate me on any given day. One woman did just that. She was the mother of a classmate, a girl, two years my junior. With me on a shortened day, and the school on a split schedule, I never saw her at Air Academy, unless I stayed late to study in the library, which I never did.

I knew Cybil from Saturday bowling. She didn't stand out, just another of sixty kids age thirteen and older bowling. Her mother, Mrs. Johnson showed up at the bowling alley every afternoon like clock work. At first, she kept her distance. Then she moved closer, eventually sitting at my overhead projector where scores were manually recorded during league play with a grease pencil. I never kept score when I practiced; I just put a line through the frame and kept on going.

I hated the interruption of my practice sessions. This was my quiet time where I worked out my personal problems.

Mrs. Johnson struck up conversations on a daily basis. We engaged as friends for weeks, her asking me stupid questions about bowling, which I'm sure she already knew the answers too. Next came cookies, brownies, cakes, and pies. Her continued appearances made me extremely uncomfortable. *What did this white woman want?* I asked Chuck, he didn't have a clue.

Finally she brings her daughter. After weeks of downright aggressive antics about how good a person her daughter was, I took Cybil on an innocent date at a bowling center away from the Academy. We laughed and joked around like any teenagers on a first date. Our relationship lasted for a year. I took Cybil to the only high school formal I would ever attend.

After one early evening date I dropped Cybil off at home. I wanted a good night's sleep. My ACT exam was scheduled for 9 a.m., the following morning. Mrs. Johnson met me later that Saturday afternoon with explicit instructions to never drop her daughter off at home. "Leave her around the corner, she can walk." What a bizarre request. My antenna should have gone off, but it didn't.

Then Mrs. Johnson told me the story of her husband, Cybil's stepfather. Born and raised in Alabama, he despised black people. Oh shit, not again.

I ran away from the relationship faster than Jessie Owens in the hundred meters. But Mrs. Johnson had other ideas. Her obsession with all things Michael Bennett continued.

Cybil babysat for families all over the Academy. When I refused to visit the homes where she babysat, Mrs. Johnson picked up her daughter, and brought her to the bowling alley, or my job, and left her with me. She masterfully manipulated the emotions of two young people knowing full well we had bonded.

Despite another warning from stepdad, our clandestine dating life continued with her mother's full support.

Mrs. Johnson even enlisted the help of those families who Cybil babysat for, to either have me pick her up, or let me stay, while Cybil watched their kids. Every white family agreed empowering the two of us even more.

Often, we'd fall asleep on the living room sofa in various stages of undress while the kids slept in the next room. On nights when the parents came home early, Cybil and I were out on the town, arriving home in the wee hours of the morning. Cybil and I dated through the summer after graduation before Mrs. Johnson finally acceded to her husband's demands, turning to enforcer-in-chief to pry us apart. I'd already grown weary of looking over my shoulder.

With a month left in school, I made the single biggest error in judgment of my young life, worse than continuing to date Cybil. I spotted two fellow students with a history of troublemaking, standing on the side of the road shooting the breeze. I didn't know the extent of their shenanigans, thinking it was more school related, like not paying attention in class, or being poor students. They had never mistreated me.

It was midnight when I encountered them as I headed home from a night of bowling. Dad always warned me nothing good happens late at night. He was about to be proven correct. The two boys waved, and I stopped, leaving the confines of my warm car.

I spotted a cassette player on the front seat and asked why they hadn't connected it to their car's Bose speaker system. The kid pointed and asked if I wanted to buy it, he had a new one already installed in the front console. I said yes, but I'd have to pay him in a few days. We agreed on a price. He allowed me to take the equipment before receiving payment. I placed the stereo in my trunk thinking Kent and I could install it later.

Days passed before I solicited Kent's help. He took one looked and recognized the stereo as one stolen from his friend's car. I told Kent where it came from. Kent reported the theft to police and both boys were promptly arrested. I'd unwittingly become an accomplice in a crime. If only I'd asked them to open their trunk. Police found dozens of stolen car stereos, including one that actually belonged to me, stolen from my car months earlier.

My receipt of stolen property, and why police hadn't contacted me, remained a mystery for a week. I'd already returned the equipment to its rightful owner.

Dad arrived at school unannounced and demanded that I open the trunk of my car. I complied, but he found nothing.

I followed Dad home where he proceeded to tear my room to pieces. He found nothing. Finally, he asked, "Where is it?" This was not the time to play games with Dad. I knew exactly what he was looking for. I told him I'd returned the stereo to its rightful owner and gave him the kid's home number to verify. He verified, like I knew he would.

Only then did Dad reveal that police investigators contacted him. Apparently, these two white boys pinned their crimes on the black kid. At the time, I had no clue they'd been on a crime spree. Police interrogated me for an hour and sent me home.

My interrogation wasn't so much an interrogation, more an interview. They needed corroboration and confirmation of my contact with these two hoodlums. The police had their eye on these boys for weeks, a fact they never disclosed to Dad. The detectives were gathering facts for criminal charges against my accusers, and looking to recover stolen merchandise. When detectives showed me their cache of ill-gotten booty, I found my own stereo.

After leaving the police station, Dad interrogated me better than the detectives; and art formed he'd mastered years ago. Then accusations started, one after another, as spit flew from his mouth. When he decided I wasn't being forthcoming, Dad drew his fist, only to be stopped by a loud squeal from Mom.

Dad had been drinking again, and failed to notice my hand was balled in a tight fist, ready to unleash two years of pent up fury. I'd put on another twenty pounds, confidant I could hold my own in any physical encounter with his thin frame. When I stood, he thought the better of it gliding off to his bedroom in a drunken stupor.

A week later police questioned me again, this time without Dad's knowledge. They went over my alibi, which they'd already confirmed, and asked if I knew more. Both detectives informed me charges were being filed against the other boys and that I might be called to testify. I said fine and walked out. The second interview took less than fifteen minutes.

I told Mom the outcome of that second interview. Keeping a secret like that from Dad, especially at the Academy, was not a good idea. We both told him. He immediately started on another one of his tirades, this time sober. He called the detectives to verify my story. They confirmed my account without revealing the details of their case. Their ambiguity and evasiveness made Dad further question my veracity. I never heard from the police again, nor was I called to testify. The two boys, as the local paper reported, were sent to jail.

The damage to my already fractured relationship with Dad proved insurmountable. A week later, Baccalaureate was held at the Air Force Academy Chapel, Dad never showed.

Graduation, slated for the following evening, at one of the big halls in the cadet area came and went, Dad a no show, preferring to drink the night away at the NCO Club. He avoided me for three days, not once offering so much as a congratulatory hug. I hated Dad and felt guilty for feeling so ill of a man who had done so much for me.

On graduation night the students were stuck in an underground stairwell for thirty minutes or more, lined up in alphabetical order. Being near the top, I could easily look down to the sea of white faces below. All were ecstatic.

I suffered silently. My agony had nothing to do with being caught up in a criminal investigation the past few weeks. Although in hindsight, being the only black male in my senior class would have confirmed some of the prevailing negativity of black males that existed at Air Academy. I was alone. The only thing I had in common with my classmates; we occupied the same space and time for another few minutes.

I couldn't help but wonder; *what would Air Academy have been like with a little infusion of color and culture?* My friends at Rutherford would all be graduating within the same week, in a ceremony I was certain would be a lot more festive, celebratory, and diverse than mine. I wept quietly on those stairs.

Most seniors made plans for graduation night weeks earlier. Several held house parties with parents dispensing alcohol to any senior regardless of age. Kent received one invitation; I received none.

Kent invited me to attend the party he'd been invited too. I reluctantly went along for the ride, only to discover my fellow graduates didn't want me around, even when a parent asked me to stay. I overheard one student say, "What's he doing here?"

Kent and I returned home after buying two cheap bottles of wine and sat on his front doorstep, wrapped in coast and blankets, drinking with his parents until sunrise.

My adult friends all took turns celebrating my graduation in the ensuring days. Some invited me to dinner; others took me out for drinks, still others baked cakes and held impromptu celebrations at the bowling alley.

Relief swept over me; grateful I'd survived Air Academy. I examined the arc of my childhood from Spain to Maine, Florida to Colorado. I left high school more confused about my identity than the day I set foot in Panama City six years earlier.

I'd been dropped into some crazy social science experiment. I was the mouse in the maze looking for that illusive piece of cheese. *What did the cheese represent? What was the expected outcome? What was the original hypothesis? Was I being prepared for something?*

Was I a white kid in black skin, or a black kid with

white sensibilities? Or did any of it matter? Whatever the answers to all my musing, the experience meant something; I just needed to figure it out.

EPILOGUE

My preoccupation with college increased dramatically after high school. I used Dad's disapproval and the experience of Air Academy to fuel my obsession, acting with a constant chip on my shoulder. The naysayers, other than Chuck, Coach, and Mom held sway over my life for too long.

I looked at Pikes Peak Community College as a gateway to higher pursuits, taking on a second job as a gas station attendant to finance what I knew to be my calling.

I earmarked every dime of additional earnings for community college, and whatever four-year university I would eventually attend. My goal seemed simple enough. Earn straight "As" at Pikes Peak, and apply for every grant, student loan, or scholarship I could find.

I wrote out a detailed plan of action that included study time, something I'd never done in high school. I altered that plan as any significant change in circumstances arose.

The Air Force Academy cadets shared the stringent

Academy entrance requirements. I planned to use that model for civilian colleges and universities.

After two months, I'd saved enough money for tuition and books for a full year at Pikes Peak. A couple of months later I had enough set aside for year two.

The mindless work of a gas station attendant provided ample opportunity to dream and study. Only two kinds of people disrupted my study time at work, wives of military officers too high society to pump their own gas, and lazy people.

I managed to continue bowling, now in adult leagues, on days I wasn't on kitchen duty, pumping gas, or studying. All five senses were functioning at maximum efficiency quenching my thirst for knowledge. My schedule was hectic, but I wouldn't have it any other way. I stayed on a perpetual adrenalin rush for weeks at a time, sleeping little.

Suddenly my fortunes started to take a turn for the worse. Dad summoned me to the house. He'd become angry about two things. First, he still paid my auto insurance and decided it was time for me to assume that responsibility. That fix was easy enough; I had the money, and found my own policy in two days.

While I knew Dad's choice for my future was enlisted military service, I never expected him to interfere with college if it didn't cost him a dime. Dad blew a gasket like only he could, after I revealed I'd attended classes at Pikes Peak for a semester. He calmed down just long enough to allow me to begin sharing my detailed plans. I would be out of his hair in less than two years. As usual, when he didn't like the tenor or direction of our conversation, he cut me off mid-sentence, essentially telling me I was foolish.

Another heated argument ensued, both of us dropping "F" bombs. Within thirty minutes I left home never to return. I stayed at a hotel just off the Academy that first night contemplating my next move. I hadn't calculated paying rent so soon. I dropped out of school for a semester using a portion of my savings to make deposits and pay rent.

Despite Mom's repeated attempts at reconciling the riff between Dad and me, we didn't speak for nearly two years, with one exception.

Two months after I left home Dad stopped by the gas station. "Your mother left me," he said. I desperately tried to be sympathetic, but I couldn't find it within me to console him. I forced myself to think about the good times, pre Academy. Those happy thoughts allowed my growing hatred to subside long enough to wrap my arms around him. I realized for the first time, Dad never intended to harm his family. Dad didn't have a malicious bone in his body when sober.

Dad wept openly in front of me for only the second time in his life---the first, when his grandfather died. Here's a senior master sergeant in full military uniform, standing in front of his eighteen-year-old son and a few customers, crying like a baby. Alcoholism and untreated PTSD was about to cost him his marriage. I didn't know what to do. Unfortunately, his two drinking buddies continued to feed his illness. Dad wasn't like them; he had a conscious.

Dad didn't know Mom had taken me to lunch earlier in the day to share the news of her leaving. She didn't need to provide a reason for the separation, I already knew. I offered to help Mom financially, but she wouldn't hear of it, preferring I focus on my own future. While I knew this day would eventually come, I never imagined it could be so painful. What few friends I had, none had come from a divorced household. I had no playbook for divorce.

Word spread quickly around the Academy. All my adult friends, black and white, reached out, embracing me, providing comfort and a place to escape when needed. Chuck wanted me back in school. In addition to building for my future, he thought the distraction would help me cope with the disintegration of my family.

Christmas 1976 was the first time our family had been separated on a holiday since Vietnam. Dad stopped by briefly and then went to his new apartment to drink. He was at critical mass and needed an intervention.

I stopped by his apartment days later to talk about counseling and Alcoholic's Anonymous. The son had become the guardian. The awkwardness of that conversation shook me to my core.

A week later, his two drinking buddies stepped in to arrange the counseling he so sorely needed. I had nothing to do with their providing assistance, but I was beyond relieved they stepped up to the plate.

The second and more lasting disruption to my college plans occurred between Christmas and New Years. I lost my job at the gas station. On a bitterly cold day, with daytime highs in the low teens and a wind chill hovering around zero, I stood watch at the gas station. Ice was a good half-inch thick, covered by a thin layer of snow. Road conditions were nearly impassable.

Stationed outside in my unheated island sanctuary,

few cars came through that day. Most people chose to stay off the roads, if they could. I averaged about five cars an hour at the self-service pump, one or two at full service. One of those cars was Mom. No way was I going to allow my mother to pump her own gas, especially in these conditions. While pumping her gas, I noticed her front tire needed air.

I directed her to an island away from the pumps and proceeded to fill her tire, when a customer arrived at the full service line. I put up one finger signifying I'd be there in a minute. The lady behind the wheel acknowledged me and indicated she'd be fine.

The assistant manager, a portly white woman, bounced from the warm confines of her office, screaming at me, " hurry up you have a customer waiting." The waiting customer rose from her warm vehicle and indicated she was fine waiting. My boss didn't realize the other customer I'd been helping was my mother. Mom jumps from her vehicle and glared, not saying a word. The boss lady went back inside. That should have ended the conversation.

With frostbite setting in, I filled up the gas tank for the waiting customer and stood inside the door, in full view of the pumps. My feet tingled; pain replacing the warming sensation as my toes thawed. I repeated this action for the next few hours. I knew one person back in Maine who had a toe amputated due to frostbite; I certainly wasn't looking to be next.

Shift over; I settled my bank for the evening, and headed for the door when my boss chewed me out for lack of attentiveness. Her stinging comments came filled with expletives and a few racial epithets that I simply couldn't allow to stand. I struck back, basically telling her to keep her fat ass in the office and let me do my job. With that, I left for home.

The following morning I filed a complaint through human resources and reported for work, where I was promptly greeted by the store manager and fired. I had an ace in the hole; Mom witnessed the initial burst of ineptitude from my boss and was actually an assistant manager herself at the BX across the street---same company.

I was reinstated after a week, only to find my hours reduced from fulltime to one day a week. Again, I levied a complaint. Since I was hired as a part time employee, they were well within their rights to limit my hours.

Recognizing I couldn't win this battle, I quit and started seeking employment opportunities in Colorado Springs. I landed another job across the street at the bank as a night janitor, but that took only two hours. Not nearly enough to compensate for a forty-hour work week loss. That cost me another semester of college. I still had my NCO Club job, but that barely paid the rent. I hated all these menial jobs, but at least I had jobs. I needed my brain free for school.

I applied for dozens of jobs and found nothing, save for one opportunity at a sporting goods store downtown. In one of the most bizarre interviews I've ever had, the company required this applicant to take a psychological exam that included an inkblot test.

Then came a lie detector test. The location of the lie detector test was a drab, nondescript office building in downtown Colorado Springs with no address on the facade. I started wondering if it belonged to the CIA. It would have made a good black ops site in plain view. What better cover.

At the time, I didn't know a lie detector test was illegal for minimum wage workers. The exam room was dark and ominous with no windows except a two-way mirror. Inside were two metal chairs and a metallic gray table.

Panic set in as I sat wondering what I'd gotten myself into. *Why did it take all of this for a sporting goods sales job?* It's not like they were selling top-secret information to the Soviet Union.

The examiner, a white male with no sense of humor wrapped some apparatus around my chest connected to a machine that made needle graph marks, like a seismograph used to measure earthquakes.

After thirty-minutes of questions like, "Had I ever stolen money from an employer," "Have you ever taken illegal drugs?" and "Did you graduate from high school?" the test was over. The employer bounced through the door and congratulated me; I'd passed. And for the record, the answers are No, No, and Yes. I never heard from the sporting goods company again. It left me to wonder if this was nothing more than a ruse to experiment with lie detectors.

With my options now severely limited, I decided a change of venue had become necessary. I called a few friends in Panama City, made arrangements for a place to live temporarily, and called Gulf Coast Community College to begin the enrollment process.

March 1977, I drove my 1972 Ford Torino to Panama City. I spent the final night with Mom at her new townhome. I woke early the next morning to the smell of bacon. We ate quietly until it was time for her to leave for work. We said our goodbyes without a tear, followed by hugs from my sisters' and the family Siamese cat. Then they were gone.

A steady stream of tears cascaded down my face for hundreds of miles forcing me to pull over due to blurred vision. I called Mom from a payphone somewhere in Texas. She admitted she cried so much, her boss sent her home for the day.

I drove forty-eight hours with no sleep, retracing the route back to Panama City exactly as Dad had driven in the opposite direction thirty months earlier. I methodically planned gas stops and the time of day I'd be driving through parts of the South, memories still fresh from seven years earlier.

Just before sunrise, on a two-lane stretch of highway just south of Hattiesburg, Mississippi, I fell asleep at the wheel. My car jumped the center median, seconds away from instant death, when my subconscious picked up the sound of a blaring horn that jolted me awake. I swerved just in time to avoid a head-on collision with an eighteen-wheeler. I found myself hugging a ditch for a couple hundred yards before gaining control and steering back onto the highway.

My pants moistened just below the zipper followed by heart palpitations so heavy, I started hyperventilating.

I found a tiny gas station managed by a couple of good-ole-boys that had just opened for business. I asked to use the restroom, which they obliged. In the meantime, they took close inventory of all my worldly possession sitting in plain view on the back seat of my car. My out of state tags certainly didn't help matters.

Next thing I know, I'm fending off threatening advances and warnings not to pass through these parts again. Their admonition reminded me of the sundown laws I'd learned about in history class. That was a time when blacks were not allowed in towns all across America after sundown. While that law hadn't been enforced for several years, they succeeded at putting the fear of God in me.

I made it to Panama City by noon, located all the old gang and partied on Panama City Beach for three days. Not much had changed except our ages. We were all adults in a state with a drinking age of eighteen and bars that stayed open until 4 a.m.

I settled at Stan's house and went about the business of finding work. I started at my old stomping grounds, the commissary, where I was quickly hired. The two Lloyds had retired. This was a temporary gig while I found something more permanent that would allow me to get a place of my own.

The father of an old girl friend hired me for yard work and other general maintenance at Tyndall's recreation center. I worked both jobs for two weeks before landing a fulltime job at a snack bar just off the flight line at Tyndall. That job lasted three months before the military decided to shutdown the facility.

The day that job ended, I was hired at Tyndall's gas station; the same job I had at the Academy with the Army Air Force Exchange Service or AAFES. AAFES was like the parent company to the BX, commissary, and various other support functions vital to military households.

My new boss delighted in someone he wouldn't have to train. He checked references and called back to the Academy all while I sat in his office waiting. The lady who had chewed me out for my lack of attentiveness provided a glowing recommendation, and spoke with me briefly over the phone, offering a very sincere apology. I started work the next day.

I went to Gulf Coast Community College and continued the enrollment process, altering my long range plans slightly to attend Florida universities, as opposed to Colorado universities, after completing my two-year program.

Despite living down South, with its steep racial divisions, Panama City felt like home. There were people my own age, black and white, who cared about me. I belonged. Many of my former Rutherford classmates were off to college, but some had remained in the area making my transition easy.

Then another bombshell shattered my plans once again. Someone at the Academy placed a code in the system basically alerting everyone I was not to be hired. My new boss tried everything, including calling AAFES headquarters in Dallas. Even Mom got involved, angry that I'd been red-flagged in the first place.

Just a month into this new job, I was let go. The Academy gas station manager, not boss lady, retroactively got the code place on my file. He later lost his job and faced jail for some illegalities.

In four months I'd blown through four jobs. The pressure mounted. Not only did I need to find work, I needed out of Stan's house. I'd begun to wear out my welcome with his family.

I searched all over Panama City, stopping at places with help wanted signs for menial labor. Any job would do---washing dishes, pumping gas, yard work---desperation had set in. I was thrown out of more places than I can count, with one hollering, "we don't hire niggers hear." They certainly didn't mind taking nigger's money. This major franchise restaurant had several black patrons sitting at its tables.

I returned to the commissary bagging groceries for tips. Just then, the gentleman who ran Tyndall Lanes proceeded to begin hammering the final nail in my coffin. Without school, I had no right to possess a military identification card, much less set foot on Tyndall Air Force Base. My old nemesis, Charlie, the bowling alley manager, saw to it that the security police obtained all necessary information to restrict me from Tyndall.

The police stopped me at the gate, called Dad in Colorado to verify I was his son, and that I'd enrolled in college. Dad refused to vouch for me having started drinking once again. With that I lost my ID card, access to Tyndall, my commissary job, and most of my close friends.

By August 1977, I was homeless. I landed a job back at the Tyndall recreation center, thanks to the kindness of an old friend for minimum wage, $2.30 an hour, twenty hours a week. I slept in my car for two months, seldom leaving the parking lot where I worked except to eat and fill up the gas tank.

In an ironic twist of fate, the hospital Dad worked at while we were stationed at Tyndall, sat directly across the street from the recreation center parking lot where I slept in my car. So as not to be observed by police, I occasionally moved my car to a corner of the hospital parking lot, what better place to hide in plain site, a hospital, open 24 hours a day. A couple of friends stepped up and offered me a sofa to sleep on a few nights a week. Survival had replaced all my college aspirations.

With holes in my only pair of shoes bounded together with duck tape and cardboard for insoles, I tried in vain to find work and found nothing.

In November 1977, the final nail in the coffin sealed my fate. A motorcycle barreled through a stoplight on busy U.S. Highway 98, slamming into the front quarter panel of my car on the passenger side, just behind the tire. The cyclist flew over the car landing in the middle of the intersection. He shattered both knees.

After an extensive investigation, I was cleared of any wrongdoing, but my home, the Ford Torino suffered extensive damage. Mom had already put me back on her insurance policy, but I couldn't afford the deductible.

I reluctantly called Mom, who had reconciled with Dad. She wired me the money for a rental car and deductible. I slept in the rental for a month. When I got my car back, it sat crooked on the frame, but at least it was operable.

I'd fallen far enough. My ego couldn't take another assault. I walked into an Air Force recruiter's office, and signed up to take the Armed Service Vocational Aptitude Battery Test (ASVAB). Three days later, I was on a bus to Gunther Air Force Base in Montgomery, Alabama. Results were back in days. I'd performed exceedingly well giving me options in terms of choosing an Air Force job.

Unsure what type of job to select, I chose a personnel

position just to get in. On November 10, 1977, on a return trip to Gunther Air Force Base, I was sworn into the United States Air Force on delayed enlistment. That presented one more challenge.

In the aftermath of the Vietnam War, troop levels had been drastically cut. I wouldn't go active until March 28, 1978. My recruiter, fully aware of my circumstances tried to help, even offering her sofa a few nights a week. I declined, feeling it wasn't proper, not to mention, she was a white woman and this was the South. For the next four months I remained homeless. Sleeping on the beach on warm nights, crashing on friend's sofas, sleeping on floors, or in my car.

One night while sleeping on the beach, I woke to find a three-foot black snake coiled around my foot seeking warmth. In the dark, I couldn't tell at first what kind of snake it was. I shook my foot violently until it slithered off.

Finally, March 15, 1978 rolled around. Over the past week, Dad and I had spoken often. It was good to hear his voice clean and sober. He had returned to AA meetings. Reconciling with Mom had done him good. I needed a place to leave my car, so we decided I would return to Colorado Springs, and leave it at home.

I left Panama City at 3 a.m., with $42 in my pocket and two peanut butter and jelly sandwiches. My recruiter arranged to have me proceed to basic training from Colorado instead of Alabama.

By 6 a.m., I pulled off the road at a rest stop in Mississippi, locked my car doors, grabbed a baseball bat from under my seat, and fell asleep. I woke after three hours to find a Mississippi Highway Patrol car parked just behind my vehicle.

I got out to stretch my legs, when the largest human I'd ever witnessed left the patrol car and walked in my direction. His arms were massive, his bulk accentuated by the bulletproof vest. This white officer easily outweighed me by seventy-five pounds and had a few inches height advantage.

We exchanged pleasantries, when he offered me a coke from his cooler, which I gladly accepted. The officer went on to explain he'd been watching over me for hours. Apparently, a couple of good-ole-boys with bad intentions were spotted near my vehicle, hovering around like lions in search of prey. This kind gentleman ran them off. We chatted a few more minutes about my impending Air Force enlistment, before he bid me a fond farewell.

By the time I arrived in Amarillo, Texas, I had $5, no food, and a half tank of gas. I made it to Trinidad, Colorado; the place Dad stopped four years earlier to marvel at the scenery. I put $4.75 in my gas tank and saved a quarter in case I got stranded and needed to make a call. I had to cover one hundred twenty eight miles on a quarter tank of gas.

I accelerated to seventy miles per hour. When I reached the crest of a hill, and there were many, I shut the engine off and coasted downward without applying the break. When my speed started to bottom out, I restarted the engine and repeated the process. This continued for fifty miles until I reached an area just south of Pueblo where the hills stopped.

I arrived at 3830 Bunkhouse Drive and ran out of gas in the driveway. A neighbor had been expecting me and extended an invitation to her home. This white lady had a feast waiting. I hadn't eaten in over twenty-four hours.

Dad arrived first. We hugged each other like a father and son should. It was our "hakuna matata" moment. I was the last person Dad needed to make amends with, having already done so with Mom and my sisters'.

I'd never seen the new home they purchased, but I liked it immediately. It was the first home the Bennett family had ever owned: a split-level, three-story house, with a huge backyard. The large living room window provided excellent unobstructed views of Pikes Peak. Dad threw a party for me, but I noticed Mom smoking a cigarette, a habit she'd kicked a decade earlier. She still didn't trust Dad. Living in fear zapped her spirit and stressed her beyond belief.

I too had my reservations. I hated the thought of not attending college, and blamed Dad, fairly, or unfairly, for my failure. I allowed Dad to think I'd capitulated, but deep down, I was still seething.

I hopped a plain to San Antonio, Texas the morning of March 28 arriving around four o'clock that afternoon. Dozens of recruits, me among them, were sworn in at the airport and whisked away to Lackland Air Force Base on the south side of town.

The murmur of the bus engines and the occasional application of the air breaks is all I remember of the trip. I'd become lost in thought, wondering what life had in store for me. I had more advantages than most, yet still managed to find myself homeless. Unlike my friend Gabe, I'd reached for the stars and missed the stars and the moon. I most certainly didn't land in the Sea of Tranquility.

My confidence had fallen off a cliff tumbling into the

abyss. Despite my failures, the Air Force provided an opportunity to start over. While that start wouldn't be on my terms, at least an opportunity was afoot. I would not let it slip away again.

My obsession with a college education never wavered. Ironically, my first duty assignment after completing basic training and technical school was a third trip to Tyndall. I spent another three-and-a-half years in Panama City.

Within a week of my arrival, I ran into an old friend, Coach Collier. Coach had moved on from Rosenwald earning his master's and PhD. Coach's new job was Director of Education at Tyndall. His responsibilities included encouraging enlisted personnel to pursue higher education.

Finally the break I'd been waiting for. Collier helped me reenroll at Gulf Coast Community College. We talked for days. I scurried over to his office for a week, buying lunch for the both of us as I explained how I found myself in such dire straits. He seemed deeply troubled, making it his mission to cure what ailed me. Of all his former students, I was arguably the most likely to succeed; yet I'd failed.

By the time I transferred from Tyndall in August 1981, I picked up enough college credits for only half of one year. The military always came first causing me to miss a few semesters of school in the performance of my sworn duties.

The same thing happened at Randolph Air Force Base, my second duty assignment. Things were moving along at an unacceptably slow pace. I took classes at the University of Texas, San Antonio, but at the rate I was able to attend, I'd be fifty before graduation.

My burning desire to complete my education drove me away from the military. June 21, 1985, I took off the uniform for the final time.

Just over seventeen years after I graduated from high school, I earned that elusive Bachelor's degree, from California State University, Northridge, in Los Angeles' San Fernando Valley, with Dad's approval and blessing. I'm not sure who was prouder, Dad, or my son, who often sat on my lap at 3 a.m., while I studied at the kitchen table.

My obsession with education at the expense of everything except my son cost me a marriage and numerous friendships, but I don't have a single regret. I love learning so much, if I could figure out a way to make a living and stay in college, I would.

I completed this story two days before Christmas 2014. Looking at recent events in New York City; Sanford, Florida; Ferguson, Missouri; Cleveland, Ohio; and Los Angeles, it pains me deeply that America hasn't found a cure for its most intransigent of illnesses---racism. This malignancy continues to find new life.

Too many seek the worst in each other, ignoring the possible. Too many exploit differences for personal gain, manipulating the naïve among us. We often appear on a path towards eradication when someone, or something, comes along to derail positive advancement. Below are some of the more egregious examples of using race as a wedge.

After the Civil War, the Reconstruction Era, while fraught with ups and downs, found progress being made, to include a few black elected officials from the South. Jim Crow and Plessey vs. Ferguson, effectively whipped out those gains, instituting a system, many could argue, was equally as harsh and unyielding as slavery.

In 1954, the Brown vs. Board of Education ending "separate but equal" began the process of dismantling Jim Crow.

The Civil Rights Movement helped usher in an era of increased, but not complete equality, culminating with President Lyndon Johnson signing both the Voting Rights Act and the Civil Rights Act.

Unfortunately, neither the Brown decision nor the two acts would be enough to keep the haters and manipulators at bay. Both President Richard Nixon and Senator Barry Goldwater used what became known as the "Southern Strategy" in the 1960s to play on the racial fears of whites. While former Alabama Governor George Wallace, and southern sympathizers received most of the blame for stoking racial flames, Nixon and Goldwater mastered the subtle tactic of hate mongering.

In the late 1970s, future President Ronald Reagan employed the same strategy to eventually win the White House. Remember the Welfare Queen, and its attachment to black women, despite the fact there are more whites on welfare than blacks. Do you remember his manipulative attacks on affirmative action?

The hyperbole of hatred works, and politicians have repeatedly used this strategy. Does anyone remember the

Willie Horton ad? I pray someone will invent a counter tactic to render the "Southern Strategy" obsolete.

The mass exodus of whites to the suburbs, and the redlining of African American homebuyers, was a systematic destruction of a more hopeful America. Business leaders made millions in the support of white flight as they built suburban neighborhoods devoid of blacks.

Blacks were victimized by predatory lenders and forced to life in substandard neighborhoods. It gives credence to the notion that pursuit of the almighty dollar, at times, brings out the worst in us.

It reminds me of the lyrics from the O'Jays hit tune *For the Love Money*. Many of you know this tune as the theme song for the television series, *The Apprentice*, hosted by Donald Trump.

> *I know money is the root of all evil,*
> *Do funny things to some people,*
> *Give me a nickel, brother can you spare a dime,*
> *Money can drive some people out of their minds*

But poverty and lack of opportunity isn't restricted to black and brown. Many whites are trapped in the same downward spiral; yet still vote for people who exacerbate their personal situations, because some leader effectively misrepresented the facts, pitting one group against another with a false choice. The actions of these leaders continue to feed the racial stratification pipeline.

Every time I hear the phrase, "post-racial" to describe the era after President Barack Obama won the presidency, I want to scream. If anything, President Obama's election picked the scab off the wound, exposing a residual cancer that no amount of chemotherapy seems capable of completely eradicating.

With that said, I am deeply grateful we've progressed far enough in our evolution to elect a black man as president. Bigotry, while dying a slow, agonizing death continues to experience life because it benefits a certain power base that doesn't have our collective best interests at heart. Wake up America, we are being manipulated.

I love multiculturalism, diversity, and cross cultural exchanges. From Spain to Maine, Florida to Colorado, my experiences made me a better person, even the hateful ones. There's a richness of life, a fullness of spirit, and a freedom that comes when we don't allow the specter of bigotry to diminish the pursuit of our goals.

My experience has taught me, in the words of President Obama "we are not as divided as our politics" and social commentary suggest. We all want the same thing: good jobs, good educations, good incomes, safe communities, etc.

Why is racial harmony and prosperity for all looked upon as mutually exclusive? We could easily have both.

I'LL END AT THE BEGINNING

No better words capture the spirit of my teenage years than an excerpt from the opening sentence in Charles Dickens' novel, *A Tale of Two Cities*. While the experience he chronicles in Paris and London during the French Revolution have nothing to do with my journey between Panama City and the Academy, his eloquent words are simply too precious to pass up as an apt description of parts of my life, if one allows for a slight reinterpretation of his words from its original meaning.

"It was the best of times, it was the worst of times, it was the age of wisdom, the age of foolishness, it was the epoch of belief, the epoch of incredulity, it was the season of Light, the season of Darkness, it was the spring of hope, the spring of despair, we had everything before us, we had nothing before us, we were all going direct to Heaven, we were all going direct the other way---in short, the period was so far like the present period, that some of its noisiest authorities insisted on its being received, for good or for evil, in the superlative degree of comparison only."

From: A TALE OF TWO CITIES
Author: CHARLES DICKENS
Published: 1859

ABOUT THE AUTHOR

MICHAEL GORDON BENNETT is founder and CEO of Bennett Global Entertainment (BGE) and BGE Strategies, a consulting, publishing, and production platform with an expertise in the areas of marketing, advertising, technology, and diversity with a special emphasis on travel, tourism, and entertainment industries. His professional accomplishments include: computer programmer and systems analyst, television and radio news producer, actor, television host, author, advertising sales, magazine writer, and over twenty years in Hollywood as an independent producer and consultant for the Travel Channel, NBC, and BET. In 2010, he was appointed to BrandUSA, the public/private partnership signed into law by President Barack Obama as part of the Travel Promotion Act. Bennett is a graduate of California State University, Northridge with a degree in journalism. He's an Air Force veteran and currently lives in Las Vegas. He has one adult son, Michael.

GUEST SPEAKER

Bennett is a much sought after speaker, host, and lecturer. One of his companies, BGE Strategies consults businesses on consumer diversity and myriad other business activities. To inquire about possible appearances, please send an email to contact@michaelgordonbennett.com or call 702-343-3906.

http://www.michaelgordonbennett.com

Made in the USA
San Bernardino, CA
15 October 2015